International Encyclopedia of Human Geography

ABOUT THE AUTHOR

Prof.Menon Shroff, is an Ecologist and Environmental Specialist with more than 28 years of academic and consulting experience. He holds a Ph.D in geography from the Univeristy of Birmingham UK and wrote the Ph.D and Master Academic Programs of Environmental Sciences for the Universidad de Guayana, Venezuela.

ABOUT THE BOOK

Human Geography is a branch of geography that focuses on the systematic study of patterns and processes that shape human interaction with the environment, with particular reference to the causes and consequences of the spatial distribution of human activity on the earth's surface. Human geography broadly differs from physical geography in that it has a greater focus on studying intangible or abstract patterns surrounding human activity and is more receptive to qualitative research methodologies. It encompasses human, political, cultural, social and economic aspects of the social sciences. Geography is concerned with place. Understanding the nature and causes of aerial differentiation on the global surface has been the geographers task since people first noticed differences between places. Through geography we seek to understand these differences in patterns of human distribution, interrelationships between human society and the physical environment, peoples use of the Earth in time and space, and how these differences are related to peoples cultures and economies. This book concentrates on the field of human geography, providing a handy introductory text on the subject. Incorporating within its folds such fields as cultural, population, historical, political, economic and urban geography, human (or social) geography is a vast and wide ranging subject.

International Encyclopedia of HUMAN GEOGRAPHY

Prof.Menon Shroff

AMIGA PRESS. INC
Delhi -110051

AMIGA PRESS. INC
H.O :- 28-A, Indra Park, Chander Nagar
Delhi :- 110051 (India)
Tel :- 011-22504028, +91-98736-57000
Email :- info@amigapress.co.in
amigapub@gmail.com
Website :- www.amigapress@co.in

This edition is published by Amiga Press.Inc

ISBN : 978-93-87295-22-3

First Published 2019

Printed and bound by Amiga Press Inc. New Delhi-India

Preface

Geography is unique in bridging the social sciences (human geography) with the natural sciences (physical geography). Human geography concerns the understanding of the dynamics of cultures, societies and economies, and physical geography concerns the understanding of the dynamics of physical landscapes and the environment.

Geography is the study of Earth, its lands, features, and inhabitants. Just about every subject, from science to sports, has its own language. Geography has its own language too. In order to understand a subject, you need to understand the terms used by that subject. Geography has many different terms. Latitude and longitude are two such terms. Latitudes are imaginary lines that circle the earth and are parallel to the equator. The equator is the zero degree latitude line. Lines of latitude are measured my degrees.

Human geography broadly differs from physical geography in that it has a greater focus on studying intangible or abstract patterns surrounding human activity and is more receptive to qualitative research methodologies. It encompasses human, political, cultural, social and economic aspects of the social sciences. While the major focus of human geography is not the physical landscape of the Earth, it is not possible to discuss human geography without going into the physical landscape with which human activities are being played out and environmental geography which is an important link between the two. Human geography is both methodologically and theoretically diverse, including feminist, marxist, post-structural approaches, among others, and using both qualitative methods (such as ethnographies and interviews) and quantitative methods (such as survey research, statistical analysis and model building).

Urban, city, and town planning integrates land use planning and transportation planning to improve the built, economic and social environments of communities. Regional planning deals with a still larger environment, at a less detailed level. Urban planning can include urban renewal, by adapting urban planning methods to existing cities suffering from decay and lack of investment. In the Neolithic period, agriculture and other techniques facilitated larger populations than the very small communities of the Paleolithic, which probably led to the stronger, more coercive governments emerging at that time.

Economic geography is a sub-discipline that uses a geographical approach to study the economy. It is a vibrant and exciting branch of geography. Its name would suggest that economic geography lies somewhere between, or at the overlap of, the disciplines of geography and economics. This is true to some extent. In fact, both geographers and economists use the term 'economic geography'. However, they mean different things by it. Indeed, it is important to stress from the outset that the approach that geographers are using to study the economy is very different from that used by most economists. A Contemporary Introduction written by Neil Coe and his colleagues, this subject guide uses the term economic geography and economic-geographical approach to describe the approach used by geographers.

Development geography is the study of the earth's geography with reference to the standard of living and quality of life of its human inhabitants. In this context, development is a process of change that affects people's lives. It may involve an improvement in the quality of life as perceived by the people undergoing change. However, development is not always a positive process. Gunder Frank commented on the global economic forces that lead to the development of underdevelopment. This is covered in his dependency theory.

This is a reference book. All the matter is just compiled and edited in nature, taken from the various sources which are in public domain.

This book concentrates on the field of human geography, providing a handy introductory text on the subject. Incorporating within its folds such fields as cultural, population, historical, political, economic and urban geography, human (or social) geography is a vast and wide ranging subject.

—Editor

Contents

1

Introduction

HUMAN GEOGRAPHY

Human geography is one of the two major subfields of geography. Human geography is the study of human use and understanding of the Earth and the process which have affected this. It is linked to both social science and the humanities.

Human geography broadly differs from physical geography in that it has a greater focus on studying intangible or abstract patterns surrounding human activity and is more receptive to qualitative research methodologies. It encompasses human, political, cultural, social and economic aspects of the social sciences. While the major focus of human geography is not the physical landscape of the Earth, it is not possible to discuss human geography without going into the physical landscape with which human activities are being played out and environmental geography which is an important link between the two. Human geography is both methodologically and theoretically diverse, including feminist, marxist, post-structural approaches, among others, and using both qualitative methods (such as ethnographies and interviews) and quantitative methods (such as survey research, statistical analysis and model building).

HISTORY

In the history of geography, geographers have often recorded and described features of the Earth that might now be considered the remit of human, rather than physical, geographers. For example Hecataeus of Miletus, a geographer and historian in ancient Greece, described inhabitants of the ancient world as well as physical features.

It was not until the 18th and 19th Centuries, however, that geography was recognised as a discrete academic discipline. The Royal Geographical Society was founded in England in 1830, although the United Kingdom did not get its first full Chair of geography until 1917. The first real geographical intellect to emerge in United Kingdom geography was Halford John Mackinder, appointed reader at Oxford University in 1887.

The National Geographic Society was founded in the USA in 1888 and began publication of the *National Geographic* magazine which became and continues to be a great popularizer of geographic information. The society has long supported geographic research and education.

One of the first examples of geographic methods being used for purposes other than to describe and theorise the physical properties of the earth is John Snow's map of the 1854 Broad Street cholera outbreak. Though a physician and a pioneer of epidemiology, the map is probably one of the earliest examples of Health geography.

However, the now fairly distinct differences between the subfields of physical and human geography developed at a later date. This connection between both physical and human properties of geography is most apparent in the theory of Environmental determinism, made popular in the 19th Century by Carl Ritter and others, and with close links to evolutionary biology of the time. Environmental determinism is the theory that a people's physical, mental and moral habits are directly due to the influence of their natural environment. However, by the mid 19th Century, environmental determinism was under attack for lacking methodological rigour associated with modern science, and later as serving to justify racism and imperialism

A similar concern with both human and physical aspects is apparent in the later Regional geography, during the later 19th and first half of the 20th Centuries. The goal of regional geography, through regionalization, was to delineate space into regions and then understand and describe the unique characteristics of each region, in both human and physical aspects. With links to possibilism and cultural ecology, some of the same notions of causal effect of the environment on society and culture, as with environmental determinism remained.

By the 1950s, however, the quantitative revolution lead to strong criticism of regional geography. Due to a perceived lack of scientific rigour in and overly descriptive nature of the discipline, and a continued separation of geography from geology and the two subfields of physical and human geography, geographers in the mid 19th Century began to apply statistical and mathematical model methods to solving spatial problems. Much of the development during the quantitative revolution is now apparent in the use of Geographic information systems, and the use of statistics, spatial modelling and positivist approaches is still important to many branches of human geography. Well-known geographers from this period are Fred K. Schaefer,

Waldo Tobler, William Garrison, Peter Haggett, Richard J. Chorley, William Bunge, and Torsten Hagerstrand.

From the 1970s a number of critiques of the positivism now associated with geography emerged. Known under the term critical geography this signalled another turning point in the discipline. Behavioural geography emerged for some time as a means to understand how people made perceived spaces and places, and made locational decisions.

More influentially, radical geography emerged in the 1970s and 1980s, drawing heavily on Marxist theory and techniques, and is associated with geographers such as David Harvey and Richard Peet.

Seeking to say something 'meaningful' about the problems recognised through quantitative methods, to provide explanations rather than descriptions, to put forward alternatives and solutions and to be politically engaged, rather than the detachment associated with positivist methods. (The detachment and objectivity of the quantitative revolution was itself critiqued by radical geographers as being a tool of capital). Radical geography and the links to Marxism and related theories remain an important part of contemporary human geography) Critical geography also saw the introduction of humanistic geography, associated with the work of Yi-Fu Tuan, which, though similar to behavioural geography, pushed for a much more qualitative approach in methodology. The changes under critical geography have lead to contemporary approaches in the discipline such as Feminist geography, New cultural geography, and the engagement with postmodern and post structural theories and philosophies.

FIELDS OF HUMAN GEOGRAPHY

The main fields of study in human geography focus around the core fields of:

Culture: Cultural geography is the study of cultural products and norms and their variation across and relations to spaces and places. It focuses on describing and analyzing the ways language, religion, economy, government, and other cultural phenomena vary or remain constant from one place to another and on explaining how humans function spatially.

Development: Development Geography is the study of the Earth's geography with reference to the Standard of living and the Quality of life of its human inhabitants, study of the location, distribution and spatial organization of economic activities across the Earth. The subject matter investigated is strongly influenced by the researcher's methodological approach.

Economic: Economic geography examines relationships between human economic systems, states, and other actors, and the biophysical environment.

Health: Health geography is the application of geographical information, perspectives, and methods to the study of health, disease, and health care.

Historical: Historical Geography is the study of the human, physical, fictional, theoretical, and "real" geographies of the past. Historical geography studies a wide variety of issues and topics. A common theme is the study of the geographies of the past and how a place or region changes through time. Many historical geographers study geographical patterns through time, including how people have interacted with their environment, and created the cultural landscape.

Political: Political geography is concerned with the study of both the spatially uneven outcomes of political processes and the ways in which political processes are themselves affected by spatial structures.

Population: Population geography is the study of the ways in which spatial variations in the distribution, composition, migration, and growth of populations are related to the nature of places.

Tourism: Tourism geography is the study of travel and tourism as an industry, as a human activity, and especially as a place-based experience.

Urban: Urban geography is the study of urban areas with specific regards to spatial and relational aspects and theories. That is the study of areas which have a high concentration of buildings and infrastructure. These are areas where the majority of economic activities are in the secondary sector and tertiary sectors. They probably have a high population density.

DEVELOPMENT GEOGRAPHY

Development geography is the study of the earth's geography with reference to the standard of living and quality of life of its human inhabitants. In this context, development is a process of change that affects people's lives. It may involve an improvement in the quality of life as perceived by the people undergoing change. However, development is not always a positive process. Gunder Frank commented on the global economic forces that lead to the development of underdevelopment. This is covered in his dependency theory.

In development geography, geographers study spatial patterns in development. They try to find by what characteristics they can measure development by looking at economic, political and social factors. They seek to understand both the geographical causes and consequences of varying development. Studies compare More Economically Developed Countries (MEDCs) with Less Economically Developed Countries (LEDCs). Additionally variations within countries are looked at such as the differences between northern and southern Italy, the Mezzogiorno.

Within development geography, sustainable development is also studied in an attempt to understand how to meet the needs of the present without compromising the needs of future generations to meet their own needs.

Quantitative Indicators

Quantitative indicators are numerical indications of development:

- Economic indicators include GNP (Gross National Product) per capita, unemployment rates, energy consumption and percentage of GNP in primary industries. Of these, GNP per capita is the most used as it measures the value of all the goods and services produced in a country, excluding those produced by foreign companies, hence measuring the economic and industrial development of the country. However, using GNP per capita also has many problems.
    - o It does not take into account the distribution of the money which can often be extremely unequal as in the UAE where oil money has been collected by a rich elite and has not flowed to the bulk of the country.
    - o GNP does not measure whether the money produced is actually improving people's lives and this is important because in many MEDCs where there are large increases in wealth over time but only small increases in happiness.
    - o The figure rarely takes into account the unofficial economy, which includes subsistence agriculture and cash-in-hand or unpaid work, which is often substantial in LEDCs. In LEDCs it is often too expensive to accurately collect this data and some governments intentionally or unintentionally release inaccurate figures.
    - o The figure is usually given in US dollars which due to changing currency exchange rates can distort the money's true street value so it is often converted using purchasing power parity (PPP) in which the actual comparative purchasing power of the money in the country is calculated.
- Social indications include access to clean water and sanitation (which indicate the level of infrastructure developed in the country) and adult literacy rate, measuring the resources the government has to meet the needs of the people.
- Demographic indicators include the birth rate, death rate and fertility rate, which indicate the level of industrialization.
    - o Health indicators (a sub-factor of demographic indicators) include nutrition (calories per day, calories from protein, percentage of population with malnutrition), infant mortality and population per

doctor, which indicate the availability of healthcare and sanitation facilities in a country.

- Environmental indications include how much a country does for the environment.

Composite Indicators

Composite or qualitative indicators combine several quantitative indicators into one figure and generally provide a more balanced view of a country. Usually they include one economic, one social and one demographic indicator.

- The HDI (Human Development Index) is now the most widely used composite indicator. A number is calculated between 0 and 1 taking into account the most important measures: GNP per capita, the adult literacy rate, the school enrollment rate and life expectancy. It was started by the United Nations in 1990 to replace GNP as a more accurate way of measuring development. A HDI between 1 and 0.8 is considered high, 0.8 and 0.6 is considered medium and 0.6 to 0.4 is considered low.

Data Example

HDI Rank	Country	GDP Per Capita (PPP US$) 2008	Human Development index (HDI) value 2006
4	Australia	35,677	0.965
70	Brazil	10,296	0.807
151	Zimbabwe	188	0.513

- Other composite measures include the PQLI (Physical Quality of Life Index) which was a precursor to the HDI which used infant mortality rate instead of GNP per capita and rated countries from 0 to 100. It was calculated by assigning each country a score of 0 to 100 for each indicator compared with other countries in the world. The average of these three numbers makes the PQLI of a country.
- The HPI (Human Poverty Index) is used to calculate the percentage of people in a country who live in relative poverty. In order to better differentiate the number of people in abnormally poor living conditions the HPI-1 is used in developing countries, and the HPI-2 is used in developed countries. The HPI-1 is calculated based on the percentage of people not expected to survive to 40, the adult illiteracy rate, the percentage of people without access to safe water, health services and the percentage of children under 5 who are underweight. The HPI-2 is calculated based on the percentage of people who do not survive to 60, the adult functional illiteracy rate and the percentage of people living below 50% of median personal disposable income.

- The GDI (Gender-related Development Index) measures gender equality in a country in terms of life expectancy, literacy rates, school attendance and income.

Qualitative Indicators

Qualitative indicators include descriptions of living conditions and people's quality of life. They are useful in analysing features that are not easily calculated or measured in numbers such as freedom, corruption or security, which are mainly non-material benefits.

Geographic Variations in Development

The updated view of the north-south divide. Blue includes G8 nations, developed/first world nations, and Europe

There is a considerable spatial variation in development rates.

Global wealth also increased in material terms, and during the period 1947 to 2000, average per capita incomes tripled as global GDP increased almost tenfold (from $US3 trillion to $US30 trillion)... Over 25% of the 4.5 billion people in LEDCs still have life expectancies below 40 years.

More than 80 countries have a lower annual per capita income in 2000 than they did in 1990. The average income in the world's five richest countries is 74 times the level in the world's poorest five, the widest it has ever been. Nearly 1.3 billion people have no access to clean water. About 840 million people are malnourished. —Stephen Codrington

The most famous pattern in development is the North-South divide.

The North-South divide is the divide which separates the rich North or the developed world, from the poor South. This line of division is not as straightforward as it sounds and splits the globe into two main parts. It is also known as the Brandt Line.

The "North" in this divide is regarded as being North America, Europe, Russia, South Korea, Japan, Australia, New Zealand and the like. The countries within this area are generally the more economically developed. The "South" therefore encompasses the remainder of the Southern Hemisphere, mostly consisting of LEDCs. Another possible dividing line is the Tropic of Cancer with the exceptions of Australia and New Zealand.

It is critical to understand that the status of countries is far from static and the pattern is likely to become distorted with the fast development of certain southern countries, many of them NICs (Newly Industrialised Countries) including India, Thailand, Brazil, Malaysia, Mexico and others.

These countries are experiencing sustained fast development on the back of growing manufacturing industries and exports.

Most countries are experiencing significant increases in wealth and standard of living. However there are unfortunate exceptions to this rule.

Noticeably some of the former Soviet Union countries has experienced major disruption of industry in the transition to a market economy. Many African nations have recently experienced reduced GNPs due to wars and the AIDS epidemic, including Angola, Congo, Sierra Leone and others.

Arab oil producers rely very heavily on oil exports to support their GDPs so any reduction in oil's market price can lead to rapid decreases in GNP. Countries which rely on only a few exports for much of their income are very vulnerable to changes in the market value of those commodities and are often derogatively called banana republics.

Many developing countries do rely on exports of a few primary goods for a large amount of their income (coffee and timber for example), and this can create havoc when the value of these commodities drops, leaving these countries with no way to pay off their debts.

Within countries the pattern is that wealth is more concentrated around urban areas than rural areas. Wealth also tends towards areas with natural resources or in areas that are involved in tertiary (service) industries and trade. This leads to a gathering of wealth around mines and monetary centres such as New York, London and Tokyo.

Aid

MEDCs (More Economically Developed Countries) can give aid to LEDCs (Less Economically Developed Countries). There are several types of aid:

- Governmental (Bilateral) aid
- International Organizational (multilateral) aid
- Voluntary aid
- Short-term/emergency aid
- Long-term/sustainable aid.

Aid can be given in several ways. Through money, materials, or skilled and learned people (e.g. teachers).

Aid has advantages. Mostly short-term or emergency aid help people in LEDCs to survive a natural (earthquake, tsunami, volcano eruption etc.) or human (civil war etc.) disaster. Aid helps make the recipient country (the country that receives aid) get more developed.

However, aid also has disadvantages. Often aid does not even reach the poorest people. Often money gained from aid is used up to make infrastructures (bridges, roads etc.), which only the rich can use. Also, the recipient country gets more dependant of aid from a donor country (the country giving aid).

2

The Nature of Geography

Geography is concerned with place. Understanding the nature and causes of aerial differentiation on the global surface has been the geographers task since people first noticed differences between places. Through geography we seek to understand these differences in patterns of human distribution, interrelationships between human society and the physical environment, peoples use of the Earth in time and space, and how these differences are related to peoples cultures and economies.

These, and other related themes, express major concerns of our time and reflect the consequences of spatial decisions. In geographys pursuit of this understanding the questions "where?," "why?," and "how?" are central. The first of these introduces the issues of location and spatial choice; the latter two signify that modern geography is not content merely to describe, but seeks to explain. Beyond these questions, geographers also ask a fourth"what if?"as a means of seeking alternatives and giving the subject an applied dimension that can assist decision makers in planning and development at a variety of geographical scales.

The idea of place is not an examinable objective but an ultimate goal, whose pursuit gives direction to geographical study. As a geographical concept it refers to the aerial context of events, objects, and actions; in other words, to the patterns resulting from human occupancy of the global surface over time. The areal context is set in space which, though measurable, has by itself no meaning. Space becomes place when humans invest it with meaning, most commonly by giving it a name and all of the associations that that name evokes. The terms place and region may, therefore, be distinguished by spatial scale, rather than by inherent differences, for both involve space that has been invested with meaning. Two important implications flow from this understanding of place: First, geography is strongly influenced by the norms of the social sciences.

The complexity and changing nature of human society seldom permit the type of precision expected in the physical sciences. Instead, the social sciences offer a variety of perspectives and methods of study by which to examine the consequences of human behaviour on the global surface. In studying the idea of place from a spatial perspective, geographers inevitably encounter the problem of change through time; for them, landscape is document. Historians, too, are concerned with change through time as they document the consequences of human behaviour.

Thus, like geographers, historians are also concerned with place. Indeed, a common concern with place brings the work of geographers and historians close together. Second, physical geographers, no less than human geographers, contribute to an understanding of place; for the concept of sitethe physical characteristics of a placeis integral to understanding aerial differentiation on the global surface. Nevertheless, geographers focus on the patterns and interactions to be found on that surface, and not primarily on the natural processes that act on it from above or below.

They recognize that interaction between humans and their environment has always been mutual, and that the growth of technology has increased the human capacity to modify the environment. That growth in technology has greatly aided geographers in their traditional tasks. It has given them increasingly refined techniques for gathering and interpreting data, whether in the field by means of GPS or by aerial and satellite imagery. Spatial relationships are at the heart of geography. Using software to analyse spatial relationships among objects being mapped, GIS, in particular, has greatly assisted geographers in depicting the character of place. Not only can they now process larger quantities of data more quickly and with greater refinement, but also they can manipulate variables and thus project alternatives that give geography an applied dimension. Finally, their work can be displayed using advanced techniques of computer-generated mapping.

The view of geography presented here is that of a core sharply focused on the concept of place one in which both physical and human elements play an important part. The subject has an applied dimension that can affect our daily lives. It can, therefore, be a powerful medium for the development of skills contributing to citizenship and cultural awareness.

HISTORICAL BACKGROUND OF GEOGRAPHY

Babylon

The oldest known world maps date back to ancient Babylon from the 9th century BC. The best known Babylonian world map, however, is the Imago Mundi of 600 BC. The map as reconstructed by Eckhard Unger shows Babylon on the Euphrates, surrounded by a circular landmass showing Assyria, Urartu and several cities, in turn surrounded by a "bitter river" (Oceanus), with seven islands arranged around it so as to form a seven-pointed star. The accompanying text mentions seven outer regions beyond the encircling ocean. The descriptions of five of them have survived. In contrast to the Imago Mundi, an earlier Babylonian world map dating back to the 9th century BC depicted Babylon as being further north from the centre of the world, though it is not certain what that centre was supposed to represent.

Greco-Roman world

The ancient Greeks saw the poet Homer as the founder of geography. His works the Iliad and the Odyssey are works of literature, but both contain a great deal of geographical information. Homer describes a circular world ringed by a single massive ocean. The works show that the Greeks by the 8th century BC had considerable knowledge of the geography of the eastern Mediterranean.

The poems contain a large number of place names and descriptions, but for many of these it is uncertain what real location, if any, is actually being referred to. Thales of Miletus is one of the first known philosophers known to have wondered about the shape of the world. He proposed that the world was based on water, and that all things grew out of it. He also laid down many of the astronomical and mathematical rules that would allow geography to be studied scientifically.

His successor Anaximander is the first person known to have attempted to create a scale map of the known world and to have introduced the gnomon to Ancient Greece. Hecataeus of Miletus initiated a different form of geography, avoiding the mathematical calculations of Thales and Anaximander he learnt about the world by gathering previous works and speaking to the sailors who came through the busy port of Miletus. From these accounts he wrote a detailed prose account of what was known of the world. A similar work, and one that mostly survives today, is Herodotus' Histories.

While primarily a work of history, the book contains a wealth of geographic descriptions covering much of the known world. Egypt, Scythia, Persia, and Asia Minor are all described in great detail. Little is known about areas further a field, and descriptions of areas such as India are almost wholly fanciful. Herodotus also made important observations about geography. He is the first to have noted the process by which large rivers, such as the Nile, build up deltas, and is also the first recorded as observing that winds tend to blow from colder regions to warmer ones.

Pythagoras was perhaps the first to propose a spherical world, arguing that the sphere was the most perfect form. This idea was embraced by Plato and Aristotle presented empirical evidence to verify this. He noted that the Earth's shadow during an eclipse is curved, and also that stars increase in height as one moves north. Eudoxus of Cnidus used the idea of a sphere to explain how the sun created differing climatic zones based on latitude. This led the Greeks to believe in a division of the world into five regions. At each of the poles was an uncharitably cold region. While extrapolating from the heat of the Sahara it was deduced that the area around the equator was unbearably hot. Between these extreme regions both the northern and southern hemispheres had a temperate belt suitable for human habitation.

Hellenistic Period

These theories clashed with the evidence of explorers, however. Hanno the Navigator had traveled as far south as Sierra Leone, and it is possible other Phoenicians had circumnavigated Africa. In the 4th century BC the Greek explorer Pytheas traveled through northwest Europe, and circled the British Isles. He found that the region was considerably more habitable than theory expected, but his discoveries were largely dismissed as fanciful by his contemporaries because of this.

Conquerors also carried out exploration, for example, Caesar's invasions of Britain and Germany, expeditions/invasions sent by Augustus to Arabia Felix and Ethiopia, and perhaps the greatest Ancient Greek explorer of all, Alexander the Great, who deliberately set out to learn more about the east through his military expeditions and so took a large number of geographers and writers with his army who recorded their observations as they moved east.

The ancient Greeks divided the world into three continents, Europe, Asia, and Libya (Africa). The Hellespont formed the border between Europe and Asia. The border between Asia and Libya was generally considered to be the Nile river, but some geographers, such as Herodotus objected to this. Herodotus argued that there was no difference between the people on the east and west sides of the Nile, and that the Red Sea was a better border.

The relatively narrow habitable band was considered to run from the Atlantic Ocean in the west to an unknown sea somewhere east of India in the east. The southern portion of Africa was unknown, as was the northern portion of Europe and Asia, so it was believed that they were circled by a sea. These areas were generally considered uninhabitable. The size of the Earth was an important question to the Ancient Greeks. Eratosthenes attempted to calculate its circumference by measuring the angle of the sun at two different locations.

While his numbers were problematic, most of the errors cancelled themselves out and he got quite an accurate figure. Since the distance from the Atlantic to India was roughly known, this raised the important question of what was in the vast region east of Asia and to the west of Europe. Crates of Mallus proposed that there were in fact four inhabitable land masses, two in each hemisphere. In Rome a large globe was created depicting this world. That some of the figures Eratosthenes had used in his calculation were considerably in error became known, and Posidonius set out to get a more accurate measurement. This number actually was considerably smaller than the real one, but it became accepted that the eastern part of Asia was not a huge distance from Europe.

Roman Period

While the works of almost all earlier geographers have been lost, many of them are partially known through quotations found in Strabo. Strabo's seventeen volume work of geography is almost completely extant, and is one of the most important sources of information on classical geography. Strabo accepted the narrow band of habitation theory, and rejected the accounts of Hanno and Pytheas as fables.

None of Strabo's maps survive, but his detailed descriptions give a clear picture of the status of geographical knowledge of the time. A century after Strabo Ptolemy launched a similar undertaking. By this time the Roman Empire had expanded through much of Europe, and previously unknown areas such as the British Isles had been explored. The Silk Road was also in operation, and for the first time knowledge of the far east began to be known.

Ptolemy's Geographia opens with a theoretical discussion about the nature and techniques of geographical inquiry, and then moves to detailed descriptions of much the known world. Ptolemy lists a huge number of cities, tribes, and sites and places them in the world. It is uncertain what Ptolemy's names correspond to in the modern world, and a vast amount of scholarship has gone into trying to link Ptolemaic descriptions to know locations. Pliny the Elder's Natural History also has parts on geography.

For the most part Ancient Greek geography was an academic field. There is little evidence that maps or charts were used for navigation. It does, however, seem that at least in Athens the people were acquainted with maps and that several were on public display. It was the Romans who made far more extensive practical use of geography and maps.

Medieval Islamic world

In the Middle East, Muslim geographers such as al-Idrisi, al-Yaqubi, al-Masudi, Ibn Khurdadhbih, Ibn al-Faqih, al-Istakhri, Ibn Battuta, Ibn Khaldun, etc. maintained the Greek and Roman techniques and developed new ones. The Islamic empire stretched from Spain to India, and Arab and Jewish traders (known as Radhanites) travelled throughout Eurasia, Africa and the Indian Ocean.

The Arabs added a great deal of knowledge to expand and correct the classical sources. There were some representatives of the West that produced geographical works of quality, such as the Syrian bishop Jacob of Edessa (633-

708), but this paled in comparison to the virtual mountain of work published by Islamic writers of the Middle Ages (who were largely responsible for the foundations of knowledge present in later Western geography). During the Muslim conquests of the seventh and early 8th centuries, Arab armies established the Islamic Arab Empire, reaching from Central Asia to the Iberian Peninsula.

An early form of globalization began emerging during the Islamic Golden Age, when the knowledge, trade and economies from many previously isolated regions and civilizations began integrating due to contacts with Muslim explorers, sailors, scholars, traders, and travellers. Subhi Y. Labib has called this period the Pax Islamica, and John M. Hobson has called it the Afro-Asiatic age of discovery, in reference to the Muslim Southwest Asian and North African traders and explorers who travelled most of the Old World, and established an early global economy across most of Asia, Africa, and Europe, with their trade networks extending from the Atlantic Ocean and Mediterranean Sea in the west to the Indian Ocean and China Seas in the east, and even as far as Japan, Korea and the Bering Strait. Arabic silver dirham coins were also being circulated throughout the Afro-Eurasian landmass, as far as sub-Saharan Africa in the south and northern Europe in the north, often in exchange for goods and slaves. In England, for example, the Anglo-Saxon king Offa of Mercia had coins minted with the Shahadah in Arabic.

These factors helped establish the Arab Empire (including the Rashidun, Umayyad, Abbasid and Fatimid caliphates) as the world's leading extensive economic power throughout the 7th–13th centuries.In the 9th century, Alkindus was the first to introduce experimentation into the Earth sciences.

An early adherent of environmental determinism was the medieval Afro-Arab writer al-Jahiz, who explained how the environment can determine the physical characteristics of the inhabitants of a certain community. He used his early theory of evolution to explain the origins of different human skin colours, particularly black skin, which he believed to be the result of the environment. He cited a stony region of black basalt in the northern Najd as evidence for his theory. In the early 10th century, Abû Zayd al-Balkhî, originally from Balkh, founded the "Balkhî school" of terrestrial mapping in Baghdad.

The geographers of this school also wrote extensively of the peoples, products, and customs of areas in the Muslim world, with little interest in the non-Muslim realms. Suhrâb, a late 10th century Muslim geographer, accompanied a book of geographical coordinates with instructions for making a rectangular world map, with equirectangular projection or cylindrical cylindrical equidistant projection. In the early 11th century, Avicenna hypothesized on the geological causes of mountains in The Book of Healing.

In mathematical geography, Abû Rayhân al-Bîrûnî, around 1025, was the first to describe a polar equi-azimuthal equidistant projection of the celestial sphere. He was also regarded as the most skilled when it came to mapping cities and measuring the distances between them, which he did for many cities in the Middle East and western Indian subcontinent. He often combined astronomical readings and mathematical equations, in order to develop methods of pin-pointing locations by recording degrees of latitude and longitude.

He also developed similar techniques when it came to measuring the heights of mountains, depths of valleys, and expanse of the horizon, in The Chronology of the Ancient Nations. He also discussed human geography and the planetary habitability of the Earth. He hypothesized that roughly a quarter of the Earth's surface is habitable by humans, and also argued that the shores of Asia and Europe were "separated by a vast sea, too dark and dense to navigate and too risky to try" in reference to the Atlantic Ocean and Pacific Ocean. At the age of 17, al-Biruni calculated the latitude of Kath, Khwarazm, using the maximum altitude of the Sun. Al-Biruni also solved a complex geodesic equation in order to accurately compute the Earth's circumference, which were close to modern values of the Earth's circumference. His estimate of 6,339.9 km for the Earth radius was only 16.8 km less than the modern value of 6,356.7 km.

In contrast to his predecessors who measured the Earth's circumference by sighting the Sun simultaneously from two different locations, al-Biruni developed a new method of using trigonometric calculations based on the angle between a plain and mountain top which yielded more accurate measurements of the Earth's circumference and made it possible for it to be measured by a single person from a single location.

By the age of 22, al-Biruni had written several short works, including a study of map projections, Cartography, which included a method for projecting a hemisphere on a plane. John J. O'Connor and Edmund F. Robertson write in the MacTutor History of Mathematics archive:

- "Important contributions to geodesy and geography were also made by al-Biruni. He introduced techniques to measure the earth and distances on it using triangulation. He found the radius of the earth to be 6339.6 km, a value not obtained in the West until the 16th century. His Masudic canon contains a table giving the coordinates of six hundred places, almost all of which he had direct knowledge."

The Arab geographer Al-Idrisi's Mappa Mundi incorporated the knowledge of Africa, the Indian Ocean and the Far East gathered by Arab merchants and explorers with the information inherited from the classical geographers to create one of the most accurate maps of the world to date. The

Tabula Rogeriana was drawn by Al-Idrisi in 1154 for the Norman King Roger II of Sicily, after a stay of eighteen years at his court, where he worked on the commentaries and illustrations of the map.

The map, written in Arabic, shows the Eurasian continent in its entirety, but only shows the northern part of the African continent. In the 14th century, Ibn Bamm◎ûm◎ah, a Moroccan, began his travels. He started as a pilgrim to Mecca, but continued his journeys for the next 30 years, covering some 73,000 miles (117,000 km).

Before returning home, he had visited most of the Muslim world and beyond, from Europe and southern Africa in the west to eastern Asia in the east. The universal use of Arabic in the Muslim world and his status as judge trained in law gave him access to royal courts at most locations he visited. Ibn Battuta (1304–1368) was a traveller and explorer, whose account documents his travels and excursions over a period of almost thirty years, covering some 73,000 miles (117,000 km).

These journeys covered most of the known Old World, extending from North Africa, West Africa, Southern Europe and Eastern Europe in the west, to the Middle East, Indian subcontinent, Central Asia, Southeast Asia and China (then the Mongol Yuan Empire) in the east, a distance readily surpassing that of his predecessors and his near-contemporary Marco Polo.

Medieval Europe

During the Early Middle Ages, geographical knowledge in Europe regressed (though it is a popular misconception that they thought the world was flat), and the simple T and O map became the standard depiction of the world. The trips of Venetian explorer Marco Polo in the 13th century, the Christian Crusades of the 12th and 13th centuries, and the Portuguese and Spanish voyages of exploration during the 15th and 16th centuries opened up new horizons and stimulated geographic writings. During the 15th century, Henry the Navigator of Portugal supported explorations of the African coast and became a leader in the promotion of geographic studies. Among the most notable accounts of voyages and discoveries published during the 16th century were those by Giambattista Ramusio in Venice, by Richard Hakluyt in England, and by Theodore de Bry in what is now Belgium.

Early modern period

Following the journeys of Marco Polo, interest in geography spread throughout Europe. From around circa 1400, the writings of Ptolemy and his Islamic successors provided a systematic framework to tie together and portray geographical information. The great voyages of exploration in 16th and 17th centuries revived a desire for both accurate geographic detail, and more solid theoretical foundations. The Geographia Generalis by Bernhardus Varenius and Gerardus Mercator's world map are prime examples of the new breed of scientific geography. The Mongols also had wide ranging knowledge of the geography of Europe and Asia, based in their governance and ruling of much of this area and used this information for the undertaking of large military expeditions.

The evidence for this is found in historical resources such as The Secret History of Mongols and other Persian chronicles written in 13th and 14th centuries. For example, during the rule of the Great Yuan Dynasty a world map was created and is currently kept in South Korea.

The Muslim Ottoman cartographer Piri Reis drawn navigational maps in his Kitab-ý Bahriye. The work includes an atlas of charts for small segments of the Mediterranean, accompanied by sailing instructions covering the sea. In the second version of the work, he included a map of the Americas. The Piri Reis map drawn by the Ottoman cartographer Piri Reis in 1513 is an early surviving map to show the Americas.

19th century

By the 18th century, geography had become recognized as a discrete discipline and became part of a typical university curriculum in Europe (especially Paris and Berlin), although not in the United Kingdom where geography was generally taught as a sub-discipline of other subjects. One of the great works of this time was Kosmos: a sketch of a physical description of the Universe, by Alexander von Humboldt, the first volume of which was published in German in 1845. Such was the power of this work that Dr Mary Somerville, of Cambridge University intended to scrap publication of her own Physical Geography on reading Kosmos.

Von Humboldt himself persuaded her to publish. In 1877, Thomas Henry Huxley published his Physiography with the philosophy of universality presented as an integrated approach in the study of the natural environment.

The philosophy of universality in geography was not a new one but can be seen as evolving from the works of Alexander von Humboldt and Immanuel Kant. The publication of Huxley physiography presented a new form of geography that analysed and classified cause and effect at the micro-level and then applied these to the macro-scale (due to the view that the micro was part of the macro and thus an understanding of all the micro-scales was need to understand the macro level). This approach emphasized the empirical collection of data over the theoretical. The same approach was also used by Halford John Mackinder in 1887.

However, the integration of the Geosphere, Atmosphere and Biosphere under physiography was soon over taken by Davisian geomorphology. Over the past two centuries the quantity of knowledge and the number of tools has exploded. There are strong links between geography and the sciences of geology and botany, as well as economics, sociology and demographics.

The Royal Geographical Society was founded in England in 1830, although the United Kingdom did not get its first full Chair of geography until 1917. The first real geographical intellect to emerge in United Kingdom geography was Halford John Mackinder, appointed reader at Oxford University in 1887. The National Geographic Society was founded in the USA in 1888 and began publication of the National Geographic magazine which became and continues to be a great popularizer of geographic information. The society has long supported geographic research and education.

20th century

In the West during the second half of the 19th and the 20th century, the discipline of geography went through four major phases: environmental determinism, regional geography, the quantitative revolution, and critical geography.

Environmental Determinism

Environmental determinism is the theory that a people's physical, mental and moral habits are directly due to the influence of their natural environment. Prominent environmental determinists included Carl Ritter, Ellen Churchill Semple, and Ellsworth Huntington.

Popular hypotheses included "heat makes inhabitants of the tropics lazy" and "frequent changes in barometric pressure make inhabitants of temperate latitudes more intellectually agile." Environmental determinist geographers attempted to make the study of such influences scientific.

Around the 1930s, this school of thought was widely repudiated as lacking any basis and being prone to (often bigoted) generalizations. Environmental determinism remains an embarrassment to many contemporary geographers, and leads to skepticism among many of them of claims of environmental influence on culture.

CLIMATE AND THE ATMOSPHERE

Climate

Climates encompasses the statistics of temperature, humidity, atmospheric pressure, wind, rainfall, atmospheric particle count and other meteorological elements in a given region over long periods of time. Climate can be contrasted to weather, which is the present condition of these same elements and their variations over periods up to two weeks. The climate of a location is affected by its latitude, terrain, and altitude, as well as nearby water bodies and their currents. Climates can be classified according to the average and the typical ranges of different variables, most commonly temperature and precipitation. The most commonly used classification scheme was originally developed by Wladimir Koppen.

The Thornthwaite system, in use since 1948, incorporates evapotranspiration in addition to temperature and precipitation information and is used in studying animal species diversity and potential impacts of climate changes. The Bergeron and Spatial Synoptic Classification systems focus on the origin of air masses that define the climate of a region.

Paleoclimatology is the study of ancient climates. Since direct observations of climate are not available before the 19th century, paleoclimates are inferred from *proxy variables* that include non-biotic evidence such as sediments found in lake beds and ice cores, and biotic evidence such as tree rings and coral. Climate models are mathematical models of past, present and future climates.

Definition

Climate (from Ancient Greek *klima,* meaning *inclination*) is commonly defined as the weather averaged over a long period of time. The standard averaging period is 30 years, but other periods may be used depending on the purpose. Climate also includes statistics other than the average, such as the magnitudes of day-to-day or year-to-year variations. The Intergovernmental Panel on Climate Change (IPCC) glossary definition is:

Climate in a narrow sense is usually defined as the "average weather," or more rigorously, as the statistical description in terms of the mean and variability of relevant quantities over a period of time ranging from months to thousands or millions of years. The classical period is 30 years, as defined by the World Meteorological Organization (WMO). These quantities are most often surface variables such as temperature, precipitation, and wind. Climate in a wider sense is the state, including a statistical description, of the climate system.

The difference between climate and weather is usefully summarized by the popular phrase "Climate is what you expect, weather is what you get." Over historical time spans there are a number of nearly constant variables that determine climate, including latitude, altitude, proportion of land to water, and proximity to oceans and mountains. These change only over periods of millions of years due to processes such as plate tectonics.

Other climate determinants are more dynamic: for example, the thermohaline circulation of the ocean leads to a 5 °C (9 °F) warming of the northern Atlantic ocean compared to other ocean basins. Other ocean currents redistribute heat between land and water on a more regional scale. The density and type of vegetation coverage affects solar heat absorption, water retention, and rainfall on a regional level. Alterations in the quantity of atmospheric greenhouse gases determines the amount of solar energy retained by the planet, leading to global warming or global cooling. The variables which determine climate are numerous and the interactions complex, but there is general agreement that the broad outlines are understood, at least insofar as the determinants of historical climate change are concerned.

Climate Classification

There are several ways to classify climates into similar regimes. Originally, climes were defined in Ancient Greece to describe the weather depending upon a location's latitude. Modern climate classification methods can be broadly divided into *genetic* methods, which focus on the causes of climate, and *empiric* methods, which focus on the effects of climate.

Examples of genetic classification include methods based on the relative frequency of different air mass types or locations within synoptic weather disturbances. Examples of empiric classifications include climate zones defined by plant hardiness, evapotranspiration, or more generally the Koppen climate classification which was originally designed to identify the climates associated with certain biomes. A common shortcoming of these classification schemes is that they produce distinct boundaries between the zones they define, rather than the gradual transition of climate properties more common in nature.

Bergeron and Spatial Synoptic

The most generic classification is that involving the concept of air masses. The Bergeron classification is the most widely accepted form of air mass classification. Air mass classification involves three letters. The first letter describes its moisture properties, with c used for continental air masses (dry) and m for maritime air masses (moist).

The second letter describes the thermal characteristic of its source region: T for tropical, P for polar, A for Arctic or Antarctic, M for monsoon, E for equatorial, and S for superior air (dry air formed by significant downward motion in the atmosphere). The third letter is used to designate the stability of the atmosphere. If the air mass is colder than the ground below it, it is labelled k. If the air mass is warmer than the ground below it, it is labelled w. While air mass identification was originally used in weather forecasting during the 1950s, climatologists began to establish synoptic climatologies based on this idea in 1973.

Based upon the Bergeron classification scheme is the Spatial Synoptic Classification system (SSC). There are six categories within the SSC scheme: Dry Polar (similar to continental polar), Dry Moderate (similar to maritime superior), Dry Tropical (similar to continental tropical), Moist Polar (similar to maritime polar), Moist Moderate (a hybrid between maritime polar and maritime tropical), and Moist Tropical (similar to maritime tropical, maritime monsoon, or maritime equatorial).

Koppen

The Koppen classification depends on average monthly values of temperature and precipitation. The most commonly used form of the Koppen classification has five primary types labelled A through E. These primary types are A, tropical; B, dry; C, mild mid-latitude; D, cold mid-latitude; and E, polar. The five primary classifications can be further divided into secondary classifications such as rain forest, monsoon, tropical savanna, humid subtropical, humid continental, oceanic climate, Mediterranean climate, steppe, subarctic climate, tundra, polar ice cap, and desert.

Rain forests are characterized by high rainfall, with definitions setting minimum normal annual rainfall between 1,750 millimetres (69 in) and 2,000 millimetres (79 in). Mean monthly temperatures exceed 18 °C (64 °F) during all months of the year. A monsoon is a seasonal prevailing wind which lasts for several months, ushering in a region's rainy season. Regions within North America, South America, Sub-Saharan Africa, Australia and East Asia are monsoon regimes. A tropical savanna is a grassland biome located in semi-arid to semi-humid climate regions of subtropical and tropical latitudes, with average temperatures remain at or above 18 °C (64 °F) year round and rainfall between 750 millimetres (30 in) and 1,270 millimetres (50 in) a year. They are widespread on Africa, and are also found in India, the northern parts of South America, Malaysia, and Australia.

The humid subtropical climate zone where winter rainfall (and sometimes snowfall) is associated with large storms that the westerlies steer from west to east. Most summer rainfall occurs during thunderstorms and from occasional tropical cyclones. Humid subtropical climates lie on the east side continents, roughly between latitudes 20° and 40° degrees away from the equator.

A humid continental climate is marked by variable weather patterns and a large seasonal temperature variance. Places with more than three months of average daily temperatures above 10 °C (50 °F) and a coldest month temperature below "3 °C (26.6 °F) and which do not meet the criteria for an arid or semiarid climate, are classified as continental.

An oceanic climate is typically found along the west coasts at the middle latitudes of all the world's continents, and in southeastern Australia, and is accompanied by plentiful precipitation year round.

The Mediterranean climate regime resembles the climate of the lands in the Mediterranean Basin, parts of western North America, parts of Western and South Australia, in southwestern South Africa and in parts of central Chile. The climate is characterized by hot, dry summers and cool, wet winters.

A steppe is a dry grassland with an annual temperature range in the summer of up to 40 °C (104 °F) and during the winter down to "40 °C ("40.0 °F).

A subarctic climate has little precipitation, and monthly temperatures which are above 10 °C (50 °F) for one to three months of the year, with permafrost in large parts of the area due to the cold winters. Winters within subarctic climates usually include up to six months of temperatures averaging below 0 °C (32 °F).

A polar ice cap, or polar ice sheet, is a high-latitude region of a planet or moon that is covered in ice. Ice caps form because high-latitude regions receive less energy in the form of solar radiation from the sun than equatorial regions, resulting in lower surface temperatures.

A desert is a landscape form or region that receives very little precipitation. Deserts usually have a large diurnal and seasonal temperature range, with high daytime temperatures (in summer up to 45 °C or 113 °F), and low night-time temperatures (in winter down to 0 °C; 32 °F) due to extremely low humidity. Many deserts are formed by rain shadows, as mountains block the path of moisture and precipitation to the desert.

Thornthwaite

Devised by the American climatologist and geographer C. W. Thornthwaite, this climate classification method monitors the soil water budget using the concept of evapotranspiration. It monitors the portion of total precipitation used to nourish vegetation over a certain area. It uses indices such as a humidity index and an aridity index to determine an area's moisture regime based upon its average temperature, average rainfall, and average vegetation type. The lower the value of the index in any given area, the drier the area is.

The moisture classification includes climatic classes with descriptors such as hyperhumid, humid, subhumid, subarid, semi-arid (values of-20 to-40), and arid. Humid regions experience more precipitation than evaporation each year, while arid regions experience greater evaporation than precipitation on an annual basis. A total of 33 percent of the Earth's landmass is considered either arid of semi-arid, including southwest North America, southwest South America, most of northern and a small part of southern Africa, southwest and portions of eastern Asia, as well as much of Australia. Studies suggest that precipitation effectiveness (PE) within the Thornthwaite moisture index is overestimated in the summer and underestimated in the winter. This index can be effectively used to determine the number of herbivore and mammal species numbers within a given area. The index is also used in studies of climate change. Thermal classifications within the Thornthwaite scheme include microthermal, mesothermal, and megathermal regimes. A microthermal climate is one of low annual mean temperatures, generally between 0 °C (32 °F) and 14 °C (57 °F) which experiences short summers and has a potential evaporation between 14 centimetres (5.5 in) and 43 centimetres (17 in). A mesothermal climate lacks persistent heat or persistent cold, with potential evaporation between 57 centimetres (22 in) and 114 centimetres (45 in). A megathermal climate is one with persistent high temperatures and abundant rainfall, with potential evaporation in excess of 114 centimetres (45 in).

Record

Modern: Details of the modern climate record are known through the taking of measurements from such weather instruments as thermometers, barometers, and anemometers during the past few centuries. The instruments used to study weather conditions over the modern time scale, their known error, their immediate environment, and their exposure have changed over the years, which must be considered when studying the climate of centuries past.

Paleoclimatology

Paleoclimatology is the study of past climate over a great period of the Earth's history. It uses evidence from ice sheets, tree rings, sediments, coral, and rocks to determine the past state of the climate. It demonstrates periods of stability and periods of change and can indicate whether changes follow patterns such as regular cycles.

Climate Change

Climate change is the variation in global or regional climates over time. It reflects changes in the variability or average state of the atmosphere over time scales ranging from decades to millions of years. These changes can be caused by processes internal to the Earth, external forces (e.g. variations in sunlight intensity) or, more recently, human activities.

In recent usage, especially in the context of environmental policy, the term "climate change" often refers only to changes in modern climate, including the rise in average surface temperature known as global warming. In some cases, the term is also used with a presumption of human causation, as in the United Nations Framework Convention on Climate Change (UNFCCC). The UNFCCC uses "climate variability" for non-human caused variations.

Earth has undergone periodic climate shifts in the past, including four major ice ages. These consisting of glacial periods where conditions are colder than normal, separated by interglacial periods. The accumulation of snow and ice during a glacial period increases the surface albedo, reflecting more of the Sun's energy into space and maintaining a lower atmospheric temperature. Increases in greenhouse gases, such as by volcanic activity, can increase the global temperature and produce an interglacial. Suggested causes of ice age periods include the positions of the continents, variations in the Earth's orbit, changes in the solar output, and vulcanism.

Climate Models

Climate models use quantitative methods to simulate the interactions of the atmosphere, oceans, land surface and ice. They are used for a variety of purposes from study of the dynamics of the weather and climate system to projections of future climate. All climate models balance, or very nearly balance, incoming energy as short wave (including visible) electromagnetic radiation to the earth with outgoing energy as long wave (infrared) electromagnetic radiation from the earth. Any imbalance results in a change in the average temperature of the earth.

The most talked-about models of recent years have been those used to infer the consequences of increasing greenhouse gases in the atmosphere, primarily carbon dioxide. These models predict an upward trend in the global mean surface temperature, with the most rapid increase in temperature being projected for the higher latitudes of the Northern Hemisphere.

Models can range from relatively simple to quite complex:

- Simple radiant heat transfer model that treats the earth as a single point and averages outgoing energy
- this can be expanded vertically (radiative-convective models), or horizontally
- finally, (coupled) atmosphere–ocean–sea ice global climate models discretise and solve the full equations for mass and energy transfer and radiant exchange.

Atmosphere

An atmosphere is a layer of gases that may surround a material body of sufficient mass, by the gravity of the body, and are retained for a longer duration if gravity is high and the atmosphere's temperature is low. Some planets consist mainly of various gases, but only their outer layer is their atmosphere.

The term stellar atmosphere describes the outer region of a star, and typically includes the portion starting from the opaque photosphere outwards. Relatively low-temperature stars may form compound molecules in their outer atmosphere. Earth's atmosphere, which contains oxygen used by most organisms for respiration and carbon dioxide used by plants, algae and cyanobacteria for photosynthesis, also protects living organisms from genetic damage by solar ultraviolet radiation. Its current composition is the product of billions of years of biochemical modification of the paleoatmosphere by living organisms.

Pressure

Atmospheric pressure is the force per unit area that is applied perpendicularly to a surface by the surrounding gas. It is determined by a planet's gravitational force in combination with the total mass of a column of air above a location. Units of air pressure are based on the internationally-recognized standard atmosphere (atm), which is defined as 101,325 Pa (or 1,013,250 dynes per cm^2).

The pressure of an atmospheric gas decreases with altitude due to the diminishing mass of gas above each location. The height at which the pressure from an atmosphere declines by a factor of e (an irrational number with a value of 2.71828..) is called the scale height and is denoted by H. For an atmosphere with a uniform temperature, the scale height is proportional to the temperature and inversely proportional to the mean molecular mass of dry air times the planet's gravitational acceleration. For such a model atmosphere, the pressure declines exponentially with increasing altitude. However, atmospheres are not uniform in temperature, so the exact determination of the atmospheric pressure at any particular altitude is more complex.

Escape

Surface gravity, the force that holds down an atmosphere, differs significantly among the planets. For example, the large gravitational force of the giant planet Jupiter is able to retain light gases such as hydrogen and helium that escape from lower gravity objects. Second, the distance from the sun determines the energy available to heat atmospheric gas to the point where its molecules' thermal motion exceed the planet's escape velocity, the speed at which gas molecules overcome a planet's gravitational grasp. Thus, the distant and cold Titan, Triton, and Pluto are able to retain their atmospheres despite relatively low gravities. Interstellar planets, theoretically, may also retain thick atmospheres.

Since a gas at any particular temperature will have molecules moving at a wide range of velocities, there will almost always be some slow leakage of gas into space. Lighter molecules move faster than heavier ones with the same thermal kinetic energy, and so gases of low molecular weight are lost more rapidly than those of high molecular weight. It is thought that Venus and Mars may have both lost much of their water when, after being photodissociated into hydrogen and oxygen by solar ultraviolet, the hydrogen escaped. Earth's magnetic field helps to prevent this, as, normally, the solar wind would greatly enhance the escape of hydrogen. However, over the past 3 billion years the Earth may have lost gases through the magnetic polar regions due to auroral activity, including a net 2% of its atmospheric oxygen. Other mechanisms that can cause atmosphere depletion are solar wind-induced sputtering, impact erosion, weathering, and sequestration — sometimes referred to as "freezing out" — into the regolith and polar caps.

Composition

Initial atmospheric makeup is generally related to the chemistry and temperature of the local solar nebula during planetary formation and the subsequent escape of interior gases. These original atmospheres underwent much evolution over time, with the varying properties of each planet resulting in very different outcomes. The atmospheres of the planets Venus and Mars are primarily composed of carbon dioxide, with small quantities of nitrogen, argon, oxygen and traces of other gases.

The atmospheric composition on Earth is largely governed by the by-products of the very life that it sustains. Earth's atmosphere contains roughly (by molar content/volume) 78.09% nitrogen, 20.95% oxygen, a variable amount (average around 0.247%, National Centre for Atmospheric Research) water vapor, 0.93% argon, 0.038% carbon dioxide, and traces of hydrogen, helium, and other "noble" gases. The low temperatures and higher gravity of the gas giants — Jupiter, Saturn, Uranus and Neptune — allows them to more readily retain gases with low molecular masses. These planets have hydrogen-helium atmospheres, with trace amounts of more complex compounds.

Two satellites of the outer planets possess non-negligible atmospheres: Titan, a moon of Saturn, and Triton, a moon of Neptune, which are mainly nitrogen. Pluto, in the nearer part of its orbit, has an atmosphere of nitrogen and methane similar to Triton's, but these gases are frozen when farther from the Sun. Other bodies within the Solar System have extremely thin atmospheres not in equilibrium. These include the Moon (sodium gas), Mercury (sodium gas), Europa (oxygen), Io (sulfur), and Enceladus (water vapor).

The atmospheric composition of an extra-solar planet was first determined using the Hubble Space Telescope. Planet HD 209458b is a gas giant with a close orbit around a star in the constellation Pegasus. The atmosphere is heated to temperatures over 1,000 K, and is steadily escaping into space. Hydrogen, oxygen, carbon and sulfur have been detected in the planet's inflated atmosphere.

Structure

Earth: The Earth's atmosphere consists, from the ground up, of the troposphere (which includes the planetary boundary layer or peplosphere as lowest layer), stratosphere (which includes the ozone layer), mesosphere, thermosphere (which contains the ionosphere), exosphere and also the magnetosphere. Each of the layers has a different lapse rate, defining the rate of change in temperature with height.

Three quarters of the atmosphere lies within the troposphere, and the depth of this layer varies between 17 km at the equator and 7 km at the poles. The ozone layer, which absorbs ultraviolet energy from the Sun, is located primarily in the stratosphere, at altitudes of 15 to 35 km. The Karman line, located within the thermosphere at an altitude of 100 km, is commonly used to define the boundary between the Earth's atmosphere and outer space. However, the exosphere can extend from 500 up to 10,000 km above the surface, where it interacts with the planet's magnetosphere.

Circulation: The circulation of the atmosphere occurs due to thermal differences when convection becomes a more efficient transporter of heat than thermal radiation. On planets where the primary heat source is solar radiation, excess heat in the tropics is transported to higher latitudes. When a planet generates a significant amount of heat internally, such as is the case for Jupiter, convection in the atmosphere can transport thermal energy from the higher temperature interior up to the surface.

Importance

From the perspective of the planetary geologist, the atmosphere is an evolutionary agent essential to the morphology of a planet. The wind transports dust and other particles which erodes the relief and leaves deposits (eolian processes). Frost and precipitations, which depend on the composition, also influence the relief. Climate changes can influence a planet's geological history. Conversely, studying surface of earth leads to an understanding of the atmosphere and climate of a planet-both its present state and its past.

For a meteorologist, the composition of the atmosphere determines the climate and its variations.

For a biologist, the composition is closely dependent on the appearance of the life and its evolution.

BRANCHES OF GEOGRAPHY

Physical geography

Physical geography (or physiography) focuses on geography as an Earth science. It aims to understand the physical lithosphere, hydrosphere, atmosphere, pedosphere, and global flora and fauna patterns (biosphere).

Human geography

Human geography is a branch of geography that focuses on the study of patterns and processes that shape human interaction with various environments. It encompasses human, political, cultural, social, and economic aspects. While the major focus of human geography is not the physical landscape of the Earth, it is hardly possible to discuss human geography without referring to the physical landscape on which human activities are being played out, and environmental geography is emerging as a link between the two. Human geography can be divided into many broad categories.

Various approaches to the study of human geography have also arisen through time and include:

- Behavioural geography
- Feminist geography
- Culture theory
- Geosophy.

Environmental geography

Environmental geography is the branch of geography that describes the spatial aspects of interactions between humans and the natural world. It requires an understanding of the traditional aspects of physical and human geography, as well as the ways in which human societies conceptualize the environment.

Environmental geography has emerged as a bridge between human and physical geography as a result of the increasing specialisation of the two sub-fields. Furthermore, as human relationship with the environment has changed as a result of globalization and technological change a new approach was needed to understand the changing and dynamic relationship. Examples of areas of research in environmental geography include emergency management, environmental management, sustainability, and political ecology.

Geomatics

Geomatics is a branch of geography that has emerged since the quantitative revolution in geography in the mid 1950s. Geomatics involves the use of traditional spatial techniques used in cartography and topography and their application to computers. Geomatics has become a widespread field with many other disciplines using techniques such as GIS and remote sensing. Geomatics has also led to a revitalization of some geography departments especially in Northern America where the subject had a declining status during the 1950s. Geomatics encompasses a large area of fields involved with spatial analysis, such as Cartography, Geographic information systems (GIS), Remote sensing, and Global positioning systems (GPS).

Regional geography

Regional geography is a branch of geography that studies the regions of all sizes across the Earth. It has a prevailing descriptive character. The main aim is to understand or define the uniqueness or character of a particular region which consists of natural as well as human elements. Attention is paid also to regionalization which covers the proper techniques of space delimitation into regions. Regional geography is also considered as a certain approach to study in geographical sciences.

Related fields

- *Urban planning, regional planning and spatial planning*: use the science of geography to assist in determining how to develop (or not develop) the land to meet particular criteria, such as safety, beauty, economic opportunities, the preservation of the built or natural heritage, and so on. The planning of towns, cities, and rural areas may be seen as applied geography.
- *Regional science*: In the 1950s the regional science movement led by Walter Isard arose, to provide a more quantitative and analytical base to geographical questions, in contrast to the descriptive tendencies of traditional geography programmes. Regional science comprises the body of knowledge in which the spatial dimension plays a fundamental role, such as regional economics, resource management, location theory, urban and regional planning, transport and communication, human geography, population distribution, landscape ecology, and environmental quality.
- *Interplanetary Sciences*: While the discipline of geography is normally concerned with the Earth, the term can also be informally used to describe the study of other worlds, such as the planets of the Solar System and even beyond. The study of systems larger than the earth itself usually forms part of Astronomy or Cosmology. The study of other planets is usually called planetary science. Alternative terms such as Areology (the study of Mars) have been proposed, but are not widely used.

TECHNIQUES OF GEOGRAPHY

As spatial interrelationships are key to this synoptic science, maps are a key tool. Classical cartography has been joined by a more modern approach to geographical analysis, computer-based geographic information systems (GIS).

In their study, geographers use four interrelated approaches:

- *Systematic*: Groups geographical knowledge into categories that can be explored globally.
- *Regional*: Examines systematic relationships between categories for a specific region or location on the planet.
- *Descriptive*: Simply specifies the locations of features and populations.
- *Analytical*: Asks why we find features and populations in a specific geographic area.

Cartography

Cartography studies the representation of the Earth's surface with abstract symbols (map making). Although other subdisciplines of geography rely on maps for presenting their analyses, the actual making of maps is abstract enough to be regarded separately.

Cartography has grown from a collection of drafting techniques into an actual science. Cartographers must learn cognitive psychology and ergonomics to understand which symbols convey information about the Earth most effectively, and behavioural psychology to induce the readers of their maps to act on the information.

They must learn geodesy and fairly advanced mathematics to understand how the shape of the Earth affects the distortion of map symbols projected onto a flat surface for viewing. It can be said, without much controversy, that cartography is the seed from which the larger field of geography grew. Most geographers will cite a childhood fascination with maps as an early sign they would end up in the field.

Geographic information systems

Geographic information systems (GIS) deal with the storage of information about the Earth for automatic retrieval by a computer, in an accurate manner appropriate to the information's purpose. In addition to all of the other subdisciplines of geography, GIS specialists must understand computer science and database systems.

GIS has revolutionized the field of cartography; nearly all mapmaking is now done with the assistance of some form of GIS software. GIS also refers to the science of using GIS software and GIS techniques to represent, analyse and predict spatial relationships. In this context, GIS stands for Geographic Information Science.

Remote sensing

Remote sensing is the science of obtaining information about Earth features from measurements made at a distance. Remotely sensed data comes in many forms such as satellite imagery, aerial photography and data obtained from hand-held sensors.

Geographers increasingly use remotely sensed data to obtain information about the Earth's land surface, ocean and atmosphere because it:

- Supplies objective information at a variety of spatial scales (local to global),
- Provides a synoptic view of the area of interest,
- Allows access to distant and/or inaccessible sites,

- Provides spectral information outside the visible portion of the electromagnetic spectrum, and
- Facilitates studies of how features/areas change over time.

Remotely sensed data may be analysed either independently of, or in conjunction with, other digital data layers (*e.g.*, in a Geographic Information System).

Quantitative methods

Geostatistics deal with quantitative data analysis, specifically the application of statistical methodology to the exploration of geographic phenomena. Geostatistics is used extensively in a variety of fields including: hydrology, geology, petroleum exploration, weather analysis, urban planning, logistics, and epidemiology.

The mathematical basis for geostatistics derives from cluster analysis, linear discriminant analysis and non-parametric statistical tests, and a variety of other subjects. Applications of geostatistics rely heavily on geographic information systems, particularly for the interpolation (estimate) of unmeasured points. Geographers are making notable contributions to the method of quantitative techniques.

Qualitative methods

Geographic qualitative methods, or ethnographical; research techniques, are used by human geographers. In cultural geography there is a tradition of employing qualitative research techniques also used in anthropology and sociology. Participant observation and in-depth interviews provide human geographers with qualitative data.

THE LANGUAGE OF GEOGRAPHY

Geography is the study of Earth, its lands, features, and inhabitants. Just about every subject, from science to sports, has its own language. Geography has its own language too. In order to understand a subject, you need to understand the terms used by that subject. Geography has many different terms. Latitude and longitude are two such terms. Latitudes are imaginary lines that circle the earth and are parallel to the equator. The equator is the zero degree latitude line. Lines of latitude are measured my degrees.

These degrees represent the degree from the equator to the poles. The north pole is located at 90 degrees or 90 degrees North Latitude; the south pole is located at -90 degrees or 90 degrees South Latitude. Longitude lines are imaginary lines that run from the north pole to the south pole. These lines are further apart at the equator and get closer together as they near the poles. Longitude is usually referenced from Greenwich, England.

This is because the 0 degree lone of longitude passes through Greenwich. This line of 0 degrees longitude is known as the prime meridian. In this context, prime means first or most important. The prime meridian is the most important meridian because all distances east or west are measured from this line. The location of the prime meridian was agreed upon by geographers from around the world. They met in 1884 in Washington, D.C. They could have chosen a different meridian to represent 0 degrees longitude, but they chose this line because it passed through the location of a famous observatory. Since many of the people were familiar with the location of Greenwich, it was chosen as the reference point for all other meridians.

There are 360 degrees around Earth, but generally, points are referenced as 180 degrees east of Greenwich (or +180 degrees) or 180 degrees west of Greenwich (or -180 degrees). Remember that latitude and longitude lines circle the earth. This means that if you were to follow the Prime Meridian (0 degrees) from Greenwich to a corresponding point on the other side of the globe, you would now be on a meridian that is 180 degrees from the Prime Meridian. Degrees can be further divided into minutes and seconds.

There are 60 seconds in a minute and 60 minutes in a degree. These additional divisions allow geographers to pinpoint a location more exactly. A hemisphere is a term that refers to half of the Earth. The hemispheres of Earth are the Western Hemisphere, the Eastern Hemisphere, the Northern Hemisphere, and the Southern Hemisphere. The Western Hemisphere is a term used to represent the half of Earth that lies to the west of the Prime Meridian.

The Eastern Hemisphere refers to the half of Earth that lies to the east of the Prime Meridian. The Northern Hemisphere refers to the half of Earth that lies north of the equator. The Southern Hemisphere refers to the half of Earth that lies south of the Equator.

These different terms provide a starting point for geographers to reference the same points by using the same terms and commonly accepted reference points. Without these agreed upon terms and reference points, geographers would have to spend a lot of time explaining the terms that they are using. These agreed upon terms allow geographers to spend more time on their studies and discussing their points instead of arguing over where a particular reference point is.

FOREST VEGETATION OF INDIA

Forest Survey of India estimates the forest cover of the country at "63.73 million ha constituting 19.39% of the geographic area of the country out of which 37.74 million ha (11.48%) is dense forest, 25.50 million ha (7.76%) open forest and 0.49 million ha (0.15%) mangroves. Madhya Pradesh accounts for the largest forest cover of the country i.e. 20.68% followed by Arunachal Pradesh (10.80%), Orissa (7.38%), Maharashtra (7.32%) and Andhra Pradesh (6.94%). The seven North-Eastern states together comprise 25.70% of the total forest cover."

An FSI report notes that the forest coverage of the country has shown a net increase of 3,3896 sq km during the period from 1997 (year of last survey conducted) to 1999. It was found out that the area of dense forest has increased by 10,098 sq.km; that of mangroves by 44 sq km. However the increase in the forest coverage is not uniform for all the states. Some states registered a net gain in the forest area while others show a declining trend.

For instance, " in Andhra Pradesh, net increase of 939 sq.km. in forest cover has occurred in 5 years (1993-98), whereas in Mizoram, loss of 437 sq.km has occurred in 4 years (1994-98). Other states where gains have been recorded are; Arunachal Pradesh, Gujarat, Haryana, Himachal Pradesh, Karnataka, Madhya Pradesh, Maharashtra Orissa, Punjab, Rajasthan Tripura, U.P., West Bengal and Delhi. The states where forest cover has declined are Assam, Bihar, Goa, Mizoram, Kerala, Manipur, Meghalaya, Nagaland, Sikkim, Andaman and Nicobar Islands and Dadar Nagar Haveli."

The FSI observes that the reasons for gains and losses are varied and many. Inclusion of established large block plantations in the forest cover, improvement in the density of forest due to Joint Forest Management and natural regeneration of mangroves have been instrumental in the increasing of forest area. Negative growth are attributed to shifting cultivation, encroachment and tree fellings.

THE CHARACTER OF GEOGRAPHY IN RELATION TO THE GENERAL NATURE OF SCIENCE

To understand the character of geography as a field in which knowledge is acquired, it is necessary to understand the essential character of the whole field of knowledge of which it is a part. We are concerned here, not with all knowledge, but with that sort of knowledge—by whatever name one chooses to call it—that is distinguished from either commonsense knowledge or from artistic perception "by the rigour with which it subordinates all other considerations to the pursuit of the ideals of certainty, exactness, universality and system".

Geography attempts to acquire knowledge of the world in which we live, both facts and relationships, which shall be as objective and accurate as possible. It seeks to present that knowledge in the form of concepts, relationships, and principles that shall, as far as possible, apply to all parts of the world. Finally it seeks to organize the dependable knowledge so obtained in logical systems, reduced by mutual connections into as small a number of independent systems as possible. It is in terms of the manner in which geography pursues these ideals that we attempt to describe its character as a field of study.

It should be noted, in general, that our definition of the kind of knowledge of which geography is a part is based not on what is known, that is, on what has been learned, but rather on the pursuit of knowledge—*i.e.*, the fundamental principles governing the manner in which the unknown is to be learned. Different branches of this "kind of knowledge" differ in the degree to which they have been able to approach the ideals stated; no branch of science can claim to have attained perfect certainty or exactness, actual universality, or complete organization of all its knowledge in a single system.

If one compares these ideals, as the fundamental requirements for that form of knowledge, which hereafter for convenience we will call "science," with the ideals of artistic perception (in whatever form one finds them stated by students of art), it is clear that there can be no logical combination of the two and no transition from one to the other. The artist certainly does not subordinate all other considerations to an ideal of exactness, nor to one of certainty. He may require that his work express a fundamental universality but that concept does not control the details of his work. Likewise he may require that an individual work of art should be organized, but does not seek a common organization of all similar works of art. In other words, we are dealing here with two essentially different approaches; both artists and geographers may attempt to acquire and present knowledge of an area of the earth, but neither can adopt the ideals of the other without sacrificing his own [*cf.* Kraft, *166*, 20 of.].

That geography seeks to make its own knowledge of the world as accurate and certain as possible is an assumption which presumably would not be questioned by professional geographers. It is not, however, a correct corollary of this assumption that geography should arbitrarily limit itself to particular kinds of facts because they appear to be subject to more accurate and certain means of measurement than others. Even if it were possible to demonstrate—as would not be the case—that the facts and relationships of immaterial phenomena could never be determined as accurately or certainly as those of either visible or material phenomena, no principle of science would require us to limit ourselves to those phenomena that could be studied somewhat more accurately and certainly, excluding those that could be studied somewhat less accurately and certainly. On the contrary, in order that our knowledge of, say, the cultural character of an area may be made as certain as possible, we are required to consider all the facts that bear upon that knowledge, whether the material products of cultural ideas or the immaterial manifestations of those ideas. Both sets of facts must, of course, be observed as accurately and certainly as possible.

Likewise these ideals admit no limitation in the specific methods of observation in geography, but rather require that we utilize all methods that will lead to more accurate and certain knowledge.

Thus, because statistical data are neither sufficiently accurate nor sufficiently detailed, we must employ the technique of field work—both direct observation and personal interview—to check and supplement the knowledge gained from statistical data. On the other hand, even if it were physically possible to make a complete field observation of every part of a region, the observations obtained reflect temporal conditions, commonly of a single season, which, as R. E. Dodge noted, may lead to erroneous generalizations concerning the continuous use of the land. Consequently the findings of field observations must be checked with statistical data, even though these were very indirectly based on observation.

The scientific ideal of certainty commands that the terms and concepts of description and relationships be made both as specific and as certain as possible—we cannot develop a sound structure on a marsh foundation in which ambiguous concepts shift their meaning whenever pressure is applied to them, and concepts apparently specific prove to be but dubious analogies.

The ideals of accuracy and certainty apply not only to the manner in which primary facts are established and to the formulation of fundamental concepts and technical terms, but also to the processes of mathematical and logical reasoning by means of which we induce relationships of observed facts, and thereby deduce further conclusions as to facts. When a single student studies a particular scientific problem, no matter how hard he strives to live up to these ideals, no matter how critically he examines his own hard work, there remains the possibility of error, whether through carelessness or through subjective influences affecting his observations and reasonings.

Since this is a generally accepted axiom in those sciences whose facts can be measured with the highest degree of accuracy and whose relatively simple phenomena make logical reasoning most certain, how much more uncertain are the findings of one student in geography! In order to make possible a higher degree of accuracy and certainty, therefore, it is a recognized principle of all science that studies should be carried on, organized, and presented in such a manner as to provide an accumulation of evidence of different students on the same problem. Every scientific study should, that is, by which we mean both that it should make use of all previous scholarly studies bearing on the problem and that it should be presented in a form usable by subsequent students.

It is one of the handicaps of the social sciences, and in part also of geography, that in much of their work it is not possible for later students to have access to the primary data used in any study; much must be taken on faith in the professional ability and reliability of the individual student.

Consequently it is all the more essential in these fields that similar studies of other students should be utilized and referred to, not as a matter of professional courtesy, but for the sake of accumulating evidence in order that results may be more certain.

Science will accept on faith from any scientist no more than is absolutely necessary. In order that subsequent students may reexamine the findings of a particular study—whether in order to utilize them further or simply to check or correct them—it is essential that there be a clear understanding of the generic concepts employed, of the methods of observation and reasoning by which the results were obtained, and, finally, of the relation of the study to the field as a whole. Obviously such a clear understanding will be easiest if the field has developed standard techniques and organization; if it has not, they must be specifically indicated in each study.

It is not the function of this paper to pass judgment on the scientific quality of work actually produced by geographers—it is their ideas about the nature of geography, and the consequences of those ideas that concern us. On the letter basis, however, it is a fair question to raise, whether the research publications in geography indicate that either geographers in general, or the editors who, to some extent, control their publications, have accepted these standards as essential to geography—standards dictated by the scientific ideals of accuracy and certainty.

With the respect to these ideals as essential principles in the pursuit of knowledge. there can be no differences among the different branches of science, but only differences in degree of attainment. Undoubtedly the attainments of geography in this respect are not of such a high degree as to tempt us to compare it with other sciences in such terms. But neither need we feel humiliated if those who choose to make such comparisons should assign our field to the "lower classes." In any competition the understanding observer will judge attainments not only in terms of degree of success but also in terms of the relative difficulties of the tasks undertaken.

The consideration of the manner in which geography may pursue the other two scientific ideals, universality and system, is of the greatest importance in understanding the character of geography as a field of study. Since these are not so readily understood as the two ideals which we have just considered, each will require detailed consideration.

3

Housing Geography

INTRODUCTION

Geography is a subject that above all helps us 'make sense of the world'. You could say that all subjects contribute to this – history, science, art... they all contribute to making sense of the world in some way. However, geography (literally, writing the world) has a particular take on this. As Ron Johnston wrote some time ago, geography studies 'the earth as the home of mankind'.

Or as Peter Taylor says, geography is the 'world subject'. You cannot take the 'geo' out of geography – the physical shape and the form the earth takes (as a whole, or in your back garden!) – and Rachel Atherton's focus on the physical world is important for the balance of this book. Neither can you take out the people who occupy the earth's *space*, and who help to shape it. In doing so, they make particular *places* through their economic, social and cultural activity.

Thus, geography takes a particular interest in the twin ideas of place and space.

The idea of 'place' Every place has a particular location and a *unique set* of physical and human characteristics.

Furthermore, the same place can be *represented* differently. Places are dynamic and subject to constant change. What we think about places is both shaped by, and shapes, our *'geographical imagination'*.

Unique – real places, with all their similarities and differences, are unique. No two places are exactly the same. This does not mean that geographers study places one after the other as singular entities. There are universal needs and global processes that impact everywhere – but they play out differently from place to place in the detail.

Represented – many places can simultaneously be represented differently. For example, a city can be described as an industrial heartland, a shopping heaven or tourist resort. Places can be represented in certain ways for specific purposes. Sometimes there are unintended consequences of representing places in certain ways: for example, what do we mean to convey by the term 'inner city'? (Dan Raven-Ellison explores these ideas of representing places to young people.)

Dynamic-places change; they have not always been like this. Geography has a role to play in teaching students to understand this, the potential of places to be different in the future.

Geographical imaginations – the ways individuals think about places depend to a large extent on the knowledge and understanding they have at their disposal – but also what they make of the images they and what they associate with the new or the strange. We all carry a great deal of 'geography' in our head. It (almost) goes without saying that the best way to study place is to do so directly – by getting 'out there' to experience and sense the world, and to try our best to interpret what we observe. (Andrew Turney focuses on young people's engagement with fieldwork as do others in parts of the chapters which follow.) The main purpose of doing this is to understand a place, or process, or feature, sometimes with a view to imagining, or envisioning, alternatives. What is this place like? What do I feel about this place? How could it change? It is this kind of thinking that David Hicks had in mind when he wrote that geography is the 'first curriculum subject to take (alternative) futures seriously'.

The Idea of 'Space'

Most phenomena (eg physical features, people, services, goods) are located and are distributed in space. They therefore have relative *locations* to each other and often *interact* with each other across space. Any *flows* or movements between these phenomena create *patterns and networks.* Spatial patterns, distributions and networks can be described and analysed, and often explained by reference to social, economic, environmental and political processes.

Location – the Ordnance Survey has estimated that 80 per cent of information can be located – that is, it can be mapped. In some ways this 'fact' alone expresses the importance of 'spatial literacy' as a part of geography – for if we can locate phenomena using coordinates, we can also study their relative locations too.

Interact – this we do by studying layers of different information and seeking relationships – interactions – between the layers. Ultimately this may lead to undertaking spatial analysis using geographic information systems (GIS). The ability to recognise, interpret and understand spatial patterns, distributions and relationships is an aspect of spatial awareness, and is nurtured through geographical enquiry.

Flows – the movement of phenomena through space, eg migration. Flows are often expressive of links that exist between locations and contribute to the pattern of networks that bind social and economic systems, eg trade links.

Patterns and networks – these are often describable and often display predic characteristics, eg as shown by gravity models, giving concrete expression to ideas such as the 'friction of distance'. Distribution patterns are often uneven, eg the distribution of wealth at a global or national scale, or within the confines of a single city. It is possible to seek explanations for the patterns described by reference to the social, economic or environmental processes at work.

Part of the power of geography is realising the limits (as well as the usefulness) of the 'spatial science' perspective – or at least its dangers. Many geographers have expressed concern over 'spatial fetishism' which may result if we think that space itself has properties (beyond the fairly obvious, like distance) leading us to imagine 'spatial processes' at work.

This is a dubious idea. There certainly are economic, social, cultural and environmental processes that operate, often with spatially differentiated outcomes. But space can be *used* too. It can be manipulated, for example, by capitalists seeking the lowest labour costs in order to maximise returns. There is no doubt that space is, in Thrift's words '(t)he fundamental stuff of human geography' and needs thinking carefully about: 'As with terms like "society" and "nature", space is not (just) a commonsense external background to human and social action.' There is a third big idea that provides geography with its fundamental architecture, influencing profoundly what we 'see' when studying place and space, and this is scale.

The idea of 'scale' Scale influences the way we represent what we see or experience. We can construct different resolutions of scale from the *personal, local* and *regional* to the *global*. In between, we have the *national* and international scales. These are very important politically and, like the others, exert great influence on the identity of individuals and groups. Choice of scale is therefore important in geographical enquiry, as is the realisation that scale resolutions are *interconnected*, as if by a single zoom lens.

Personal – the personal scale refers to personal space – the 'bubble' in which people are sometimes said to live – the world they inhabit in their person, and how they perceive the world.

Local – this is sometimes expressed as the *scale of experience*, and in school geography has given rise to 'locality studies' in which the focus of study is the daily lives of people – where they live, the work they do, where they shop and play.

Regional – this is a wider frame of reference, often resting on administrative concerns (such as the planning regions of England), but sometimes strongly associated with identity and linked to landscape or heritage (including, for example, former economic activity such a heavy engineering or mining). Many geographers would argue that regions provide a fundamental unit of study for geography, enabling us to classify and organise the world for descriptive and analytical purposes.

National – this has been expressed as the *scale of ideology*, in the sense that this is the political context in which people live as citizens in a relationship with a state or government. The borders of nations change, frequently as a result of violent conflict. Territories are often disputed, not least when valuable resources are at stake, such as oil or water. Even the idea can be debated in geography, for idea of 'nation' is not straightforward – and does not always coincide with 'state'. Thus, most children in English schools today express multiple identities. Although 'British' may be on their passports, they may think of themselves, for example, as Bangladeshi, English, Irish, Jamaican, Pakistani, Scottish or Welsh – or European, Asian, Islamic... or more likely a combination of these categories (and many more besides).

Global – the global scale has become ever more present in people's minds since the Apollo photographs of 1969 – and now with Google Earth. The global scale has been dubbed the *scale of reality* in the sense that economic, environmental, political and social processes operate on a global scale. We cannot fully understand High Street shopping in our locality, or industrial change in a region or country, without comprehending the global context in which decisions are made.

Interconnectedness – virtually any topic, when studied geographically, benefits from a 'scaled' approach. In essence this implies study at a range of scales so that ideas of global interconnectedness can be developed.

Place, space and scale are arguably the three really big ideas that underpin school geography. Opening up these ideas a little, as in the above, quickly shows their scope and potential. We can see the relevance of being able to 'think geographically' to anyone living in the world and wanting to understand and respond to the challenges facing them during the 21st century.

Over the years there have been many authoritative appeals for the spirit and purpose of geography. Often these are made slightly defensively: it is so obvious what the power of geography is, so why doesn't everyone see it! One reason for this is the confused identity geography has, particularly between the *academic* discipline (in all its diversity and seemingly anarchic specialisms), *school* geography (with its clear imperative to serve educational aims and purposes) and the subject that resides in the *popular* imagination (emphasising factual knowledge and sustained through quiz shows and such like).

GEOGRAPHY – MEANING AND DEFINITIONS

Geography is the study of the Earth and its lands, features, inhabitants, and phenomena. A literal translation would be "to describe or write about the

Earth". The first person to use the word "geography" was Eratosthenes (276-194 B.C.). Four historical traditions in geographical research are the spatial analysis of natural and human phenomena (geography as a study of distribution), area studies (places and regions), study of man-land relationship, and research in earth sciences. Nonetheless, modern geography is an all-encompassing discipline that foremost seeks to understand the Earth and all of its human and natural complexities—not merely where objects are, but how they have changed and come to be.

As "the bridge between the human and physical sciences," geography is divided into two main branches—human geography and physical geography. Traditionally, geographers have been viewed the same way as cartographers and people who study place names and numbers. Although many geographers are trained in toponymy and cartology, this is not their main preoccupation.

Geographers study the spatial and temporal distribution of phenomena, processes and features as well as the interaction of humans and their environment. As space and place affect a variety of topics such as economics, health, climate, plants and animals, geography is highly interdisciplinary.

> *"...mere names of places...are not geography...know by heart a whole gazetteer full of them would not, in itself, constitute anyone a geographer. Geography has higher aims than this: it seeks to classify phenomena (alike of the natural and of the political world, in so far as it treats of the latter), to compare, to generalize, to ascend from effects to causes, and, in doing so, to trace out the great laws of nature and to mark their influences upon man. This is 'a description of the world'—that is Geography. In a word Geography is a Science—a thing not of mere names but of argument and reason, of cause and effect." —William Hughes, 1863*

Geography as a discipline can be split broadly into two main sub fields: human geography and physical geography. The former focuses largely on the built environment and how space is created, viewed and managed by humans as well as the influence humans have on the space they occupy. The latter examines the natural environment and how the climate, vegetation & life, soil, water, and landforms are produced and interact. As a result of the two subfields using different approaches a third field has emerged, which is environmental geography. Environmental geography combines physical and human geography and looks at the interactions between the environment and humans.

IMPORTANCE OF GEOGRAPHY AND ITS PLACE IN CURRICULUM

At present geography is one of the important subjects in school curriculum. Geography derives a lot of material from such subjects as Biology,

Anthropology, Sociology, Economics, Mathematics, Chemistry and other sciences. The subject matter of geography includes study of natural environment of man and also the study of social and cultural environment. Thus geography has a very wide scope unparalleled by any other subject.

Geography is a science and an art. It tries to train and develop good citizens who may be able to solve various social economic and political problems of the country. The importance of geography can be understood more clearly by considering the effect of geography teaching on man as a human being, as an administrator, as a politician etc. We shall also have to consider the practical importance of geography, Economic importance geography, political and social importance, cultural and intellectual importance etc. The importance of geography is discussed under various heads in the following pages.

(i) *Importance of Geography for Administrators and Politicians:* To run the administration efficiently it is essential for the administrator to have a thorough knowledge of the geography of the country. In the absence of a knowledge of geographical conditions of a country it becomes difficult to run the administration efficiently. Geographical factors affect the Economic, political and social life of the inhabitants of an area. From a knowledge of geography it becomes easier to know about inter-dependence of people of various countries. In the present age no country can live without taking help from other countries and to have a proper and coordial relationship the knowledge of geography is quite helpful. The administrators in a developed country are on the look out for a country where their finished and manufactured goods may find a good market. In this adventure the knowledge of geographical conditions of a country are quite handy to the administrator. Such a knowledge can help the administrator to establish beneficial relationship with other countries and their neighbouring world.

(ii) *Political Importance:* To gain in political importance the knowledge of geography of other countries is essential for any country and even for an individual. It is only by the knowledge of geographical conditions that we develop sympathy for any particular country. For example if you happen to live in a fertile country it would not be difficult for you to imagine the plight of a fellow being living in a desert. Thus the knowledge of geography helps to bring about the world together and in this way it helps to solve a number of political problems. Thus knowledge of geography is of political importance.

(iii) *Practical Importance:* A knowledge of geography is quite handy to prepare the students to face various problems of life. If a student is familiar with the natural conditions of a country, its climate, vegetation, natural resources, mineral wealth etc., then it becomes easier for him to plan his future. Such a knowledge can be of much help to would be industrialists of a country and a student of geography interested in setting up an industry after the completion of his education can make a better selection for the location of his industrial unit keeping in mind the natural resources needed. The knowledge of geography is also helpful to an individual in developing social, political and economic relationships with the other countries. Thus we find that the knowledge of geography has a practical utility.

(iv) *Cultural and Intellectual Importance of Geography:* A knowledge of geography helps us in acquiring the knowledge about cultural and intellectual life of a particular country and in this way it becomes easier to carry out a proper study of the cultural life of whole world.

The knowledge of geography also helps a student in developing his power of imagination and also encourages him to find out cause and effect of various phenomenon. When a student of geography learns about the mountains, rivers, forests etc. then a image of all these things is formed before him. When ever he actually comes across any of these things he can identify them and discern them easily. Such a knowledge helps the student to know about the cultures and civilisation of different countries.

Geographical factors also influence the intellectual life of a country so we can say that geography has an intellectual importance. In the words of Fairgrieve, *"The real value of geography lies in the fact that it helps man to place himself in the world to learn his true position and duties".*

(v) *Economic Importance:* Geography has its economical importance as well. Knowledge of geography helps us to know about various natural resources of a country or a region in a country. Such a knowledge can be used for the economic progress of a country or a region. We flourish in the world only if we have economic prosperity.

(vi) *Social Importance:* A knowledge of geography helps a student in developing a proper social outlook. A proper social outlook develops a feeling of brotherhood for the nationals of other countries and makes a student broad minded. He no more remains self-centred and he develops a feeling of world citizenship. Thus a knowledge of geography has *a* social importance.

(vii) *Importance for Earning a Livelihood:* We spend a major part of our life in earning our livelihood and the knowledge of geography can help us to a large extent in this. Such a knowledge is also helpful to us to utilise our leisure time in a beneficial way. It is the knowledge that we gained in geography about the things and conditions prevailing around us that help us in this. The knowledge of geography has given us the knowledge of various sources that are available and which could be profitable tapped to earn our livelihood.

(viii) *Natural Curiosity:* We have a natural curiosity to know more and more about the life style of people in other lands and countries. The knowledge of geography helps to satisfy this natural curiosity and also throws light on the various factors that influence our life style. Thus geography has a important role in satisfying our natural curiosities.

(ix) *Importance in Understanding Other Subjects:* A knowledge of geography helps us in understanding various other subjects (e.g. sociology, economics, Anthropology, Biology etc.) For example a knowledge of geography helps in understanding history because it provides the proper perspective. Various historical events have been influenced by geographical factors. The development of civilisation began in India and Egypt because of geographical reasons.

Geographical factors also influence the political system in a country. The prevalence of democracy in Switzerland is due to geographical factors. To acquire a thorough and proper knowledge of political science the knowledge of geography is essential. The social life and structure of society in a country is governed to a large extent by various geographical factors prevailing in that country. A knowledge of geography also helps to properly understand the subject matter of sociology. Thus we find that a knowledge of geography is important in understanding and acquiring the knowledge of various social sciences. Thus we find that geography occupies an important place in various fields of life. A knowledge of geography also inculcates a spirit of patriotism and internationalism. Because of this geography occupies an important place in primary, secondary and higher education. President Eisenhower of America called Geography the foundation of humanity. P.E. James gives the following reasons for the importance of geography.

(i) Geography helps us to have a proper picture of man and his environment.

(ii) Geography gives us information about various types of climates, natural conditions, mineral wealth etc. of the various nations.

(iii) With the knowledge of geography we can read and discern the maps, sketches, diagrams etc.

(iv) It develops our power of observation.

In view of Fairgrieve the two principles that make the knowledge of geography impertinent and important are as under:

We spend about 2/3rd of our life in dealing with our neighbours and countryman. In this period we perform the duties as good citizens. The knowledge of geography helps us in performance of these duties. A knowledge of geography comes handy to know about the economic needs of the people of other countries and such a knowledge helps the industrialists, agriculturists, politicians etc. in better performance of their job.

HOUSE

A house is a home, shelter, building or structure that is a dwelling or place for habitation by human beings. The term includes many kinds of dwellings ranging from rudimentary huts of nomadic tribes to free standing individual structures.

In some contexts, "house" may mean the same as dwelling, residence, home, abode, lodging, accommodation, or housing, among other meanings. The social unit that lives in a house is known as a household.

Most commonly, a household is a family unit of some kind, though households can be other social groups, such as single persons, or groups of unrelated individuals. Settled agrarian and industrial societies are composed of household units living permanently in housing of various types, according to a variety of forms of land tenure. English-speaking people generally call any building they routinely occupy "home". Many people leave their houses during the day for work and recreation, and return to them to sleep or for other activities.

History

The English word *house* is derived from the proto-Germanic *hud-dos*, thought possibly to be a derivative of the verbal root *hûd* 'to hide'. Terms in other languages show varying derivations.

The oldest house in the world is approximately from 10,000 BC and was made of mammoth bones, found at Mezhirich near Kiev in Ukraine. It was probably covered with mammoth hides. The house was discovered in 1965 by a farmer digging a new basement six feet below the ground.

Architect Norbert Schoenauer, in his book *6,000 Years of Housing*, identifies three major categories of types of housing: the "Pre-Urban" house, the "Oriental Urban" house, and the "Occidental Urban" house.

Types of Pre-Urban houses include temporary dwellings such as the Inuit igloo, semi-permanent dwellings such as the pueblo, and permanent dwellings such as the New England homestead. "Oriental Urban" houses include houses of the ancient Greeks and Romans, and traditional urban houses in China, India, and Islamic cities. "Occidental Urban" houses include medieval urban houses, the Renaissance town house, and the houses, tenements and apartments of the 19th and 20th centuries. Houses of that time were generally made of simple and raw materials (rocks, sticks, woven cloth, etc.)

Structure

The developed world in general features three basic types of house that have their own ground-level entry and private open space, and usually on a separately titled parcel of land:

- Single-family detached houses – free-standing on all sides.
- Semi-detached houses (duplexes) – houses that are attached, usually to only one other house via a party wall.
- Terraced house (UK), also known as a *row house* or *townhouse* – attached to other houses, possibly in a row, each separated by a party wall.

In addition, there are various forms of attached housing where a number of dwelling units are co-located within the same structure, which share a ground-level entry and may or may not have any private open space, such as apartments (a.k.a. flats) of various scales. Another type of housing is movable, such as houseboats, caravans, and trailer homes.

In the United Kingdom, 27% of the population live in terraced houses and 32% in semi-detached houses, as of 2002. In the United States as of 2000, 61.4% of people live in detached houses and 5.6% in semi-detached houses, 26% in row houses or apartments, and 7% in mobile homes.

Function

Some houses transcend the basic functionality of providing "a roof over one's head" or of serving as a family "hearth and home". When a house becomes a display-case for wealth and/or fashion and/or conspicuous consumption, we may speak of a "great house".

The residence of a feudal lord or of a ruler may require defensive structures and thus turn into a fort or a castle. The house of a monarch may come to house courtiers and officers as well as the royal family: this sort of house may become a palace.

Moreover, in time the lord or monarch may wish to retreat to a more personal or simple space such as a villa, a hunting lodge or a dacha. Compare the popularity of the holiday house or cottage, also known as a crib.

In contrast to a relatively upper class or modern trend to ownership of multiple houses, much of human history shows the importance of multi-purpose houses. Thus the house long served as the traditional place of work (the original cottage industry site or "in-house" small-scale manufacturing workshop) or of commerce (featuring, for example, a ground floor "shop-front" shop or counter or office, with living space above). During the Industrial Revolution there was a separation of manufacturing and banking from the house, though to this day some shopkeepers continue (or have returned) to live "over the shop".

INSIDE THE HOUSE

Layout

Ideally, architects of houses design rooms to meet the needs of the people who will live in the house. Such designing, known as "interior design", has become a popular subject in universities.

Feng shui, originally a Chinese method of situating houses according to such factors as sunlight and micro-climates, has recently expanded its scope to address the design of interior spaces with a view to promoting harmonious effects on the people living inside the house. Feng shui can also mean the "aura" in or around a dwelling. Compare the real-estate sales concept of "indoor-outdoor flow".

The square footage of a house in the United States reports the area of "living space", excluding the garage and other non-living spaces. The "square metres" figure of a house in Europe reports the area of the walls enclosing the home, and thus includes any attached garage and non-living spaces.

Parts

Many houses have several rooms with specialized functions. These may include a living/eating area, a sleeping area, and (if suitable facilities and services exist) washing and lavatory areas. In traditional agriculture-oriented societies, domestic animals such as chickens or larger livestock (like cattle) often share part of the house with human beings.

Most conventional modern houses will at least contain a bedroom, bathroom, kitchen (or kitchen area), and a living room.

A typical "foursquare house" (as pictured) occurred commonly in the early history of the United States of America where they were mainly built, with a staircase in the centre of the house, surrounded by four rooms, and connected to other sections of the house (including in more recent eras a garage).

The names of parts of a house often echo the names of parts of other buildings, but could typically include:

Atrium

In modern architecture, an atrium (plural atria) is a large open space, often several storeys high and having a glazed roof and/or large windows, often situated within an office building and usually located immediately beyond the main entrance doors. Atria are popular with companies because they give their buildings "a feeling of space and light", but have been criticised by fire inspectors as they could allow fire to spread to a building's upper storeys more quickly.

History

The Latin word *atrium* referred to the open central court, from which the enclosed rooms led off, in the type of large ancient Roman house known as a domus.

The impluvium was the shallow pool sunken into the floor to catch the rainwater. Some surviving examples are beautifully decorated. The opening in the ceiling above the pool called for some means of support for the roof. And it is here where one differentiates between five different styles of atrium. As the centrepiece of the house the atrium was the most lavishly furnished room. Also, it contained the little chapel to the ancestral spirits (lararium), the household safe (arca) and sometimes a bust of the master of the house. The term was also used for a variety of spaces in public and religious buildings, mostly forms of arcaded courtyards, larger versions of the domestic spaces. Byzantine churches were often entered through such a space (as are many mosques, though the term is not usually used for Islamic architecture.

Tallest Atrium

As of 2007, Dubai's Burj Al Arab, has the tallest atrium. The Burj Al Arab was built to impress and to iconize the urban development in the city of Dubai.

Largest Atrium

The Luxor Hotel, in Las Vegas, Nevada, has the largest atrium in the world at 29 million cubic feet (820,000 m^3).

Glazed Atrium

The 19th century brought the industrial revolution with great advances in iron and glass manufacturing techniques. Courtyards could then have horizontal glazing overhead, eliminating some of the weather elements from the space and giving birth to the modern atrium.

One of the main public spaces at Federation Square, Melbourne, Australia is called The Atrium and is a street-like space, 5-stories high with glazed walls and roof. The structure and glazing pattern follow the system of fractals used to arrange the panels on the rest of the facades at Federation Square.

Attic

An attic is a space found directly below the pitched roof of a house or other building. As attics fill the space between the ceiling of the top floor of a building and the slanted roof, they are known for being awkwardly shaped spaces with exposed rafters and difficult-to-access corners. While some attics are converted into bedrooms or home offices, complete with windows and staircases, most attics remain hard to get to and neglected, and are typically used for storage. Attics can also help control temperature in a house by providing a large mass of unmoving air. Hot air rising from lower floors of a building often gets trapped in the attic, further compounding their reputation for in hospitability. However in recent years many attics have been insulated to help decrease heating costs since on average, uninsulated attics account for 15% of the total energy loss in a typical house.

In some places "attic" is used more specifically to apply to lofts which have boarded floors and ceilings, and usually windows or skylights, and then "loft" is kept to mean a dark, unboarded roof-space which lacks these features.

Alcove

Alcove (through the Spanish, *alcoba*, from the Arabic, *al-*, the, and *qubbah*, a vault) is an architectural term for a recess in a room, usually screened off by pillars, balustrades or drapery.

Usage : Though their apartment lacked a dining room, an *alcove* adjacent to the living room made for an adequate ambience for dinner.

In geography and geology, the term Alcove is used for a wind-eroded depression in the side of a cliff of a homogenous rock type, famous from sandstones of the Colorado Plateau like the Navajo Sandstone.

GEOGRAPHY OF A HOUSE

A nursery is usually, in American connotations, a bedroom within a house or other dwelling set aside for an infant or toddler. A typical nursery would contain a crib (or similar type of bed), a table or platform for the purpose of changing diapers (also known as a changing table), as well as various items required for the care of the child (such as baby powder and medicine). A nursery is generally designated for the smallest bedroom in the house, as a baby requires very little space until at least walking age; the premise being that the room is used almost exclusively for sleep.

However, the room in many cases could remain the bedroom of the child well into his or her teenage years, or until a younger sibling is born, and the parents decide to move the older child into another larger bedroom, if one should be available.

In Victorian and Edwardian times, for the wealthy and mid-tier classes, a nursery was a suite of rooms at the top of a house, including the night nursery, where the children slept, and a day nursery, where they ate and played, or a combination thereof. The nursery suite would include some bathroom facilities and possibly a small kitchen.

The nurse (nanny) and nursemaid (assistant) slept in the suite too, to be within earshot of the sleeping children. The schoolroom might also be adjacent, but the governess, whose job it was to teach the children, would not be part of the nursery; she would have her own bedroom, possibly in another wing. Fictional portrayals of nurseries abound, for example in the writings of Kipling and E. Nesbit; perhaps the most famous nursery is that in *Mary Poppins*, or the nursery in J.M. Barrie's *Peter Pan*.

Box-room/Storage Room

Many houses are built to contain a box-room (box room or boxroom) that is easily identifiable, being smaller than the others. The small size of these rooms limits their use, and they tend to be used as a small single bedroom, small child's bedroom, or as a storage room.

Traditionally, and often seen in country houses and larger suburban houses up until the 1930s in Britain, the box room was literally for the storage of boxes, trunks, portmanteaux, and the like, rather than for bedroom use.

Conservatory

A conservatory is a glass and metal structure traditionally found in the garden of a large house or public park. Modern conservatories are smaller, can be made of PVC, and are often added to houses for home improvement purposes.

The traditional nineteenth century conservatory was a large greenhouse used for growing tender and rare plants, or, less often, for birds and rare animals – sometimes with the plants and animals living together. An orangery is similar to a large greenhouse or conservatory and was used originally to winter citrus trees and house exotic plants.

Many cities, especially those in cold climates and with large European populations, have built municipal conservatories to display tropical plants and hold flower displays. This type of conservatory was popular in the early nineteenth century, and by the end of the century people were also giving them a social use (e.g., tea parties). Conservatory architecture varies from typical Victorian glasshouses to modern styles, such as geodesic domes. Many were large and impressive structures and are included in the list below.

Smaller garden conservatories became popular in the second half of the twentieth century, as places which are part-greenhouses, for conserving plants, and part-recreational, as a solarium or sunroom. They are often used as an extra room rather than for horticulture.

In the UK, a conservatory can also refer to a smaller glass enclosure attached to a house. In other parts of the world this is referred to as a sunroom. In the UK there is a legal definition of a conservatory, it is a building that has at least 50% of its side wall area glazed and at least 75% of its roof glazed with translucent materials, either polycarbonate sheeting or glass.

DINING ROOM

A dining room is a room for consuming food. In modern times it is usually adjacent to the kitchen for convenience in serving, although in medieval times it was often on an entirely different floor level. Historically the dining room is furnished with a rather large dining table and a number of dining chairs; the most common table shape is generally rectangular with two armed end chairs and an even number of un-armed side chairs along the long sides.

History

In the Middle Ages, upper class Britons and other European nobility in castles or large manor houses dined in the Great Hall. This was a large multi-function room capable of seating the bulk of the population of the house.

The family would sit at the head table on a raised dais, with the rest of the population arrayed in order of diminishing rank away from them. Tables in the great hall would tend to be long trestle tables with benches. The sheer number of people in a Great Hall meant it would probably have had a busy, bustling atmosphere. Suggestions that it would also have been quite smelly and smoky are probably, by the standards of the time, unfounded. These rooms had large chimneys and high ceilings and there would have been a freeflow of air through the numerous door and window openings.

It is true that the owners of such properties began to develop a taste for more intimate gatherings in smaller 'parlers' or 'privee parlers' off the main hall but this is thought to be due as much to political and social changes as to the greater comfort afforded by such rooms. In the first instance, the Black Death that ravaged Europe in the 14th Century caused a shortage of labour and this had led to a breakdown in the feudal system. Also the religious persecutions following the dissolution of the monasteries under Henry VIII made it unwise to talk freely in front of large numbers of people.

Over time, the nobility took more of their meals in the parlour, and the parlour became, functionally, a dining room (or was split into two separate rooms). It also migrated farther from the Great Hall, often accessed via grand ceremonial staircases from the dais in the Great Hall. Eventually dining in the Great Hall became something that was done primarily on special occasions.

Toward the beginning of the 18th Century, a pattern emerged where the ladies of the house would withdraw after dinner from the dining room to the drawing room. The gentlemen would remain in the dining room having drinks. The dining room tended to take on a more masculine tenor as a result.

Modern Dining Rooms in North America

A typical North American dining room will contain a table with chairs arranged along the sides and ends of the table, as well as other pieces of furniture, (often used for storing formal china), as space permits. Often tables in modern dining rooms will have a removable leaf to allow for the larger number of people present on those special occasions without taking up extra space when not in use. Although the "typical" family dining experience is at a wooden table or some sort of kitchen area, some choose to make their dining rooms more comfortable by using couches or comfortable chairs.

In modern American and Canadian homes, the dining room is typically adjacent to the living room, being increasingly used only for formal dining with guests or on special occasions. For informal daily meals, most medium size houses and larger will have a space adjacent to the kitchen where table and chairs can be placed, larger spaces are often known as a dinette while a smaller one is called a breakfast nook. Smaller houses and condos may have a breakfast bar instead, often of a different height than the regular kitchen counter (either raised for stools or lowered for chairs). If a home lacks a dinette, breakfast nook, or breakfast bar, then the kitchen or family room will be used for day-to-day eating.

This was traditionally the case in England, where the dining room would for many families be used only on Sundays, other meals being eaten in the kitchen.

In Australia, while the use of the dining room is still prevalent, family meals are also often eaten at a breakfast counter or in front of the television in the lounge.

FAMILY ROOM OR DEN

A family room is an informal, all-purpose room in a house similar to a living room. The family room is designed to be a place where family and guests gather for group recreation like talking, reading, watching TV, and other family activities. Often, the family room is located adjacent to the kitchen, and at times, flows into it with no visual breaks· A family room often has doors leading to the back yard and specific outdoor living areas such as a deck, garden, or terrace.

The distinction between a family room, a living room, and a recreation room may be fluid. In homes with more than one, the living room is usually the more formal room, often reserved for guests, special occasions, and the display of items such as antiques or artwork.

The recreation room is typically in the basement and used for games and playtime. In homes with only one, the terms are generally synonymous. It is not uncommon for someone who grew up calling such a room by only one term to have no idea of the distinction between the two. In floorplans, a "great room" is where the living room and family room are combined into one high-ceilinged room adjacent to the kitchen.

URBAN HOUSING

An urban area is characterized by higher population density and vast human features in comparison to areas surrounding it. Urban areas may be cities, towns or conurbations, but the term is not commonly extended to rural settlements such as villages and hamlets. Urban areas are created and further developed by the process of urbanization. Measuring the extent of an urban area helps in analyzing population density and urban sprawl, and in determining urban and rural populations (Cubillas 2007).

Unlike an urban area, a metropolitan area includes not only the urban area, but also satellite cities plus intervening rural land that is socio-economically connected to the urban core city, typically by employment ties through commuting, with the urban core city being the primary labour market.

In fact, urbanized areas agglomerate and grow as the core population/ economic activity center within a larger metropolitan area or envelope. Metropolitan areas tend to be defined using counties or county sized political units as building blocks. Counties tend to be stable political boundaries; economists prefer to work with economic and social statistics based on metropolitan areas. Urbanized areas are a more relevant statistic for determining per capita land usage and densities (Dumlao & Felizmenio 1976).

DEFINITIONS

They vary somewhat amongst different nations. European countries define urbanized areas on the basis of urban-type land use, not allowing any gaps of typically more than 200 meters, and use satellite imagery instead of census blocks to determine the boundaries of the urban area. In less developed countries, in addition to land use and density requirements, a requirement that a large majority of the population, typically 75%, is not engaged in agriculture and/or fishing is sometimes used.

Australia

In Australia, urban areas are referred to as "urban centres" and are defined as population clusters of 1000 or more people, with a density of 200 or more persons per square kilometre.

Canada

In Canada, an urban area is an area that has more than 400 people per square kilometre and has more than 1,000 people. If two or more urban areas are within two kilometres of each other, they are merged into a single urban area. The boundaries of an urban area are not influenced by municipal or even provincial boundaries.

China

In China, an urban area is an urban district, city and town with a population density higher than 1,500 people per square kilometre. As for urban districts with a population density lower than 1,500 people per square kilometre, only the population that lives in streets, town sites, and adjacent villages is counted as urban population.

France

In France, an urban area is a zone (*aire urbaine*) encompassing an area of built-up growth (called an "urban unit" (*unité urbaine*)-close in definition to the North American urban area) and its commuter belt (*couronne périurbaine*). Although the official INSEE translation of *aire urbaine* is "urban area", most North Americans would find the same as being similar in definition to their metropolitan area.

Japan

In Japan urbanized areas are defined as contiguous areas of densely inhabited districts (DIDs) using census enumeration districts as units with a density requirement of 4,000 inhabitants per square kilometre (10,000 /sq mi).

New Zealand

Statistics New Zealand defines New Zealand urban areas for statistical purposes as a settlement with a population of a thousand people or more.

Norway

Statistics Norway defines urban areas ("tettsteder") similarly to the other Nordic countries. Unlike in Denmark and Sweden, the distance between each building has to be of less than 50 meters, although exceptions are made due to parks, industrial areas, rivers, and similar. Groups of houses less than 400 metres from the main body of an urban area are included in the urban area.

Poland

In Poland, official "urban" population figures simply refer to those localities which have the status of towns (*miasta*). The "rural" population is that of all areas outside the boundaries of these towns. This distinction may give a misleading impression in some cases, since some localities with only village status may have acquired larger and denser populations than many smaller towns.

Sweden

Urban areas in Sweden (*tätorter*) are statistically defined localities, totally independent of the administrative subdivision of the country. There are 1,940 such localities in Sweden, with a population ranging from 200 to 1,252,000 inhabitants.

United Kingdom

The United Kingdom's Office for National Statistics produced census results from urban areas since 1951, since 1981 based upon the extent of irreversible urban development indicated on Ordnance Survey maps. The definition is an extent of at least 20 hectares and at least 1,500 census residents. Separate areas are linked if less than 200 metres apart. Included are transportation features. The largest urban area is Greater London, followed by the West Midlands county, Greater Manchester, Greater Glasgow and Merseyside.

United States

In the United States there are two categories of urban area. The term *urbanized area* denotes an urban area of 50,000 or more people. Urban areas under 50,000 people are called *urban clusters*. Urbanized areas were first delineated in the United States in the 1950 census, while urban clusters were added in the 2000 census. There are 1,371 urban areas and urban clusters with more than 10,000 people.

The U.S. Census Bureau defines an urban area as: "Core census block groups or blocks that have a population density of at least 1,000 people per square mile (386 per square kilometer) and surrounding census blocks that have an overall density of at least 500 people per square mile (193 per square kilometer)."

The concept of Urbanized Areas as defined by the U.S. Census Bureau is often used as a more accurate gauge of the size of a city, since in different cities and states the lines between city borders and the urbanized area of that city are often not the same.

For example, the city of Greenville, South Carolina has a city population under 60,000 but an urbanized area over 300,000, while Greensboro, North Carolina has a city population over 200,000 but an urbanized area population of around 270,000 — meaning that Greenville is actually "larger" for some intents and purposes, but not for others, such as taxation, local elections, etc.

The largest urban area in the United States is that of New York City, with its city proper population exceeding 8 million and its metropolitan area population almost 19 million. The next four largest urban areas in the U.S. are those of Los Angeles, Chicago, Miami and Philadelphia. About 70 percent of the population of the United States lives within the boundaries of urbanized area (210 out of 300 million). Combined, these areas occupy about 2 percent of the United States. The majority of urbanized area residents are suburbanites;

core central city residents make up about 30 percent of the urbanized area population (about 60 out of 210 million).

FIREPLACE (FOR WARMTH DURING WINTER; GENERALLY NOT FOUND IN WARMER CLIMATES)

A fireplace is an architectural structure to contain a fire for heating and, especially historically, for cooking. A fire is contained in a firebox or firepit; a chimney or other flue directs gas and particulate exhaust to escape. Fireplaces are a central household feature, as the flames and crackling sounds are comforting, even when not necessary for heat or cooking. Fireplace mantels are a focus for interior decoration.

Types of Fireplace

A. Cool air enters.

B. The cool air is heated and is released.

C. Smoke is released.

A fireplace may have: a foundation, a hearth, a firebox, a fireplace mantel, an ashdump door, a chimney crane, a cleanout door, a grate, a lintel, a lintel bar, overmantel, a chimney breast, a damper, a smoke chamber, a throat, a flue, a chimney chase, a crown, a cap, a shroud, or a spark arrestor.

Fireplace types:

- Masonry (brick or stone fireplaces and chimneys. This type of fireplace is popular due to its nostalgic qualities.
- Manufactured ("prefab") fireplaces with sheet metal fire boxes.

Masonry and prefab fireplaces can be fueled with wood, natural gas, biomass and lp/propane fuel sources.

- Ventless Fireplaces (duct free/rom-venting fireplaces) that are fueled by either gel, LP/bottled gas or natural gas. Some states and local counties have laws and ordinances regarding these types of fireplaces. They require the least installation and are the most efficient fireplace. The gas burning version of a vent free fireplace while using less fuel, burns that fuel at close to 100% efficiency. They must be sized appropriately to the area to be heated. Aside from the heat output there are also air quality control problems due to the amount of moisture they release into the room air, and oxygen sensor and carbon monoxide sensors are safety essentials.

Chimney/flue types:

- Masonry (brick or stone fireplaces and chimneys) with or without tile lined flue. Unreinforced masonry chimneys do not stand up to earthquakes well.

- Reinforced concrete chimneys. Fundamental flaws (the difference in thermal expansion rates between steel rebar and concrete which caused the chimney flues to crack when heated) bankrupted the US manufacturers and obsoleted the technique.This is evidenced by vertical cracks on the exterior of the chimney.
- Metal-lined flue: Double or triple walled metal pipe running up inside a new or existing wood framed or masonry chase

Newly constructed flues may feature a chase cover, a cap, and a spark arrestor at the top to keep small animals out and sparks from exiting the chimney cavity.

History

Ancient fire pits were sometimes built in the ground in the center of a hut or dwelling. Smoke escaped through holes in the roof. Smoke would be blown outside or back into the room. Chimneys, invented much later, partially fixed this problem, venting smoke outside.

In 1678 Prince Rupert, nephew of Charles I, raised the grate of the fireplace, improving the airflow and venting system. The 1700s saw two important developments in the history of fireplaces. Ben Franklin developed a convection chamber for the fireplace that greatly improved the efficiency of fireplaces and wood stoves. He also improved the airflow by pulling air from a basement and venting out a longer area at the top. In the later 1700s, Count Rumford designed a fireplace with a tall, shallow firebox that was better at drawing the smoke up and out of the building. The shallow design also improved greatly the amount of radiant heat projected into the room. Rumford's design is the foundation for modern fireplaces.

One famous tradition in the United States during the Great Depression was President Franklin Delano Roosevelt's "fireside chats", weekly radio addresses in which he made use of the family gathering time to state his views.

Many homes no longer have open fireplaces, their inefficient heating replaced by central heating, or electric heaters, its social function by the home entertainment center. Some fireplaces have been closed off not allowing them to be used. Some have been made unable to be used by feeding a telephone, television antenna, cable TV or satellite TV wire down them. For homeowners that want the ambiance of a fireplace without the energy loss they have a few options. They can install into a new home or addition a high efficiency gas or wood fireplace. They do not have the appeal of a true open fireplace, but offer the fireplace effect while adding true heating value to the home. For people with existing fireplaces, the alternative to simply closing them up is to install a high efficiency gas, wood or biomass fireplace insert. Some governments have a partial ban on solid fuel burning fireplaces due to air pollution. Ventless fireplaces have received attention recently: they are free standing, requiring no chimney and no hearth. Prefabricated fireplaces are popular because of their lower construction cost and safer and more reliable operation. Brick or stone fireplaces can be designed to meet exact specifications for opening size, depth, and facing material. They cost more to build and require more maintenance.

FOYER

A foyer is a large, vast room or complex of rooms (in a theatre, opera, concert hall, showroom, cinema, etc.) adjacent to the auditorium. It is a repose area for spectators and place of venues, especially used before performance and during intermissions, but also as a place of celebrations or festivities after performance. Usually a foyer is a large, specially designed hall, but sometimes it is a corridor surrounding the main hall. It is furnished and big enough to enable spectators to stroll, get together and rest. Foyers are commonly adorned with art works, permanent or temporary exhibitions related to the activity of the institution, and a refreshment room or buffet. Moreover, the foyer can be the main place of some events such as vernissage, meetings with the artists, actors' benefit, etc.

A foyer in a house is usually a small entry area or room by the front door. Other public rooms such as the living room, dining room, and family room typically attach to it, along with any main stairway. It was initially intended as an "airlock", separating the fireplace-heated rooms from the (colder, in winter) front entrance, where cold air infiltration made for cold drafts and low temperatures. It is commonly used for outer garment and umbrella storage for both residents and guests.

Social Housing

In social housing a *Foyer* is a service that combines housing for homeless young people with other services such as guidance and support.

The Foyer movement started in France, but is now gaining popularity in other countries. The first Foyers in the UK were launched in 1992 and as of 2008 there are well over 100 in operation.

4

Rural and Urban Geography

RURAL URBAN CONTRAST

Many families and individuals find themselves, at least at some point, questioning the advantages of rural versus urban life. Quality of life is one of the central issues to consider in any comparison between rural versus urban living. While a case can be made for either location as being the best place to live, it is worthwhile to consider how these two options, rural versus urban, are similar and different. Important factors such as the capacity to make general choices, diversity, health, and employment concerns all influence both sides of the comparison and although each both rural and urban living offer great benefits, they both have a seemingly equal number of drawbacks. Rural and urban areas are generally similar in terms of terms of human interaction but differ most widely when diversity and choice are issues.

There are a number of positive as well as negative factors that contribute the overall quality of life in urban centres and if there is any general statement to be made about urban living, it is that there is a great deal of diversity and choice. In urban areas, there are many more choices people can make about a number of aspects of their daily lives. For instance, in urban areas, one is more likely to be able to find many different types of food and this could lead to overall greater health since there could be a greater diversity in diet. In addition, those in urban areas enjoy the opportunity to take in any number of cultural or social events as they have a large list to choose from. As a result they have the opportunity to be more cultured and are more likely to encounter those from other class, cultural, and ethnic groups.

Parents have a number of choices available for the education of their children and can often select from a long list of both public and private school districts, which leads to the potential for better education. It is also worth noting that urban areas offer residents the possibility to choose from a range of employment options at any number of companies or organizations. Aside form this, urbanites have better access to choices in healthcare as well and if they suffer from diseases they have a number of specialists to choose from in their area. According to one study conducted in Canada, "rural populations show poorer health than their urban counterparts, both in terms of general health indicators (i.e. standardized mortality, life expectancy at birth, infant mortality) and in terms of factors such as motor vehicle accidents and being overweight" (Pampalon 421). This could be the result of less reliance on vehicles in urban areas as well as greater emphasis on walking. Despite the conclusions from this study, however, there are a number of drawbacks to urban living as well. Although the life expectancy in cities may be higher, pollution (noise and atmospheric) is an issue that could impact the overall quality of life. In addition to this, overpopulation concerns can also contribute to a decrease in the standard of living.

Rural places do not offer the same level of choice and in very isolated areas and one might be forced to commute long distances to find even a remote selection of the diversity found in urban centres. Still, despite this lack of choice, there are a number of positive sides to rural living in terms of quality of life.

For instance, living in a rural area allows residents to enjoy the natural world more easily instead of having to go to parks. In addition, people do not have to fight with the daily stresses of urban life such as being stuck in traffic, dealing with higher rates of crime, and in many cases, paying higher taxes.

These absences of stressors can have a great effect on the overall quality of life and as one researcher notes, "People living in rural and sparsely populated areas are less likely to have mental health problems than those living in urban areas and may also be less likely to relapse into depression or mental illness once they have recovered from these in more densely populated areas".

The lack of daily stress found in cities from external factors (traffic, long lines, feeling caged, etc) has much to do with this. While there may not be a large number of stores and restaurants to choose from, those in rural areas have the benefit of land upon which to grow their own food, which is much healthier. Although urban populations have large numbers of social networks and networking opportunities, rural communities offer residents the ability to have long-lasting and more personal relationships since they encounter the same people more frequently. While there are not as many schools to choose from and sometimes rural schools are not funded as well as some others, children can grow up knowing their classmates and experience the benefits of smaller classrooms.

One of the drawbacks to living in a rural area, however, is that unlike urban areas, residents do not have the best opportunity to choose from a range of employment options. While they can commute to larger towns, this gets expensive and is not as convenient as working close to their residence. In general, if there is any statement to be made about the quality of life of rural living, it is that there is a greater ability to connect with people and the landscape. The quality of life in urban areas is similar to that in rural areas in that both involve a high degree of socialization, even if on a cursory level. Where they differ most noticeably is in the availability of choices and diversity, especially when vital factors (healthcare, education, and employment options) are concerned.

CHANGE IN INDIAN RURAL LIFE

In many ways independence from colonial rule in 1947 marked the beginning of a new phase in the history of Indian agriculture. Having evolved out of a long struggle against colonial rule with the participation of the people from various social categories, the Indian state also took over the task of supervising the transformation of its stagnant and backward economy to make sure that the benefits of economic growth were not monopolized entirely by a particular section of society. It is with this background that development emerged as a strategy of economic change and an ideology of the new regime.

However at the micro-level the structures that evolved during colonial rule still continued to exist. The local interests that had emerged over a long period of time continued to be powerful in the Indian countryside even after the political climate had changed. According to Daniel Thorner the earlier structure of land relations and debt dependencies where a small section consisting of few landlords and money lenders were dominant continued to prevail in the Indian countryside. The nature of property relations, the local values that related social prestige negatively to physical labour and the absence of any surplus with the actual cultivator for investment on land ultimately perpetuated stagnation. This complex of legal, economic and social relations typical of Indian countryside served to produce an effect that Thorner described as a built-in depressor.

RURAL RELIGION

Many Indian villages have Brahmanic temples within them, however the religious focus is mainly on the shrines of the village's goddess and god. Rural Indians inhabit a world full of divine and semi-divine beings; tree spirits (yakshas), ghosts (bhootas), puranic, local, personal and ancestral gods who co-exist in a complex hierarchy. As well as public shrines to the gods, every Hindu home has a domestic shrine and a veneration of sacred trees and snakes were both attested to millennia ago and still play a important part in religious practice and belief today.

Unlike in orthodox puranic Hinduism villagers have direct access to the local gods and do not require the intercession of a priest. The Goddess also plays a larger role in local religion and rural religion is centred on specific places of perceived spiritual power. The shrines themselves are relatively simple affairs. They are usually covered and often enclosed on three sides by a low wall. Shrines with buildings on them are quite rare. The simplest form of shrine can consist of a pile of stones by a riverbank or in a field, where, at some point in the past a spirit had made its presence known. Villages often have a number of shrines to different deities located at the edge of the village. In South India the most visually striking shrines are those dedicated to the god Aiyanar. Aiyanar is a Brahmanised pre-Aryan deity and is regarded as a benign being concerned with the welfare of the village community rather than that of the individual. Shrines to Aiyanar are used on special occasions and can therefore sometimes look neglected. Aiyanars power is dependent on three subordinate gods named Karrupu, Muniyan and Maturaiviran who are regarded as impure spirits.

Aiyanars shrines sometimes contain huge brightly painted terracotta statues of these subordinate gods. Throughout India, a part of ritual practice involves making offerings of food, flowers, incense or terracotta figures, mainly of animals, to the deities. Life size terracotta horses are offered to Aiyanar and are believed to serve the god in the spirit world and carry him around the village at night as he protects it. The horses are renewed from time to time but the old ones are kept so the shrines often contain a small herd. Devotional terracottas are made by professional potters of the Kumhars caste and have a long history going back to the Harrapan culture of 2,500 BCE. The skill of a potter is believed to be a gift of the Gods and the potters are understood to possess a kind of magical power.

Another widely worshipped God in South India is Murukan (the Tamil name of Kartikeya). Murukan is invoked for protection and is a god of war associated with the planet Mars. In village shrines, Murukan is represented by a spear. In areas where he is regarded as the offspring of Shiva and Parvati, a trisul (or trident, an emblem of Shiva) can be found next to the spear. Offerings of ghee or fruit are skewered on to the blade tips although human hair is considered to be the most auspicious offering to Murukan. In addition to the type of offerings made to the male gods the village goddesses can require placating with live offerings. Where Goddess shrines contain anthropomorphic images of the deity, they are usually roughly carved in stone or wood, garlanded with flowers and sometimes dressed in clothing.

An unpaid priest and his assistants have the duty to maintain the shrines (at the community's expense) and to propitiate the deity to ward off communal bad luck and disease. Individual villagers, regardless of caste, can approach the village deity directly as and when they have a need. At specific times of year and during crisis a festival is held in honour of the Goddess. The main feature of these festivals is the sacrifice of an animal, at one time buffalo sacrifice was widely practised, nowadays the victim is more likely to be a goat or chicken. In Northern India the blood from such sacrifices is shunned because it is regarded as impure.

In the South the opposite is true, the blood is liberally flecked and smeared over the altar and devotees, as there is a strong belief in the power of the impure. The meaning of the sacrifice appears to be to release the power of the Goddess into the community. As the Goddess is regarded as both destructive and creative it is not considered wise to allow her presence in the village for very long. Spirit possession is also a feature of the Goddess festival as are severe penances such as hook hanging, fire walking and fire swallowing. Brahmins discourage the practice of animal sacrifice and not all villages Goddesses demand it. Examples of 'vegetarian' Goddesses in Tamil Nadu, include Antal and Sapta Kannimar, while in Orissa Ma Ksetrapala prefers cannabis. Widely known Goddesses such as Mariyamman in Tamil Nadu and Sitala in North India are relived differently from one area or village to the next and offering vary according to their perceived character. In parts of South India Goddess shrines are located to the north of the village. This is significant as the north is associated with spiritual knowledge and disease and so emphasises the innate duality of the Goddess. Western scholars have tended to portray village Goddesses as sinister or malicious and venerate or placated through fear, however they are best described as ambivalent and are the objects of intense devotion.

Snake veneration is also an important part of Indian religion. An important festival called the Nagapanchami is held at the start of the rainy season in August and it is a common sight to see Naga worship all over India by those hoping to be blessed with children. The Nagas are a race of serpents whose origins are described in the Mahabharata and the Varaka Purana. As divine beings they are depicted in human, half human and fully serpent form. In rural areas snakes are commonly found near ant hills and termite mounds, both of which are regarded as the entrances to the otherworld. The mounds are frequently marked with ash and offerings of milk or eggs are made to the resident Naga. Particularly impressive mounds can thatched roofs supported by posts placed over the, similar to some Goddess shrines. Like the dragons of European mythology Nagas are seen as guardians of the otherworld and of treasure. There is also an association between snakes and trees, both being symbols of fertility and the roots of trees, like the termite mound, is seen as an entrance to the otherworld. In South India women desiring children erect snake stones under sacred tress. These stones have stylised cobras carved on them represent the Goddess Nakamal (snake virgin) and are immersed in water for several months to empower them then erected under Nim, or Pipal trees, accompanied by prayer and ritual.

In North India Manasa is invoked for protection against snakebite and to cure infertility and is represented by an earthen snake image, the branch of a tree or a water pot. As mentioned above, trees are considered to be symbols of fertility however overlying this aspect of folk religion is the Vedic concept of the tree as the axis of the Cosmos. The Rg Veda relates how sacrificial offerings were tied to a tree so that the energies released would travel upwards to the realm of Gods. Sacred trees can be found in villages, within a temple complex or shrine and in forests. The tree spirits or Yaksha (male) Yakshini (female) was worshipped in very early times, however much of the reverence shown to them has been transferred to the river Goddesses. The Yaksha is still recognised but villagers can make offerings to their ancestors, local Gods and puranic deities through the tree. The Pipal tree, for example, is believed to be the home of the elder sister of Laksmi, a Goddess named Nairrti, who seems to be a Brahmanised village Goddess. Nairrti could be described as Laksmi's dark side, as she represents misfortune. The Pipal is not touched except on Saturday when Nairrti is believed to visit Laksmi. Shrines to Nairrti are found outside villages. The Gond tribe venerates pairs of trees simply as "man" and "woman". The shade of a tree is also considered sacred. The ancient art of mediumship under sacred trees, especially those in the grounds of temples and shrines is still a common occurrence. In forests trees can be found stained and garlanded with beads, representing Bana Durga (Forest Durga) and shrines to forest Kali can be found under pairs of trees. The trees are given a similar reverence and type of offerings as those given to the Gods.

Sacred spaces are created in the home, often an entire room is used as a place of worship. Offerings of food and incense are made to the Gods, who are represented by the statues made from brass, wood or stone. The help of the deity is sought mainly but not exclusively by the women of the house for a range of personal and domestic issues.

The custom of making a sacred vow or Vrat to the deity forms the basis for many domestic rituals. The custom of Vrat originates in part from the Artharvaveda, the last of the four great Vedas which contains spells and incantations derived from folk religion. The knowledge of Vrat rituals is said to have been spread throughout India by magician priests who were accompanied by a sacred prostitute and a musician as they toured villages in brightly painted carts.

The success of the ritual relies upon an implicit belief in magic and the focusing of intent, empowered by gesture and incantation to raise energy. The nature of the rituals varies according to the individual, although they do usually involve recitation of mantras and the making of magical drawings. The ritual may also need repeating on a monthly or seasonal basis. Finally a vow is made to the deity to perform an austerity, usually fasting for a fixed period, for example every Monday for sixteen weeks, or to provide gifts when the outcome is known.

Rural religion and in particular the local Goddess has tended to be ignored or denigrated by both Indian and Western scholars and regarded as a subject not worthy of serious scholarly investigation. This brief article hopes to have shown that rural religion and the day to day worship of local Gods and Goddesses forms the basis of religious activity in India and provides Hinduism with much of its continuity with India's ancient past.......

CHALLENGES FOR URBAN DEVELOPMENT

In the present context, it will be a mammoth task for the Urban Local Bodies to extend the coverage of water supply, sanitation. Due to burgeoning urban population growth, the big cities viz., metropolitan (million plus) and mega cities are under severe strain particularly in terms of making access to infrastructure services to the inhabitants. Overall the urban dwellers in the country have low access to infrastructure services such as water supply, sanitation, power supply and solid waste disposal. The availability of, at least, minimum level of these services is considered necessary for a conducive human settlement and habitat. In addition to the absolute shortage of services in urban areas, there is the problem of inequitable distribution across the states and different income strata of population.

The deficiencies in services in urban areas are absorbed by the low-income and poorer parts of the population. Infrastructure inadequacies and inequitable distribution are accompanied by the absence of efficient and effective management, which has led to service leakages and financial losses and have, consequently, had an adverse impact on urban productivity and economic growth. Improvements in productivity and efficiency are essential to make continued economic growth possible with growing population, Urbanisation and industrialization and increasingly degraded resource base.

Urban Planning and Management

Master Plan/ Development Plan is an important instrument for urban planning and development. The existing status of Master Plans in India needs to be reviewed.

Experience of implementing the Master Plans has not been encouraging because of weak data base, financial constraints, lack of resource mobilization, over ambitious plan proposals, lack of integration between spatial planning proposals with economic development plans and inadequate legislative support. In the Master Plan for cities, vegetable markets, firewood depots, building material markets and such other heavy markets should be located in the periphery of the town in conforming zone. It should suggest steps for covering the open drains, shifting of dairies from the city and other measures for improving the sanitary condition so that cities are free from flies/mosquitoes and cattle menace. Master Plans, instead of being rigid and static, should be made feasible and dynamic to incorporate the changing situations. The existing Town Planning Acts/City Development Act do not have adequate provision for redevelopment/reconstruction/urban renewal. As such there is a need to have Model Urban Renewal Act in India to tackle the problems of core areas specifically which will also be helpful in achieving the envisaged goals under JNNURM.

Finance

- Financing of infrastructure facilities like water supply, sewerage, drainage, solid waste management and power supply requires huge amount of investment.
- Urban Local Bodies are not in a position to afford huge investments due to their weak financial base.
- There has not been much rationality in pricing infrastructure/ services in most of the million plus cities of the country.
- Existing tariff structure for different core services is not sufficient to meet the production/ operation/ maintenance costs.
- Subsidization of services further worsens the financial condition of the implementing agencies.
- With inadequate return from the provision of services and also huge gap between demand and supply of the services the Urban Local Bodies are not able to cope up with the pressure.
- Urban Local Bodies have to struggle to get the State and Central Govt. grants and are unable to expand the availability of services commensurating the growth of population and related demand for the services.

Though the urban water supply and sanitation sector had remained as an important area of concern, but allocation of funds made right from the First Five Year Plan onwards has remained almost of the order of 1.00% to 1.5% of the total public sector outlay. In the Ninth Plan, this, however, could be stepped up to 2.17%. The tentative 10th Plan outlay for urban water supply and sanitation sector was ₹.18749.20 crore, which is only 1.3% of total public sector outlay.

Governance

It may be pertinent to mention that in the backdrop of recent changes introduced in the system of urban governance and planning, there have been wider implications on the pattern of urban growth. During the 1950s and 1960s, physical planning controls on location of economic activities and urban land-use, imposed through Master Plans, etc., were more of a restrictive nature and flexibility had limited scope.

The Urban governance in the country today has been characterized by fragmentation of responsibility, incomplete devolution of functions to the elected bodies, lack of adequate financial resources, unwillingness to progress towards municipal autonomy, adherence to outdated methods in property taxation and hesitation in the matter of levy of user charges, property tax recovery, levy or withdrawal of octroi, role of parastatals on water supply and sanitation services, etc. Experience shows that functional autonomy can become a reality only when financial strength supports it. Therefore, the States need to play a catalytic role, in particular, the parastatal agencies and Development Authorities, need to adopt a supportive role towards the elected bodies rather than take over functions, which statutorily belong to ULBs.

The Master Plan document incorporating the zoning regulations and development control regulations were perceived as static, whereas the large cities especially the million plus experienced large scale conversion of agricultural land into urban uses thereby leading to spurt in construction activities. Further, in most of the metropolitan cities rampant violation of building bye laws have become a common feature. The presence of unauthorized and haphazard development within the city limits as well as in the fringes put a question mark on the urban governance. Further the cumbersome processes involved in getting clearances in the construction activity affected the transparency in the governance.

Further, the financing of infrastructure facilities like water supply, sewerage, drainage, solid waste management, power supply requires huge amount of investment and the ULB's just are not in a position to afford huge investments due to their poor financial base. They are not able to plan infrastructure networks in an efficient manner, conducive to desired spatial pattern as well as keep them cost effective. Also, there has not been much rationality in pricing infrastructure/ services in most of the million plus cities of the country. The existing tariff structure for different core services has not been sufficient to meet the production/ operation/ maintenance costs.

The subsidization of services further worsens the financial condition of the implementing agencies. With the inadequate return from the provision of services and also huge gap between demand and supply of the services the Local Bodies are not able to cope up with the pressure. The problem of lack of urban governance could only be overcome as the ULB's undertake reforms appropriately and work for attaining transparency and simplification of procedures. Hence, the cumbersome process involved in approval of Building plans and issuance of completion certificate have to be simplified with the introduction of single window clearance. Various city administrations have realised the need for the same and this has also lead to liberalization in the development control regulations and the processes associated with them.

Infrastructure and Service Delivery

- *Water:*
  - According to 54th round of National Sample Survey, 70% of urban households reported being served by tap and 21% by Tube well or hand pump.
  - 66% of urban households reported having their principal source of water within their premises while 32% had it within 0.2 Km.
  - 41% had sole access to their principal source of drinking water and 59% were sharing a public source.
- *Sewerage:*
  - The 54th round of NSS reported 26% of households having no latrines, 35% using septic tank and 22% using sewerage system.
  - 43% of households in urban areas either had no latrines or no connection to a septic tank or sewerage.
  - In urban areas sewerage connections varied from a low 48% to a high 70%.
  - Out of 300 Class I cities, about 70 have partial sewerage system and sewage treatment facilities.
  - According to Central Pollution Control Board, the waste water generated in 300 Class I cities is about 15800 million litres a day while the treatment facilities exist for hardly 3750 million litres per day.
- *Solid Waste:*
  - 71% of urban households reported removal of household waste by household members themselves, 14% by Local Authorities, 12% by private agreement among residents.
  - 47% of urban households reported removing of their wastes to community dumping spot and 30% to individual dumping spot.
  - The solid waste generated by the million plus cities ranges from 1200 metric tones per day in cities like Ahmedabad and Pune to a maximum of 5000-5500 metric tones per day in cities like Delhi and Mumbai.
  - Out of total waste generated in the million plus cities hardly 30% is treated before disposal.
  - The per capita solid waste generation ranges from 300 gm in Bangalore to 500-550 gm in Mumbai and Delhi.

- *Urban Transport:*
  - Fare structure of city transport in most of the million plus cities is highly subsidized.
  - Public Transport Authorities have to resort to deficit financing and have very little incentive to be cost affective.
  - Road network of the million plus cities has problems like inefficient use, poor maintenance, poor traffic management and poor enforcement of regulations on parking and encroachments on right-of-way.
  - High proportion of traffic is slow moving.
  - High traffic volumes and low road capacities lead to high volume/ capacity ratios for most of the road networks in million plus cities.
  - The share of public transport in mega cities is Mumbai 88%, Kolkata 79%, Chennai 67% and Delhi 62%.
  - The share of urban suburban railway is Mumbai (44%). Kolkata (14%), Chennai (16%) and Delhi (1%).
  - With the introduction of metro in Delhi, the share of passenger trips by metro is likely to increase substantially with the completion of phase I and II.

Transport

India is one of the emerging urban economies in the world with roughly 60% of the country's GDP coming from the urban areas. Rapid Urbanisation with economic growth has generated corresponding increase in travel demand. However, neither the transport infrastructure development has kept pace with the increased travel, nor the investment strategy has been appropriately focused to provide efficient access and mobility to citizens.

Due to lack of efficient, comfortable and reliable public transport coupled with buoyant economic growth of about 10%, most of the cities in the country are already witnessing a rapid growth of personal vehicles. This coupled with the declining share of public transport has led to severe problems of congestion and its consequent costs in the form of travel delays, loss of productivity, air quality deterioration, noise pollution and increasing road fatalities. It is not only posing a serious threat to sustainability of urban areas but also impacting India's energy security with increased consumption of petroleum fuel.

If cities are to be the engines of economic growth that power India's development in the 21st century, transportation systems have to be their lifeline. Immediate proactive measures are needed to deal with the emerging situation. The only emerging solution is to invest sincerely in public transport, pedestrianisation and non motorized vehicles (NMVs) now or pay very heavily later since the continuous growth in number of personalized mode will also require very high constant investments in terms of road infrastructure to accommodate the increased number of vehicles on road.

In the light of these trends the Government of India has announced a National Urban Transport Policy in April 2006. The policy focuses on the need to "Move people - Not vehicles". It seeks to do this by encouraging improvements in public transport and facilities for the use of non-motorised modes. It suggests greater involvement of the private sector and innovative financing mechanisms to enhance efficiency and reduce the impact on the public budget. It seeks to encourage the use of cleaner technologies. It seeks to create better awareness amongst the people so that there is support for the initiatives that need to be taken and also for some of the compromises that people may need to make. It emphasizes the need to build capacity to undertake good urban transport planning, both at the institutional and individual level.

Vision and Objectives

According to the Registrar General population projection about 37 million persons will be added in the urban areas during the Eleventh Plan period. In view of the stronger relation between Urbanisation and economic growth, the states with higher growth rate may also register higher Urbanisation level. Recognizing the interdependence between Urbanisation and economic growth, the vision in Eleventh Plan should be to develop the cities in a sustainable manner, so that they could provide required infrastructure support for the sustained economic growth and also absorb the benefits of expanding economic activities. Urban Development should contribute in achieving the national goals and objectives of the economic development envisaging about 10% of economic growth rate.

The vision and objectives of urban development should focus on increasing the efficiency and productivity of cities by deregulation and development of land market, dismantling the public sector monopoly over urban infrastructure, creating conditions for the private sector to invest in urban economic infrastructure, establishing autonomous regulatory framework to oversee the functioning of the public and private sector, strengthening urban local governments, reducing incidence of poverty and deprivation in cities and towns and consolidating fragmented programmes and schemes under one umbrella like JNNURM. In this context, JNNURM with reform agenda is a unique mission.

The implementation of the mission in right perspective will create environment for cities to become efficient, equitable and accountable. Any statutory or procedural bottleneck in implementation of JNNURM need to be sorted out so that cities become major partner in the process of economic and social development and inclusive growth. Comprehensive planning and effective monitoring are, therefore, essential to take the JNNURM to its logical conclusion so that financial and functional efficiencies of urban local bodies are improved.

Improvement of the urban environment through creation of basic infrastructure like water supply, sanitation etc. in order to bring down the rate of morbidity and mortality, and financial losses by way of controlling water borne diseases, which will facilitate enhancement of productivity and overall economic development of the country. Inadequate availability of drinking water, improper treatment of sewage, uncollected solid waste etc. severely affect the quality of life. The 11th plan aims at tackling all such urban issues with a view to providing safe drinking water and adequate sanitation facilities to the entire urban population leading to improvement in urban environment.

Strategies and Action Plans

The strategy in the Eleventh Plan should lay emphasis on faster, broad-based and inclusive growth. The policies and action plan in urban development should be in consonance with putting the economic development on a sustainable growth trajectory with a growth rate of about 10% by the end of the plan period. In urban areas, apart from improving the urban infrastructure services, productive employment opportunities need to be created at a faster pace than before. It should reduce intra-city disparities by ensuring access to basic physical and social infrastructure services to all.

The steps initiated as part of the National Common Minimum Programme during the Tenth Five Year Plan need to be strengthened and consolidated further in the Eleventh Plan. The key element of the strategy in urban development is inclusive growth by providing access to the basic facilities and services to all in urban areas. In the long run good infrastructure in city/ town determine the level of development of economic opportunities in the future. The private sector has a critical role in achieving the objectives of faster and more inclusive growth. The urban areas need to provide conducive environment where all sectors and groups participate in an equitable manner for sustainable growth of towns and cities.

Development from Above

Keeping in view the national level policies and goals for economic and urban development, there is a need to follow the concept of integrated development planning linking the development plans from national to local levels in an hierarchical framework. At the national level a National Urbanisation Policy is overdue and the time is ripe to formulate a long term National Urbanisation Policy indicating the emerging pattern of Urbanisation and measures to channelise the future urban growth in an equitable and sustainable manner. Within the broad framework of National Urbanisation Policy, Regional Development Plan at the State level may be formulated as a broad policy and vision document for development of urban and rural growth centers in an integrated manner.

At the district and metropolitan area levels, the District Development Plan and Metropolitan Development Plan, as envisaged under 74th Constitution Amendment Act, should be prepared by DPC and MPC indicating the potentials and growth perspective of various settlements as part of urban–rural continuum. At local level, City Development Plans, Ward and Local Area Plans indicating vision of the cities, priorities of development, investment requirements, resource mobilization, land use and location of facilities and services alongwith development promotion regulations may be prepared by Urban Local Bodies for achieving the objectives of planned development.

GEOGRAPHY AND URBAN PLANNING

Urban, city, and town planning integrates land use planning and transportation planning to improve the built, economic and social environments of communities. Regional planning deals with a still larger environment, at a less detailed level. Urban planning can include urban renewal, by adapting urban planning methods to existing cities suffering from decay and lack of investment. In the Neolithic period, agriculture and other techniques facilitated larger populations than the very small communities of the Paleolithic, which probably led to the stronger, more coercive governments emerging at that time.

The pre-Classical and Classical periods saw a number of cities laid out just as to fixed plans, though many tended to develop organically. Designed cities were characteristic of the Mesopotamian, Harrapan, and Egyptian civilizations of the third millennium BCE. Distinct characteristics of urban planning from remains of the cities of Harappa, Lothal, and Mohenjo-daro in the Indus Valley Civilization (in modern-day northwestern India and Pakistan) lead archeologists to conclude that they are the earliest examples of deliberately planned and managed cities.

The streets of many of these early cities were paved and laid out at right angles in a grid pattern, with a hierarchy of streets from major boulevards to residential alleys. Archaeological evidence suggests that many Harrapan houses were laid out to protect from noise and enhance residential privacy; many also had their own water wells, probably for both sanitary and ritual purposes.

These ancient cities were unique in that they often had drainage systems, seemingly tied to a well-developed ideal of urban sanitation. The Greek Hippodamus has been dubbed the "Father of City Planning" for his design of Miletus; Alexander commissioned him to lay out his new city of Alexandria, the grandest example of idealized urban planning of the ancient Mediterranean world, where the city's regularity was facilitated by its level site near a mouth of the Nile. The Hippodamian, or grid plan, was the basis for subsequent Greek and Roman cities. The ancient Romans used a consolidated scheme for city planning, developed for military defense and civil convenience.

The basic plan consisted of a central forum with city services, surrounded by a compact, rectilinear grid of streets, and wrapped in a wall for defence. To reduce travel times, two diagonal streets crossed the square grid, passing through the central square.

A river usually flowed through the city, providing water, transport, and sewage disposal. Many European towns, such as Turin, preserve the remains of these schemes, which show the very logical way the Romans designed their cities.

They would lay out the streets at right angles, in the form of a square grid. All roads were equal in width and length, except for two, which were slightly wider than the others. One of these ran east–west, the other, north–south, and intersected in the middle to form the centre of the grid.

All roads were made of carefully fitted flag stones and filled in with smaller, hard-packed rocks and pebbles. Bridges were constructed where needed. Each square marked by four roads was called an insula, the Roman equivalent of a modern city block. Each insula was 80 yards (73 m) square, with the land within it divided. As the city developed, each insula would eventually be filled with buildings of various shapes and sizes and crisscrossed with back roads and alleys. Most insulae were given to the first settlers of a Roman city, but each person had to pay to construct his own house.

The city was surrounded by a wall to protect it from invaders and to mark the city limits. Areas outside city limits were left open as farmland. At the end of each main road was a large gateway with watchtowers. A portcullis covered the opening when the city was under siege, and additional watchtowers were constructed along the city walls. An aqueduct was built outside the city walls. The collapse of Roman civilization saw the end of Roman urban planning, among other arts. Urban development in the Middle Ages, characteristically focused on a fortress, a fortified abbey, or a (sometimes abandoned) Roman nucleus, occurred "like the annular rings of a tree", whether in an extended village or the centre of a larger city. Since the new centre was often on high, defensible ground, the city plan took on an organic character, following the irregularities of elevation contours like the shapes that result from agricultural terracing.

The ideal of wide streets and orderly cities was not lost, however. A few medieval cities were admired for their wide thoroughfares and orderly arrangements, but the juridical chaos of medieval cities (where the administration of streets was sometimes passed down through noble families), and the characteristic tenacity of medieval Europeans in legal matters prevented frequent or large-scale urban planning until the Renaissance and the early-modern strengthening of central government administration, as European (and soon after, North American) society transited from city-states to what we would recognize as a more modern concept of a nation-state.

Florence was an early model of the new urban planning, which took on a star-shaped layout adapted from the new star fort, designed to resist cannon fire.

This model was widely imitated, reflecting the enormous cultural power of Florence in this age; "[t]he Renaissance was hypnotized by one city type which for a century and a half— from Filarete to Scamozzi— was impressed upon utopian schemes: this is the star-shaped city".

Radial streets extend outward from a defined centre of military, communal or spiritual power. Only in ideal cities did a centrally planned structure stand at the heart, as in Raphael's Sposalizio (Illustration) of 1504.

As built, the unique example of a rationally planned quattrocento new city centre, that of Vigevano (1493–95), resembles a closed space instead, surrounded by arcading. Filarete's ideal city, building on Leone Battista Alberti's De re aedificatoria, was named "Sforzinda" in compliment to his patron; its twelve-pointed shape, circumscribable by a "perfect" Pythagorean figure, the circle, took no heed of its undulating terrain in Filarete's manuscript. This process occurred in cities, but ordinarily not in the industrial suburbs characteristic of this era which remained disorderly and characterized by crowding and organic growth.

Following the 1695 bombardment of Brussels by the French troops of King Louis XIV, in which a large part of the city centre was destroyed, Governor Max Emanuel proposed using the reconstruction to completely change the layout and architectural style of the city. His plan was to transform the medieval city into a city of the new baroque style, modeled on Turin, with a logical street layout, with straight avenues offering long, uninterrupted views flanked by buildings of a uniform size.

This plan was opposed by residents and municipal authorities, who wanted a rapid reconstruction, did not have the resources for grandiose proposals, and resented what they considered the imposition of a new, foreign, architectural style.

In the actual reconstruction, the general layout of the city was conserved, but it was not identical to that before the cataclysm. Despite the necessity of rapid reconstruction and the lack of financial means, authorities did take several measures to improve traffic flow, sanitation, and the aesthetics of the city. Many streets were made as wide as possible to improve traffic flow.

In the 1990s, the University of Kentucky voted the Italian town of Todi as the ideal city and "most livable town in the world", the place where man and nature, history and tradition, come together to create a site of excellence. In Italy, other examples of ideal cities planned just as to scientific methods are Urbino, Pienza, Ferrara, San Giovanni Valdarno, and San Lorenzo Nuovo. Many Central American civilizations also planned their cities, including sewage systems and running water.

In Mexico, Tenochtitlan was the capital of the Aztec empire, built on an island in Lake Texcoco in what is now the Federal District in central Mexico. At its height, Tenochtitlan was one of the largest cities in the world, with over 200,000 inhabitants. Shibam in Yemen features over 500 tower houses, each rising 5 to 11 storeys high, with each floor being an apartment occupied by a single family. The city has some of the tallest mudbrick houses in the world, some over 100 feet (30 meters) high. In the developed countries of Western Europe, North America, Japan, and Australasia, planning and architecture can be said to have gone through various paradigms or stages of consensus in the last 200 years. Firstly, there was the industrialised city of the 19th century, where building was largely controlled by businesses and wealthy elites.

Around 1900, a movement began for providing citizens, especially factory workers, with healthier environments. The concept of the garden city arose and several model towns were built, such as Letchworth and Welwyn Garden City in Hertfordshire, UK, the world's first garden cities. These were small in size, typically providing for a few thousand residents. In the 1920s, the ideas of modernism began to surface in urban planning. Based on the ideas of Le Corbusier and using new skyscraper-building techniques, the modernist city stood for the elimination of disorder, congestion, and the small scale, replacing them with preplanned and widely spaced freeways and tower blocks set within gardens.

There were plans for large-scale rebuilding of cities in this era, such as the Plan Voisin, which proposed clearing and rebuilding most of central Paris. No large-scale plans were implemented until after World War II, however. Throughout the late 1940s and 1950s, housing shortages caused by wartime destruction led many cities to subsidize housing blocks. Planners used the opportunity to implement the modernist ideal of towers surrounded by gardens.

The most prominent example of an entire modernist city is Brasilia in Brazil, constructed between 1956 and 1960. By the late 1960s and early 1970s, many planners felt that modernism's clean lines and lack of human scale sapped vitality from the community, blaming them for high crime rates and social problems. Modernist planning fell into decline in the 1970s when the construction of cheap, uniform tower blocks ended in most countries, such as

Britain and France. Since then many have been demolished and replaced by other housing types. Rather than attempting to eliminate all disorder, planning now concentrates on individualism and diversity in society and the economy; this is the post-modernist era. Minimally planned cities still exist. Houston is a large city (with a metropolitan population of 5.5 million) in a developed country without a comprehensive zoning ordinance.

Houston does, however, restrict development densities and mandate parking, even though specific land uses are not regulated. Also, private-sector developers in Houston use subdivision covenants and deed restrictions to effect land-use restrictions resembling zoning laws. Houston voters have rejected comprehensive zoning ordinances three times since 1948. Even without traditional zoning, metropolitan Houston displays large-scale land-use patterns resembling zoned regions comparable in age and population, such as Dallas. This suggests that non-regulatory factors such as urban infrastructure and financing may be as important as zoning laws in shaping urban form.

SUBURBANIZATION OF GEOGRAPHY

Suburbanization (or suburbanisation) is a term used to describe the growth of areas on the fringes of major cities. It is one of the many causes of the increase in urban sprawl. Many residents of metropolitan regions work within the central urban area, choosing instead to live in satellite communities called suburbs and commute to work via automobile or mass transit.

Others have taken advantage of technological advances to work from their homes, and chose to do so in an environment they consider more pleasant than the city. These processes often occur in more economically developed countries, especially in the United States, which is believed to be the first country in which the majority of the population lives in the suburbs, rather than in the cities or in rural areas. Proponents of containing urban sprawl argue that sprawl leads to urban decay and a concentration of lower income residents in the inner city.

Causes and effects

Suburbanization can be linked to a number of different push and pull factors. Push factors include the congestion and population density of the cities, pollution caused by industry and high levels of traffic and a general perception of a lower quality of life in inner city areas. Pull factors include more open spaces and a perception of being closer to "nature", lower suburban house prices and property taxes in comparison to the city, and the increasing number of job opportunities in the suburban areas.

Improvements in transportation infrastructure encourage suburbanization, as people become increasingly able to live in a suburb and commute in to the nearby town or city to work. Developments in railways, bus routes and roads are the main improvements that make suburbanization more practical.

The increase in the number and size of highways is a particularly significant part of this effect. Government policies can have a significant effect on the process. In the United States, for instance, policies of the Federal government in the post-World War II era, such as the building of an efficient network of roads, highways and superhighways, and the underwriting of mortgages for suburban one-family homes, had an enormous influence on the pace of suburbanization in that country. In effect, the government was encouraging the transfer of the middle-class population out of the inner cities and into the suburbs, sometimes with devastating effects on the viability of the city centres

However, some argue that the effect of Interstate Highway Systems on suburbanization is overstated. Researchers of this vein believe city centre populations would have declined even in the absence of highway systems, contending that suburbanization is a long-standing and almost universal process. They primarily argue that as incomes rise, most people want the range and choice offered by automobiles. In addition, there is no significant evidence directly linking the development of highway systems to declining urban populations. Insurance companies also fueled the push out of cities, as in many cases, it redlined inner-city neighbourhoods, denying mortgage loans there, and instead offering low rates in the suburban areas.

More recently, some urban areas have adopted "green belt" policies which limit growth in the fringe of a city, in order to encourage more growth in the urban core. It began to be realised that a certain amount of population density in the centre city is conducive to creating a good, working urban environment. Race also played a role in American suburbanization. During World War I, the massive migration of African Americans from the South resulted in an even greater residential shift towards suburban areas. The cities became seen as dangerous, crime-infested areas, while the suburbs were seen as safe places to live and raise a family, leading to a social trend known in some parts of the world as white flight.

This phenomenon runs counter to much of the rest of the world, where slums mostly exist outside the city, rather than within them. With the increasing population of the older, more established suburban areas, many of the problems which were once seen as purely urban ones have manifested themselves there as well.

Some social scientists suggest that the historical processes of suburbanization and decentralization are instances of white privilege that have contributed to contemporary patterns of environmental racism. Recent developments in communication technology, such as the spread of broadband services, the growth of e-mail and the advent of practical home video conferencing, has enabled more people to work from home rather than commuting. Although this can occur either in the city or in the suburbs, the effect is generally decentralizing, which works against the largest advantage of the centre city, which is easier access to information and supplies due to centralization.

Similarly, the rise of efficient package express delivery systems, such as (in the United States) FedEx and UPS, which take advantage of computerization and the availability of an efficient air transportation system, also eliminates some of the advantages that were once to be had from having a business located in the city. Industrial, warehousing, and factory land uses have also moved to suburban areas.

Cheap telecommunications removes the need for company headquarters to be within quick courier distance of the warehouses and ports. Urban areas suffer from traffic congestion, which creates costs in extra driver costs for the company which can be reduced if they were in a suburban area near a highway. As with residential, lower property taxes and low land prices encourage selling industrial land for profitable brownfield redevelopment. Suburban areas also offer more land to use as a buffer between industrial and residential and retail space to avoid NIMBY sentiments and gentrification pressure from the local community when residential and retail is adjacent to industrial space in an urban area. Suburban municipalities can offer tax breaks, specialized zoning, and regulatory incentives to attract industrial land users to their area, such as City of Industry, California. The overall effect of these developments is that businesses as well, and not just individuals, now see an advantage to locating in the suburbs, where the cost of buying land, renting space, and running their operations, is cheaper than in the city.

This continuing dispersal from a single city centre has led to other recent phenomena in American suburbs, the advent of edge cities and exurbs, arising out of clusters of office buildings built in suburban commercial centres around shopping malls and higher density developments. With more and more jobs for suburbanites being located in these areas rather than in the main city core that the suburbs grew out of, traffic patterns, which for decades centred on people commuting into the centre city to work in the morning and then returning home in the evening, have become more complex, with the volume of intra-suburban traffic increasing tremendously. By 2000, half of the US population lived in suburban areas.

Effects on psychological health

Historically it was believed that living in highly urban areas resulted in social isolation, social disorganization, and psychological problems, and that living in suburbs would be more conducive to overall happiness, due to lower population density, lower crime, and a more stable population. A study based on data from 1974, however, found this not to be the case, finding that people living in suburbs had neither greater satisfaction with their neighbourhood nor greater satisfaction with the quality of their lives as compared to people living in urban areas.

GEOGRAPHY AND URBAN AREAS

Census statistics for urban areas are produced both because of the widespread interest in information for areas *per se* (as they are more readily identifiable as the traditional towns and cities of Great Britain than are administrative areas, most of which comprise a mixture of both urban and rural land), and for the complementary purpose of dividing the country.s population between those living in urban areas and those living in rural areas.

Furthermore, the Statistical Office of the European Communities (SOEC) requested member countries to define large urban agglomerations (of 100,000 or more population) after the 1980 round of censuses. This part of the Report covers the concept of an urban area and some of the variety of ways in which such areas may be defined. The definitions used for urban areas identified in this listing differ between areas in England and Wales and areas in Scotland.

The concept

The traditional concept of a town or city would be a free-standing built-up area with a service core with a sufficient number and variety of shops and services, including perhaps a market, to make it recognisably urban in character.

It would have administrative, commercial, educational, entertainment and other social and civic functions and, in many cases, evidence of being historically well established. A local network of roads and other means of transport would focus on the area, and it would be a place drawing people for services and employment from surrounding areas. It would often be a place known beyond its immediate vicinity. Urban areas in Britain are, however, more complex. On one hand, historically free-standing towns have, over the years, grown and coalesced into continuously built-up areas, and subsidiary central places have developed as suburbs and satellite towns. This was recognised in the definition of conurbations used in the 1951 Census8. At the other extreme, some historic towns have stagnated and have lost central place functions.

General definitions of urban areas

An obvious way to define a town is in terms of its administrative boundary-that is, the area administered by a city, borough or town council. This is the method that had been followed in censuses in Great Britain up to and including 1971. In England and Wales, until re-organisation of local government in 1974, the division of the country between boroughs, urban districts and rural districts provided an approximate urban/rural split, and in Scotland, until reorganisation in 1975, the division between cities, burghs and district councils provided a similar split.

But there were serious disadvantages in the use of such administrative boundaries. They tended to change only infrequently and thus often did not reflect the development of a town. Sometimes the boundary lay well beyond the town.s built-up area (over-bounding) and included tracts of rural countryside. More often they lay within the built-up area (under-bounding) and so included only part of the totality of the urban area.

The local government boundaries established after reorganisation in the mid-1970s, and in use at the time of the 1991 Census, were almost entirely unsuited for the definition of urban areas because many districts had been deliberately drawn up to bring together towns and the surrounding rural countryside into single administrative units.

There are, however, at least three other approaches to defining an urban area. It may be defined either in terms of the built-up area (the.bricks and mortar. approach); or, alternatively, it may be defined in terms of the areas for which it provides services and facilities-the functional area. The functional area may embrace not only the built-up area but also free-standing settlements outside the urban area together with tracts of surrounding countryside if the population in these surrounding areas depends on the urban centre for services and employment.

A third method is to use density (either of population or of buildings) as an indicator of urbanisation. However, implementation of any of these approaches involves some arbitrary decisions in drawing up boundaries because, in practice, towns tend to merge physically and functionally with neighbouring towns and their hinterlands. The first attempt to define urban areas in a census was made after the 1951 Census and a limited range of statistics was published in the General Report from that Census.

After the 1966 Sample Census, the then Ministry of Housing and Local Government produced an analysis of de facto urban areas But neither of these provided a suitable base for statistics for urban and rural areas to be produced from later censuses. A new initiative was therefore necessary for the 1981 Census. The request from SOEC for member countries to define large urban agglomerations after the 1980 round of censuses, coincided with research at the then OPCS and the Department of Environment (DoE) into new methods of defining urban areas.

In England and Wales, two methods were considered:the first based on a combination of population density and land use; and the second on the extent of urban development indicated on Ordnance Survey (OS) maps. The latter was selected as it met the needs of both OPCS and DoE and enabled internationally comparable statistics to be produced for SOEC and the United Nations.

Basically, the same criteria were adopted for defining urban areas in the 1991 Census. In Scotland, the method used was a mix of the.bricks and mortar. approach and the population density methods described in paragraph 1.8. The definition of an urban area in England and Wales Generally, the terminology.urban. and.rural. has no fundamental definitional basis. The starting point in the definition of urban areas in England and Wales in this Report is the identification of areas with land use which is irreversibly urban in character. The definition used to identify urban land use is modelled on the developed areas classification produced by DoE, which, in turn, is based on the National Land Use Classification.

Land included as urban land comprises

- Permanent structures and the land on which they are situated (built-up site); for this purpose,.land. is defined as the ground covered by a permanent structure and any ground enclosed by, or closely associated with, such a structure;
- Transportation corridors (such as roads, railways and canals) which have built-up sites on one or both sides, or which link up built-up sites which are less than 50 metres apart;
- Transportation features such as airport and operational airfields, railway yards, motorway service areas and car parks;
- Mine buildings (but mineral workings and quarries are excluded); and
- Any area completely surrounded by built-up sites. Areas such as playing fields and golf courses are excluded unless they are completely surrounded by built-up sites.

The prerequisite for the recognition of an urban area is that the area of urban land should extend for 20 hectares or more. Separate areas of urban land are linked if less than 50 metres apart. Land between built-up sites is not regarded as urban unless it satisfies one of the conditions. The critical factor in the recognition of an urban area is a minimum population of approximately 1,000 persons.

However, as there was no prior information on the 1991 populations of areas of urban land, a proxy threshold was applied by excluding areas with less than four 1991 Census Enumeration Districts (EDs). This resulted in the exclusion of some areas of urban land with more than 1,000 population, but very few above 2,000. A rule recommended by the United Nations and used by a number of European Community members states is that areas of urban land of 20 or more hectares that are less than 200 metres apart are linked to form a continuous urban area. Major urban agglomerations, such as Greater London and the metropolitan counties, are sub-divided in order to provide a more useful set of statistics and to enable some comparisons to be made with previously published census data. Some smaller urban agglomerations are also subdivided where appropriate, and, where possible, previously separate urban centres, where urban land has since merged, are also subdivided.

Identification of urban areas in England and Wales

The first stage was the updating, by Ordnance Survey (OS) of the 1981 set of 1:10,000 scale transparent overlays depicting the extent of urban land as defined by the criteria above as at 1 April 1991. These overlays were updated at OS headquarters from information supplied by each of their local field offices, making use of local intelligence including recent urban development which might not have been fully surveyed. The second stage was for OS to digitise the boundaries of the areas of urban land, including the subdivisions used in 1981. A computer analysis of the digitised boundaries and the population-weighted centroids of the 1991 Census EDs was then carried out.

This process identified those ED centroids within or near the boundary of each area of urban land. An ED was then defined as urban if its centroid was either within the area of urban land or within a buffer zone of 150 metres of it. From detailed inspection of a sample of areas, this buffer zone minimised the misclassification of EDs as rural when they were really urban in character, or vice versa.

Those areas of urban land with four or more such EDs were then classified as urban areas. Inspections were carried out on newly emerging urban areas in 1991, and on any 1981 urban areas that had apparently disappeared, to confirm that the treatment of these areas had been correct; similarly with those areas in 1981 that had merged or split.

URBAN PLANNING

Urban, city, and town planning integrates land use planning and transportation planning to improve the built, economic and social environments of communities. Regional planning deals with a still larger environment, at a less detailed level.

Urban planning can include urban renewal, by adapting urban planning methods to existing cities suffering from decay and lack of investment.

History

Agriculture and other techniques facilitated larger populations than the very small communities of the Paleolithic. They may have led to stronger, more coercive governments at the same time. The pre-Classical and Classical ages saw a number of cities laid out according to fixed plans, though many tended to develop organically. Designed cities were characteristic of the Mesopotamian, Harrapan, and Egyptian civilizations of the third millennium BCE.

Distinct characteristics of urban planning from remains of the cities of Harappa, Lothal, and Mohenjo-daro in the Indus Valley Civilization (in modern-day northwestern India and Pakistan) lead archeologists to conclude that they are the earliest examples of deliberately planned and managed cities.The streets of many of these early cities were paved and laid out at right angles in a grid pattern, with a hierarchy of streets from major boulevards to residential alleys. Archaeological evidence suggests that many Harrapan houses were laid out to protect from noise and enhance residential privacy; many also had their own water wells, probably for both sanitary and ritual purposes. These ancient cities were unique in that they often had drainage systems, seemingly tied to a well-developed ideal of urban sanitation.

The Greek Hippodamus (c. 407 BC) has been dubbed the "Father of City Planning" for his design of Miletus; Alexander commissioned him to lay out his new city of Alexandria, the grandest example of idealized urban planning of the Mediterranean world, where the city's regularity was facilitated by its level site near a mouth of the Nile. The Hippodamian, or grid plan, was the basis for subsequent Greek and Roman cities.

The ancient Romans used a consolidated scheme for city planning, developed for military defence and civil convenience. The basic plan consisted of a central forum with city services, surrounded by a compact, rectilinear grid of streets, and wrapped in a wall for defence. To reduce travel times, two diagonal streets crossed the square grid, passing through the central square. A river usually flowed through the city, providing water, transport, and sewage disposal. Many European towns, such as Turin, preserve the remains of these schemes. The Romans had a very logical way of designing their cities. They laid out the streets at right angles, in the form of a square grid. All roads were equal in width and length, except for two, which formed the center of the grid and intersected in the middle. One ran east–west, the other north–south. They were slightly wider than the others. All roads were made of carefully fitted stones and smaller, hard-packed stones. Bridges were constructed where needed. Each square marked by four roads was called an *insula,* the Roman equivalent of a modern city block.

Each insula was 80 yards (73 m) square, with the land within it divided. As the city developed, each insula would eventually be filled with buildings of various shapes and sizes and crisscrossed with back roads and alleys. Most insulae were given to the first settlers of a Roman city, but each person had to pay to construct his own house.

The city was surrounded by a wall to protect it from invaders and to mark the city limits. Areas outside city limits were left open as farmland. At the end of each main road was a large gateway with watchtowers. A portcullis covered the opening when the city was under siege, and additional watchtowers were constructed along the city walls. An aqueduct was built outside the city walls.

The collapse of Roman civilization saw the end of Roman urban planning, among other arts. Urban development in the Middle Ages, characteristically focused on a fortress, a fortified abbey, or a (sometimes abandoned) Roman nucleus, occurred "like the annular rings of a tree", whether in an extended village or the center of a larger city. Since the new center was often on high, defensible ground, the city plan took on an organic character, following the irregularities of elevation contours like the shapes that result from agricultural terracing.

The ideal of wide streets and orderly cities was not lost, however. A few medieval cities were admired for their wide thoroughfares and orderly arrangements, but the juridical chaos of medieval cities (where the administration of streets was sometimes passed down through noble families), and the characteristic tenacity of medieval Europeans in legal matters prevented frequent or large-scale urban planning until the Renaissance and the strengthening of all central governments, from city-states to the kings of France, characteristic of that epoch.

Florence was an early model of the new urban planning, which took on a star-shaped layout adapted from the new star fort, designed to resist cannon fire. This model was widely imitated, reflecting the enormous cultural power of Florence in this age; "[t]he Renaissance was hypnotized by one city type which for a century and a half— from Filarete to Scamozzi— was impressed upon utopian schemes: this is the star-shaped city". Radial streets extend outward from a defined center of military, communal or spiritual power.

Only in ideal cities did a centrally planned structure stand at the heart, as in Raphael's *Sposalizio* (*Illustration*) of 1504. As built, the unique example of a rationally planned *quattrocento* new city center, that of Vigevano (1493–95), resembles a closed space instead, surrounded by arcading.

Filarete's ideal city, building on Leone Battista Alberti's *De re aedificatoria*, was named "Sforzinda" in compliment to his patron; its twelve-pointed shape, circumscribable by a "perfect" Pythagorean figure, the circle, took no heed of its undulating terrain in Filarete's manuscript. This process occurred in cities, but ordinarily not in the industrial suburbs characteristic of this era, which remained disorderly and characterized by crowding and organic growth.

Following the 1695 bombardment of Brussels by the French troops of King Louis XIV, in which a large part of the city center was destroyed, Governor Max Emanuel proposed using the reconstruction to completely change the layout and architectural style of the city. His plan was to transform the medieval city into a city of the new baroque style, modeled on Turin, with a logical street layout, with straight avenues offering long, uninterrupted views flanked by buildings of a uniform size.

This plan was opposed by residents and municipal authorities, who wanted a rapid reconstruction, did not have the resources for grandiose proposals, and resented what they considered the imposition of a new, foreign, architectural style. In the actual reconstruction, the general layout of the city was conserved, but it was not identical to that before the cataclysm. Despite the necessity of rapid reconstruction and the lack of financial means, authorities did take several measures to improve traffic flow, sanitation, and the aesthetics of the city. Many streets were made as wide as possible to improve traffic flow.

In the 1990s, the University of Kentucky voted the Italian town of Todi as the ideal city and "most livable town in the world", the place where man and nature, history and tradition, come together to create a site of excellence. In Italy, other examples of ideal cities planned according to scientific methods are Urbino, Pienza, Ferrara, San Giovanni Valdarno, and San Lorenzo Nuovo.

Many Central American civilizations also planned their cities, including sewage systems and running water. In Mexico, Tenochtitlan was the capital of the Aztec empire, built on an island in Lake Texcoco in what is now the Federal District in central Mexico. At its height, Tenochtitlan was one of the largest cities in the world, with over 200,000 inhabitants.

Shibam in Yemen features over 500 tower houses, each rising 5 to 11 storeys high, with each floor being an apartment occupied by a single family. The city has some of the tallest mudbrick houses in the world, some over 100 feet (30 meters) high.

In the developed countries of Western Europe, North America, Japan, and Australasia, planning and architecture can be said to have gone through various paradigms or stages of consensus in the last 200 years. Firstly, there was the industrialised city of the 19th century, where building was largely controlled by businesses and wealthy elites. Around 1900, a movement began for providing citizens, especially factory workers, with healthier environments. The concept of the garden city arose and several model towns were built, such as Letchworth and Welwyn Garden City in Hertfordshire, UK, the world's first garden cities. These were small in size, typically providing for a few thousand residents.

In the 1920s, the ideas of modernism began to surface in urban planning. Based on the ideas of Le Corbusier and using new skyscraper-building techniques, the modernist city stood for the elimination of disorder, congestion, and the small scale, replacing them with preplanned and widely spaced freeways and tower blocks set within gardens. There were plans for large-scale rebuilding of cities in this era, such as the *Plan Voisin* (based on Le

Corbusier's Ville Contemporaine), which proposed clearing and rebuilding most of central Paris. No large-scale plans were implemented until after World War II, however. Throughout the late 1940s and 1950s, housing shortages caused by wartime destruction led many cities to subsidize housing blocks. Planners used the opportunity to implement the modernist ideal of towers surrounded by gardens. The most prominent example of an entire modernist city is Brasilia in Brazil, constructed between 1956 and 1960.

Reaction

By the late 1960s and early 1970s, many planners felt that modernism's clean lines and lack of human scale sapped vitality from the community, blaming them for high crime rates and social problems.

Modernist planning fell into decline in the 1970s when the construction of cheap, uniform tower blocks ended in most countries, such as Britain and France. Since then many have been demolished and replaced by other housing types. Rather than attempting to eliminate all disorder, planning now concentrates on individualism and diversity in society and the economy; this is the post-modernist era.

Minimally planned cities still exist. Houston is a large city (with a metropolitan population of 5.5 million) in a developed country without a comprehensive zoning ordinance. Houston does, however, restrict development densities and mandate parking, even though specific land uses are not regulated. Also, private-sector developers in Houston use subdivision covenants and deed restrictions to effect land-use restrictions resembling zoning laws. Houston voters have rejected comprehensive zoning ordinances three times since 1948. Even without traditional zoning, metropolitan Houston displays large-scale land-use patterns resembling zoned regions comparable in age and population, such as Dallas. This suggests that non-regulatory factors such as urban infrastructure and financing may be as important as zoning laws in shaping urban form.

Sustainable Development and Sustainability

Sustainable development and sustainability influence today's urban planners. Some planners argue that modern lifestyles use too many natural resources, polluting or destroying ecosystems, increasing social inequality, creating urban heat islands, and causing climate change. Many urban planners, therefore, advocate sustainable cities.

However, sustainable development is a recent, controversial concept. Wheeler, in his 1998 article, defines sustainable urban development as "development that improves the long-term social and ecological health of cities and towns." He sketches a 'sustainable' city's features: compact, efficient land use; less automobile use, yet better access; efficient resource use; less pollution and waste; the restoration of natural systems; good housing and living environments; a healthy social ecology; a sustainable economy; community participation and involvement; and preservation of local culture and wisdom.

Because of political and governance structures in most jurisdictions, sustainable planning measures must be widely supported before they can affect institutions and regions. Actual implementation is often a complex compromise. Collaborative Strategic Goal Oriented Programming (CoSGOP) is a collaborative and communicative way of strategic programming, decision-making, implementation, and monitoring oriented towards defined and specific goals. It is based on sound analysis of available information, emphasizes stakeholder participation, works to create awareness among actors, and is oriented towards managing development processes. It was adopted as a theoretical framework for analyzing redevelopment processes in large urban distressed areas in European cities.

Background of CoSGOP'

CoSGOP is derived from goal-oriented planning (Gesellschaft für Technische Zusammenarbeit-GTZ 1988), which was oriented towards the elaboration and implementation of projects based on a logical framework, which was useful for embedding a specific project in a wider development frame and defining its major elements. This approach had weaknesses: its logical rules were strictly applied and the expert language did not encourage participation. CoSGOP introduced a new approach characterized by communication with and active involvement of stakeholders and those to be affected by the program; strategic planning based on the identification of strengths and weakness, opportunities and threats, as well as on scenario-building and visioning; the definition of goals as the basis for action; and long-term, flexible programming of interventions by stakeholders.

Elements of CoSGOP

CoSGOP is not a planning method but a process model. It provides a framework for communication and joint decision-making, in a structured process characterized by feedback loops. It also facilitates stakeholder learning. The essential elements of CoSGOP are analysis of stakeholders (identifying stakeholders' perceptions of problems, interests, and expectations); analysis of problems and potentials (including objective problems and problems and potentials perceived by stakeholders); development of goals, improvement priorities, and alternatives (requiring intensive communication and active stakeholder participation); specification of an improvement program and its main activities (based on priorities defined with the stakeholders); assessment of possible impacts of the improvement program; definition and detailed specification of key projects and their implementation; continuous monitoring of improvement activities, feedback, and adjustment of the programme (including technical and economic information and perceptions of stakeholders).

Application

CoSGOP has been applied in European cross-border policy programming, as well in local and regional development programming. In 2004, the CoSGOP model was applied in the LUDA Project, starting with an analysis of the European experience of urban regeneration projects.

Collaborative Planning in the United States

Collaborative planning arose in the US in response to the inadequacy of traditional public participation techniques to provide real opportunities for the public to make decisions affecting their communities. Collaborative planning is a method designed to empower stakeholders by elevating them to the level of decision-makers through direct engagement and dialogue between stakeholders and public agencies, to solicit ideas, active involvement, and participation in the community planning process. Active public involvement can help planners achieve better outcomes by making them aware of the public's needs and preferences and by using local knowledge to inform projects. When properly administered, collaboration can result in more meaningful participation and better, more creative outcomes to persistent problems than can traditional participation methods. It enables planners to make decisions that reflect community needs and values, it fosters faith in the wisdom and utility of the resulting project, and the community is given a personal stake in its success.

Experiences in Portland and Seattle have demonstrated that successful collaborative planning depends on a number of interrelated factors: the process must be truly inclusive, with all stakeholders and affected groups invited to the table; the community must have final decision-making authority; full government commitment (of both financial and intellectual resources) must be manifest; participants should be given clear objectives by planning staff, who facilitate the process by providing guidance, consultancy, expert opinions, and research; and facilitators should be trained in conflict resolution and community organization.

5

Culture Geography

INTRODUCTION

Cultural geography is a sub-field within human geography. Cultural geography is the study of cultural products and norms and their variations across and relations to spaces and places. It focuses on describing and analysing the ways language, religion, economy, government and other cultural phenomena vary or remain constant, from one place to another and on explaining how humans function spatially.

Areas of study

The areas of study of cultural geography are very broad.

Among many applicable topics within the field of study are:

- Globalization has been theorised as an explanation for cultural convergence.
- Westernization or other similar processes such as modernization, americanization, islamization and others.
- Theories of cultural hegemony or cultural assimilation via cultural imperialism.
- Cultural areal differentiation, as a study of differences in way of life encompassing ideas, attitudes, languages, practices, institutions and structures of power and whole range of cultural practices in geographical areas.
- Study of cultural landscapes.
- Other topics include spirit of place, colonialism, post-colonialism, internationalism, immigration, emigration and ecotourism.

History

Though the first traces of the study of different nations and cultures on Earth can be dated back to ancient geographers such as Ptolemy or Strabo, cultural geography as academic study firstly emerged as an alternative to the environmental determinist theories of the early Twentieth century, which had believed that people and societies are controlled by the environment in which they develop.

Rather than studying pre-determined regions based upon environmental classifications, cultural geography became interested in cultural landscapes. This was led by Carl O. Sauer, at the University of California, Berkeley. As a result, cultural geography was long dominated by American writers. Sauer defined the landscape as the defining unit of geographic study. He saw that cultures and societies both developed out of their landscape, but also shaped them too.

This interaction between the 'natural' landscape and humans creates the 'cultural landscape'. Sauer's work was highly qualitative and descriptive and was surpassed in the 1930s by the regional geography of Richard Hartshorne, followed by the quantitative revolution.

Cultural geography was generally sidelined, though writers such as David Lowenthal continued to work on the concept of landscape. In the 1970s, the critique of positivism in geography caused geographers to look beyond the quantitative geography for its ideas. One of these re-assessed areas was also cultural geography.

New cultural geography

Since the 1980s, a "new cultural geography" has emerged, drawing on a diverse set of theoretical traditions, including Marxist political-economic models, feminist theory, post-colonial theory, post-structuralism and psychoanalysis.

Drawing particularly from the theories of Michel Foucault and performativity in western academia, and the more diverse influences of postcolonial theory, there has been a concerted effort to deconstruct the cultural in order to make apparent the various power relations.

A particular area of interest is that of identity politics and construction of identity.

Examples of areas of study include:

- Feminist geography
- Children's geographies
- Some parts of Tourism geography
- Behavioural geography
- Sexuality and space
- Some more recent developments in Political geography

Some within the 'new cultural geography' have turned their attention to critiquing some of its ideas, seeing its views on identity and space as static. It has followed the critiques of Foucault made by other 'poststructuralist' theorists such as Michel de Certeau and Gilles Deleuze. In this area, non-representational geography and population mobility research have dominated. Others have attempted to incorporate these critiques back into the new cultural geography.

CULTURAL DIVERSITY

Ethnic origins, religions, and languages are the major sources of cultural diversity. India is a country incredible for its diversity, biological and cultural. It is the natural resources that attracted to the subcontinent many streams of people at different times, from different directions; bringing together a great diversity of human genes and human cultures. Thus the bulk of the Indian population represents racial admixture in varying degrees. Unlike several other lands where the dominant human cultures have tended to absorb or eliminate others, in India the tendency has been to nurture diversity, which has been favoured by the diversity of the country's ecological regimes. Powerful kingdoms and enumerable dynasties, contributed to the shaping of India's cultural regions. An important source of diversity among the people of India is the cultural identity of particular communities and regions.

Despite maintaining distinct identities several jatis, sects, and communities have organic links with other segments of the population of the region, which develops a cultural persona over time. Indian civilization has had a pluralistic character from the start. The pluralistic and composite ethos of Indian civilization, which began evolving during the Vedic period, was supplemented by the rise of Buddhism and Jainism, and was further reinforced during the early medieval period, which witnessed the early zenith in the Bhakti Movement. This composite tradition attained primacy during the late medieval period.

Linguistic and philological evidences demonstrate the incorporation and adaptation of regional features into the mainstream of Sanskritic culture distinctly. Certain kinds of echo formations, which are characteristic of the Austric family of languages, found their way into the Indo-Aryan speeches. The presence of non-Aryan elements, especially Proto-Dravidian, in vocabulary, syntax and phoenetics in Vedic Sanskrit is now fairly well established. The later Vedic texts indicate an even greater admixture of non-Aryan words. The Vedic society was internally differentiated and it was pluralistic. It was a synthesis of Aryan and non-Aryan, including tribal elements. Since its very beginning Hinduism has been a "mosaic of distinct cults, deities, sects and ideas". Most records reveal that totemic deities such as fish, tortoise and boar were made into incarnations of Vishnu. Shiva was formed by a fusion of the Vedic Rudra with some non-Aryan deity. Shiva in its tribal and folk form is observable in several parts of peninsular India, including plains of northeast India, particularly in Assam -north-Bengal regions. Enough material exists which confirm the fact that Brahmanism immersed the deities of tribespeople and 'low-castes'. The popularity of the saga of Jagannath cult in Orissa and that of Viththala in Maharashtra testify this. Similarly, serpent worship and phallus worship, which later found their way into classical Hinduism, were taken over from local communities.

Unorthodox sects and cults, such as Shakta and the Tantric tradition, incorporated several esoteric features from indigenous, including tribal cultures. Thus, some interrelated critical foundations of unity may be delineated at the pan-Indian level. We may categorize them first as the Sanskritic Hinduism at the social structural levels and through a system of pilgrimage centres. Then we may consider a composite cultural tradition born out of the protracted interaction and exchange between Hindus and Muslims and adherents of other faiths through the length and breadth of the country.

In this context one may notice social reforms and humanistic tendency as exemplified in the Sufi and Bhakti Movements. The secular-democratic philosophy, which is enshrined in the Constitution of the country and a Gandhian vision of Indianness, which was well founded during freedom movement, are manifestation and demonstration of our composite culture in modern India. Since the late medieval period India witnessed a creative synthesis of Hindu and Islamic civilizations and thus grew a composite tradition, a pluralistic synthesis of the Indo-Islamic tradition including inter-faith convergence. There are two interrelated dimensions of the Indo-Islamic tradition.

On the one hand, it manifested itself in syncretistic traditions of music, art, literature and architecture, and on the other, it found expression in folklore, dress patterns, food habits, names and surnames. If we turn to rural landscape we discover the distribution of material traits at the regional level indicating a certain complementarities in that it is marked by both local differentiation and interpenetration. Not only that a cluster or complex of material traits at the regional level unites different parts and communities, different communities have brought with them often innovations into regions of their adoption and internalized them effectively, though a proper mapping of same is unlikely to be accomplished shortly. This phenomenon is seldom subjected to a critical examination in a diachronic framework anywhere. Language is an important attribute of a population, and has great relevance and significance in a multi-lingual and multi-ethnic country like India. The language literature generated by census over the last more than one hundred years has thrown much light on the ethnic and the linguistic characteristics of the population. The total number of mother tongues returned in 1961 and 1971 censuses was around

3,000, in 1981 around 7,000 and in 1991, it was more than 10,000. Tribal languages cannot be dismissed as dialects; many of them have a growing literature and at least two have their own scripts. Their multiplicity is baffling. Consider the case of Nagaland, formerly a district but now a State. It has as many as twenty different languages. The Kohima station of All India Radio used to broadcast in twenty-five languages, besides Nagamese, the lingua-franka. The pan-Indian, civilizational dimension of cultural pluralism and syncretism encompasses ethnic diversity and admixture, linguistic heterogeneity as well as fusion, and variations as well as synthesis in customs, behavioural patterns, beliefs and rituals. The process of synthesis and integration has been extensively at work at the regional level. Though each group or community has a distinctive identity and ethos of its own, it does not exist in a social vacuum.

Rather, it forms part of an extended and dynamic network. Often, interaction, exchange and integration characterize inter-community relations. The sharing of space, regional ethos and cultural traits cut across religions and sectarian differences and bind the local people together. It is now revealed and established more vividly those cultural and religious practices in diverse eco-cultural zones of India have historically converged and people shared common traditions extensively. Thus, we witness a fine balancing between pluralism and syncretism pervading the base of Indian culture. While enough literature exists on this aspect of cultural manifestation in historical writings, not much is known about the religious syncretism and its stretch in contemporary India.

Cultural Diversity is our everyday reality

The international migration rate is growing fast every year. The "International Migration Report 2002" of the United Nations Department of Economic and Social Affairs, the number of migrants has doubled since the 1970s. The report also says that around 175 million persons are residing away from the country of their birth and one in every 10 persons in the developed regions is a migrant. Also, more migrants are coming from countries ever farther away. While the reasons for migration vary, one thing is sure: we live in an increasingly heterogeneous society.

Cultural Diversity reflects the respect of fundamental rights

Culture is a set of distinctive spiritual, material, intellectual and emotional features of society or a social group. It encompasses, in addition to art and literature, lifestyles, ways of living together, values systems, traditions and beliefs. Respecting and safeguarding culture is a matter of Human Rights.

Cultural Diversity presupposes respect of fundamental freedoms, namely freedom of thought, conscience and religion, freedom of opinion and expression, and freedom to participate in the cultural life of one's choice.

Cultural Diversity is our collective strength

The Johannesburg Declaration on Sustainable Development acknowledges that our rich diversity, which is our collective strength, should be used to ensure sustainable development. Cultural Diversity, indeed, is not just a natural fact that we need simply recognize and respect. It is about plurality of knowledge, wisdom and energy which all contribute to improving and moving the World forward.

CULTURAL LANDSCAPE

The cultural landscape is the environment around us which has been shaped by our interactions with all the constituent parts of that environment—the trees, plants, weather, houses, cars, other people, bugs, and a rather large number of other elements. In the twenty-first century, we are made quite aware of some of the problems involved in our relationship with our environments—many people are also in a position to enjoy their environmental interactions considerably.

Although the study of the cultural landscape has many social and political goals, at a most basic level, it is an attempt to understand the processes by which we engage our environments, with the most obvious goals of adding insight to these processes so that we might better understand both the possibilities and problems involved. I find the cultural landscape fascinating for a number of reasons.

The record that our creative interactions with the circumstances of everyday life leaves around us interests me aesthetically, morally, and practically: I read in the landscape a tremendous number of stories about what people have done in the past and what they have hoped for the future; I am continually delighted by the complexity and beauty of cultural and natural systems; and I find a great sense of equanimity in the ongoing adaptation and resiliance of both these natural and cultural systems in the face of disruption, change and stresses that serve as constant reminders that the unknown is always much larger than the known. Ongoing, active involvement with the processes of the cultural landscape around me seems to me one of the best ways I have to remain engaged with both the culture and the environment of which I am a part.

The modernization of the built environment has brought problems which our culture has often responded to with an attitude of escape; I find in my interest and interaction with the cultural landscape a compelling way to engage these problems at a scale appropriate to what is plausibly achieved in everydaylife. Many of the most pressing issues of culture and environment at the turn of the twenty-first century are themselves products of or exacerbated by our sense of the natural environment as a medium for escape—and our sense of culture as something from which we need escape! Attention to the cultural landscape not only allows us to gain insights into the way we do and might behave in our environments, but also provides us access to an understanding of our environments that includes us as part of the landscape, and that helps us to understand the natural environment not only as something apart from us which our modernization has exploited furiously, but also as a series of processes of which we are part, and within which we have had a long history.

This rich sense of our constant participation in the processes which surrounds us not only helps us see continuity along with change in the context of modernization and globalization, but it also helps us to get a sense of the profoundly social nature of our environmental experience.

CULTURAL LEVELING

Cultural leveling is the process by which different cultures approach each other as a result of travel and communication. Cultural leveling within the United States has been driven by mass market media such as radio and television broadcasting and nation wide distribution of magazines and catalogs. Some of these means and effects are considered artifacts of the Machine Age of the 1920s and 1930s.

CULTURAL MAPPING

"Cultural mapping" (also known as cultural resource mapping or cultural landscape mapping) is the label organisations and peoples (including UNESCO) concerned about safeguarding cultural diversity give to a wide range of research techniques and tools used to 'map' distinct peoples' tangible and intangible cultural assets within local landscapes around the world

- In its Universal Declaration on Cultural Diversity, UNESCO notes the importance of States adopting inclusive ways of encouraging cultural diversity...

The term 'cultural mapping' is also used to describe the use of 'cultural mapping' type research methods, tools, and techniques to identify, describe, portray, promote, and plan future use of particular region's or cities combined cultural assets and resources:

- A broadly-based mapping exercise for purposes of investigating or creating an identity profile of the community is enriching, informative and useful [...] The process of mapping by itself draws attention to the existence and importance of cultural resources. The results point out problems to be solved or strengths to build upon.

CULTURAL PRACTICE

Cultural practice generally refers to the manifestation of a culture or sub-culture, especially in regard to the traditional and customary practices of a particular ethnic or other cultural group. In the broadest sense, this term can apply to any person manifesting any aspect of any culture at any time. However, in practical usage it commonly refers to the traditional practices developed within specific ethnic cultures, especially those aspects of culture that have been practiced since ancient times. The term is gaining in importance due to the increased controversy over "rights of cultural practice", which are protected in many jurisdictions for indigenous peoples and sometimes ethnic minorities. It is also a major component of the field of cultural studies, and is a primary focus of international works such as the United Nations declaration of the rights of indigenous Peoples. Cultural practice is also a subject of discussion in questions of cultural survival. If an ethnic group retains its formal ethnic identity but loses its core cultural practices or the knowledge, resources, or ability to continue them, questions arise as to whether the culture is able to actually survive at all. International bodies such as the United Nations Permanent Forum on Indigenous Issues continually work on these issues, which are increasingly at the forefront of globalization questions.

INTERCULTURAL COMPETENCE

Intercultural competence is the ability of successful communication with people of other cultures. A person who is interculturally competent captures and understands, in interaction with people from foreign cultures, their specific concepts in perception, thinking, feeling and acting. Earlier experiences are considered, free from prejudices; there is an interest and motivation to continue learning.

Cross-cultural competence

Cross-cultural competence, another term for inter-cultural competence, has generated its own share of contradictory and confusing definitions, due to the wide variety of academic approaches and professional fields attempting to achieve it for their own ends. One author identified no fewer than eleven different terms with some equivalence to 3C: cultural savvy, astuteness, appreciation, literacy or fluency, adaptability, terrain, expertise, competency, awareness, intelligence, and understanding.

Organizations from fields as diverse as business, health care, government security and developmental aid agencies, academia, and non-governmental organizations have all sought to leverage 3C in one guise or another, often with poor results due to a lack of rigorous study of the phenomenon and reliance on "common sense" approaches based on the culture developing the 3C models in the first place. The U.S. Army Research Institute, which is currently engaged in a study of the phenomenon, defines 3C as: "A set of cognitive, behavioural, and affective/motivational components that enable individuals to adapt effectively in intercultural environments".

Cross-cultural competence does not operate in a vacuum, however. One theoretical construct posits that 3C, language proficiency, and regional knowledge are distinct skills that are inextricably linked, but to varying degrees depending on the context in which they are employed. In educational settings, Bloom's affective and cognitive taxonomies serve as an effective framework to describe the overlap area between the three disciplines: at the receiving and knowledge levels 3C can operate with near independence from language proficiency or regional knowledge, but as one approaches the internalizing and evaluation levels the required overlap area approaches totality.

The development of intercultural competence is mostly based on experiences one comes across while communicating with different cultures. While interacting with people from other cultures they face certain obstacles which are caused due to differences in the cultural understanding between the two people in question. Such experiences motivate people to work on skills that can help them put forward their point of view in front of an audience belonging to a completely different cultural ethnicity and background.

An issue that comes forward, especially for people who live in countries which is not their country of origin is that of which culture they should follow. Should they try to fit in and adapt to the culture surrounding them, or should they hold on to their culture and try to avoid interacting with the culture surrounding them? This issue is one faced by most people today. Globalization has caused the immigration rates to sky rocket for most of the developed and developing countries, and hence people come to these countries in order to find employment and settle down in such countries where they are constantly surrounded by a culture which does not belong to them. International students are another part of the population that faces this dilemma. They have to make a choice about whether they are willing to modify their cultural boundaries in order to adapt to the culture around them or whether they hold on to their culture and surround themselves by people from their own country.

The people who decide to live by the latter rule are the students which face most problems in their university life and face constant culture shocks, while the students who live by the former rule face less problems and interact more with the domestic students. They end up increasing their knowledge about the culture which is followed by the domestic students and modify their own culture to inculcate certain aspects from the culture surrounding them in order to help them blend successfully in the society.

EARTH IN CULTURE

The cultural perspective on the Earth, or world, varies by society and time period. Religious beliefs often include a creation belief as well as personification in the form of a deity. The exploration of the world has modified many of the perceptions of the planet, resulting in a viewpoint of a globally-integrated ecosystem. Unlike the remainder of the planets in the Solar System, mankind didn't perceive the Earth as a planet until the sixteenth century.

Etymology

Unlike the other planets in the Solar System, in English, Earth does not directly share a name with an ancient Roman deity. The name Earth derives from the eighth century Anglo-Saxon word erda, which means ground or soil. It became eorthe later, and then erthe in Middle English. These words are all cognates of Jörð, the name of the giantess of Norse myth. Earth was first used as the name of the sphere of the Earth in the early fifteenth century. The planet's name in Latin, used academically and scientifically in the West during the Renaissance, is the same as that of Terra Mater, the Roman goddess, which translates to English as Mother Earth.

Planetary Symbol

The standard astronomical symbol of the Earth consists of a cross circumscribed by a circle. This symbol is known as the wheel cross, sun cross, Odin's cross or Woden's cross. Although it has been used in various cultures for different purposes, it came to represent the compass points, earth and the land.

Another version of the symbol is a cross on top of a circle; a stylized globus cruciger that was also used as an early astronomical symbol for the planet Earth.

Religious Beliefs

Earth has often been personified as a deity, in particular a goddess. In many cultures the mother goddess is also portrayed as a fertility deity. To the Aztec, Earth was called Tonantzin-"our mother"; to the Incas, Earth was called Pachamama-"mother earth".

The Chinese Earth goddess Hou Tu is similar to Gaia, the Greek goddess personifying the Earth. To Hindus it is called Bhuma Devi, the Goddess of Earth. In Norse mythology, the Earth giantess Jörð was the mother of Thor and the daughter of Annar. Ancient Egyptian mythology is different from that of other cultures because Earth is male, Geb, and sky is female, Nut. Creation myths in many religions recall a story involving the creation of the world by a supernatural deity or deities. A variety of religious groups, often associated with fundamentalist branches of Protestantism or Islam, assert that their interpretations of the accounts of creation in sacred texts are literal truth and should be considered alongside or replace conventional scientific accounts of the formation of the Earth and the origin and development of life.

Such assertions are opposed by the scientific community as well as other religious groups. A prominent example is the creation-evolution controversy.

Physical Form

In the ancient past there were varying levels of belief in a flat Earth, with the Mesopotamian culture portraying the world as a flat disk afloat in an ocean. The spherical form of the Earth was suggested by early Greek philosophers; a belief espoused by Pythagoras. By the Middle Ages-as evidenced by thinkers such as Thomas Aquinas-European belief in a spherical Earth was widespread.

Prior to circumnavigation of the planet and the introduction of space flight, belief in a spherical Earth was based on observations of the secondary effects of the Earth's shape and parallels drawn with the shape of other planets.

Modern perspective

The technological developments of the latter half of the 20th century are widely considered to have altered the public's perception of the Earth. Before space flight, the popular image of Earth was of a green world. Science fiction artist Frank R. Paul provided perhaps the first image of a cloudless blue planet on the back cover of the July 1940 issue of Amazing Stories, a common depiction for several decades thereafter. Earth was first photographed from space by Explorer 6 in 1959. Yuri Gagarin became the first human to view Earth from space in 1961.

The crew of the Apollo 8 was the first to view an Earth-rise from lunar orbit in 1968. In 1972 the crew of the Apollo 17 produced the famous "Blue Marble" photograph of the planet Earth from cislunar space. This became an iconic image of the planet as a marble of cloud-swirled blue ocean broken by green-brown continents. NASA archivist Mike Gentry has speculated that "The Blue Marble" is the most widely distributed image in human history. A photo taken of a distant Earth by Voyager 1 in 1990 inspired Carl Sagan to describe the planet as a "Pale Blue Dot." Since the 1960s, Earth has also been described as a massive "Spaceship Earth," with a life support system that requires maintenance, or, in the Gaia hypothesis, as having a biosphere that forms one large organism. Over the past two centuries a growing enviro-nmental movement has emerged that is concerned about humankind's effects on the Earth. The key issues of this socio-political movement are the conservation of natural resources, elimination of pollution, and the usage of land. Although diverse in interests and goals, environmentalists as a group tend to advocate sustainable management of resources and stewardship of the environment through changes in public policy and individual behaviour. Of particular concern is the large-scale exploitation of non-renewable resources. Changes sought by the environmental movements are sometimes in conflict with commercial interests due to the additional costs associated with managing the environmental impact of those interests.

CULTURAL TRAVEL

Cultural Travel is a type of travel that emphasizes experiencing life within a foreign culture, rather than from the outside as a temporary visitor. Cultural travellers leave their home environment at home, bringing only themselves and a desire to become part of the culture they visit. Cultural travel goes beyond cultural exploration or discovery; it involves a transformation in way of life. This definition was first used by Gary Langer "Travel to Learn".

Transitions Abroad. A way of describing travel that requires a "transition" to a new level of understanding of and appreciation for a foreign culture. The term is often distorted and misused by travel agents, tour operators and international tourism organizations.

Culture primarily has to do with people and less with places or things. So visiting museums, touring ancient structures, attending festivals, and eating local food does not provide the same experience as becoming a member of the culture itself. The antithesis of cultural travel is tourism, where people bring their home environment with them wherever they go and apply it to whatever they see.

CULTURAL TOURISM

'Cultural tourism' is the subset of tourism concerned with a country or region's culture, specifically the lifestyle of the people in those geographical areas, the history of those peoples, their art, architecture, religion(s), and other elements that helped shape their way of life. Cultural tourism includes tourism in urban areas, particularly historic or large cities and their cultural facilities such as museums and theatres. It can also include tourism in rural areas showcasing the traditions of indigenous cultural communities, and their values and lifestyle. It is generally agreed that cultural tourists spend substantially more than standard tourists do. This form of tourism is also becoming generally more popular throughout the world, and a recent OECD report has highlighted the role that cultural tourism can play in regional development in different world regions. Cultural tourism has been defined as 'the movement of persons to cultural attractions away from their normal place of residence, with the intention to gather new information and experiences to satisfy their cultural needs'.

Destinations

One type of cultural tourism destination is living cultural areas. For an indigenous culture that has stayed largely separated from the surrounding majority, tourism can present both advantages and problems. On the positive side are the unique cultural practices and arts that attract the curiosity of tourists and provide opportunities for tourism and economic development.

On the negative side is the issue of how to control tourism so that those same cultural amenities are not destroyed and the people do not feel violated. Other destinations include historical sites, modern urban districts, theme parks and country clubs, coastal or island ecosystems, and inland natural areas. Only a handful of people take part in these holiday trips each year as opposed to the thousands of people who go on package holidays.

CULTURAL REGION

Cultural Region –places and regions provide the essence of geography. A culture region is a geographical unit based on characteristics and functions of culture. Three types of culture regions are recognized by geographers: formal, functional, and vernacular.

Formal Culture Region

Formal Culture Region- an area inhabited by people who have one or more cultural traits in common, such as language, religion or system of livelihood. It is an area that is relatively homogeneous with regard to one or more cultural traits.

The geographer who identifies a formal culture region must locate cultural borders. Because cultures overlap and mix, such boundaries are rarely sharp, even if only a single cultural trait is mapped.

For this reason, we find cultural border zones rather than lines. These zones broaden with each additional cultural trait that is considered, because no two traits have the same spatial distribution. As a result, instead of having clear borders, formal culture regions reveal a centre or core where the defining traits are all present. Away from the central core, the characteristics weaken and disappear. Thus, many formal culture regions display a core-periphery pattern.

Functional Culture Regions

Functional Culture Regions- the hallmark of a formal culture region is cultural homogeneity. It is abstract rather than concrete. By contrast, a functional culture region need not be culturally homogeneous; instead, it is an area that has been organized to function politically, socially, or economically as one unit. A city, an independent state, a precinct, a church diocese or parish, a trade area or a farm. Functional culture regions have nodes, or central points where the functions are coordinated and directed.

Example: City halls, national capitals, precinct voting places, parish churches, factories, and banks. In this sense, functional regions also possess a core-periphery configuration, in common with formal culture regions. Many functional regions have clearly defined borders that include all land under the jurisdiction of a particular urban government; clearly delineated on a regional map by a line distinguishing between one jurisdiction and another.

Vernacular Culture Regions

Vernacular Culture Regions- is one that is perceived to exist by its inhabitants, as evidenced by the widespread acceptance and use of a special regional name. Some vernacular regions are based on physical environmental features; others find their basis in economic, political, or historical characteristics. Vernacular regions, like most culture regions, generally lack sharp borders, and the inhabitants of any given area may claim residence in more than one such region.

It grows out of people's sense of belonging and identification with a particular region. Ex: one popular region in the US "Dixie". They often lack the organization necessary for functional regions, although they may be centred around a single urban node, and they frequently do not display the cultural homogeneity that characterizes formal regions.

CHILDREN'S STREET CULTURE

Children's street culture refers to the cumulative culture created by young children. Collectively, this body of knowledge is passed down from one generation of urban children to the next, and can also be passed between different groups of children. It is most common in children between the ages of seven and twelve. It is strongest in urban working class industrial districts where children are traditionally free to "play out" in the streets for long periods without supervision.

Difference from mass media culture

Children's street culture is invented and largely sustained by children themselves, although it may come to incorporate fragments of media culture and toys in its activities. It is not to be confused with the commercial media-culture produced for children, although it may overlap.

Location and play materials

Young children's street culture usually takes place on quiet backstreets and sidewalks, and along routes that venture out into local parks, playgrounds, scrub and wasteland, and to local shops. It can often incorporate many found and scavenged materials such as old car seats, tyres, planks, bricks, etc. Sometimes found materials will be combined to create objects. Play will often incorporate crazes.

It also imposes imaginative status on certain parts of the urban realm. In summer children may use scavenged materials to create a temporary and semi-hidden 'den' or 'hideout' or 'HQ' in a marginal area near their homes, that serves as an informal meeting and relaxation place during the summer. An urban area that looks faceless or neglected to an adult may have deep 'spirit of place' meanings in children's street culture.

History and research

Although it varies from place to place, research shows that it appears to share many commonalities across many cultures. It is a traditional phenomenon that has been closely investigated and documented in the western world during the 20th century by anthropologists and folklorists such as Iona Opie; street photographers such as Roger Mayne, Helen Levitt, David Trainer, Humphrey Spender and Robert Doisneau; urbanists such as Colin Ward and Robin Moore, as well as being described in countless novels of childhood. The research of Robin Moore stresses children's need for 'marginal' unsupervised areas 'within running distance' of homes.

There are now two academic journals devoted to this area, the Journal of Children's Geographies and Play and Folklore. It has occasionally been central to feature films, such as the Our Gang series, Ealing's Hue and Cry and some Children's Film Foundation films. Since the advent of distractions such as video games, and television, concerns have been expressed about the vitality-or even the survival-of children's street culture.

Children's urban legends

Many informal groups of small children will develop some level of superstitious beliefs about their local area. For instance:- they will believe that there are certain places that are 'unlucky' to step on or touch or that an old woman is a 'witch', or that an abandoned house is 'haunted'. But in some extreme circumstances a consistent mythos may emerge among young children, and across a large area.

One example dates from 1997, The Miami New Times published Lynda Edwards' report "Myths Over Miami", which describes a huge consistent mythology spreading among young homeless children in the American South.

The story has been picked up and reprinted many times on internet blogs and websites.

There is no known verification or confirmation that the mythology she describes actually exists, but these "secret stories" are clearly based on known elements of street culture, such as labeling certain places "haunted" or recycling legends of dangerous spirits such as Mary Worth. The object was the basis for Mercedes Lackey's novel Mad Maudlin, co-written with Rosemary Edghill.

CIVILIZATION AND COLONIALISM GEOGRAPHY

Civilization is a sometimes controversial term which has been used in several related ways. Primarily, the term has been used to refer to human cultures which are complex in terms of technology, science, politics and division of labour. Such civilizations are generally urbanized.

In classical contexts civilized peoples were called this in contrast to "barbarian" peoples, while in modern contexts civilized peoples have been contrasted to "primitive" peoples. In modern academic discussions however, there is a tendency to use the term in a more neutral way to mean approximately the same thing as "culture" and can refer to any human society associated with any particular geographical location at a particular time, historical or current.

Still, even when used in this second sense, the word is often restricted to apply only to societies that have attained a particular level of advancement, especially the founding of cities, with the word "city" defined in various ways. The level of advancement of a civilization is often measured by its progress in agriculture, long-distance trade, occupational specialization, and urbanism. Aside from these core elements, civilization is often marked by any combination of a number of secondary elements, including a developed transportation system, writing, standards of measurement, contract and tort-based legal systems, characteristic art styles, monumental architecture, mathematics, science, sophisticated metallurgy, politics, and astronomy.

Colonialism

Colonialism is the establishment, maintenance, acquisition and expansion of colonies in one territory by people from another territory. Colonialism is a process whereby sovereignty over the colony is claimed by the metropole and the social structure, government, and economics of the colony are changed by colonists-people from the metropole. Colonialism is a set of unequal relationships: between the metropole and the colony, and between the colonists and the indigenous population.

The term colonialism normally refers to a period of history from the late 15th to the 20th century when European nation states established colonies on other continents. In this period, the justifications for colonialism included various factors such as the profits to be made, the expansion of the power of the metropole and various religious and political beliefs. Colonialism and imperialism were ideologically linked with mercantilism. Collins English Dictionary defines colonialism as "the policy of acquiring and maintaining colonies, especially for exploitation."

The Merriam-Webster Dictionary offers four definitions, including "something characteristic of a colony" and "control by one power over a dependent area or people." The Stanford Encyclopedia of Philosophy "uses the term 'colonialism' to describe the process of European settlement and political control over the rest of the world, including Americas, Australia, and parts of Africa and Asia." It discusses the distinction between colonialism and imperialism and states that "[g]iven the difficulty of consistently distinguishing between the two terms, this entry will use colonialism as a broad concept that refers to the project of European political domination from the sixteenth to the twentieth centuries that ended with the national liberation movements of the 1960s."

In his preface to Jürgen Osterhammel's Colonialism: A Theoretical Overview, Roger Tignor says, "For Osterhammel, the essence of colonialism is the existence of colonies, which are by definition governed differently from other territories such as protectorates or informal spheres of influence." In the book, Osterhammel asks, "How can 'colonialism' be defined independently from 'colony?'"

He settles on a three-sentence definition:

- Colonialism is a relationship between an indigenous majority and a minority of foreign invaders. The fundamental decisions affecting the lives of the colonized people are made and implemented by the colonial rulers in pursuit of interests that are often defined in a distant metropolis. Rejecting cultural compromises with the colonized population, the colonisers are convinced of their own superiority and their ordained mandate to rule.

Cosmopolitanism

Cosmopolitanism is the belief that everyone exists in a globally constructed ethical-political order. The purpose of this paper is to unpack this definition. Such a definition, I believe, strikes at the core of many iterations of cosmopolitanism today. But it is not my intention to provide an intellectual history of the term here. Rather, I will seek to explicate my own understanding of the term in relation to our contemporary epoch.

Many forms of cosmopolitanism today come from a Kantian liberal perspective, basing their conceptions of cosmopolitanism on Kant's articulation of the term. Alternatively, I will seek to provide an interpretation of cosmopolitanism through going to the roots of the word in its first articulations in ancient Greek discourse. Cosmopolitanism has meet with much criticism and skepticism in some circles. And such a concept is indeed frightening if it is not critically evaluated in terms of the global era in which we live. This is why we will discuss the global context in which the term "cosmopolitanism" gains meaning today.

After examining this context, I shall begin to unpack my own understanding of the term through looking back at the term's etymological origins. And finally, I will complete the explication of my definition through applying the arguments of the previous part to the global context and laying out some of its normative implications.

The Global Era, Or, Why Should We Care

The increased interconnection of people on a global scale has problematized the ethical-political boundaries associated with the nation-state. Such boundaries are by no means obsolete. But as processes of globalization bring people into new relationships with those beyond their national borders, those borders have increasingly become points of reflection and contention.

Undoubtedly, people have been closely interconnected for thousands of years. And each era has struggled to construct economic, moral, and political frameworks to mediate such interconnections. During the modern era, the international state system was devised in Europe to contain economic and political decision-making under a sovereign authority. Such developments generated struggles to create and sustain ethical-political attitudes framed in terms of national solidarity. Sometimes these ethical-national characteristics were "pre-political," as in the case of Germany; others, such as France, were actively constructed in service of political unification. But in each case, they served to create normative ideals for ethical-political unity.

International laws, customs, and treaties, served as the framework to adjudicate relations with other sovereign nations. Thus with the onset of modernity, the international state system became the primary normative institutional framework to contain ethical-political relationships. And despite it's imperfect realization at times, this system has become global in scope. The international state system was conceived over three hundred years ago against the existing socio-political context in Europe. Yet, it has been argued that, today, globalization has significantly altered the ways in which people interact across these political boundaries. The globalization of organized violence, global economic trade and finance, multinational/transnational corporate organization, increased migrations and cultural transmissions across borders, and the potential for global environmental catastrophe have called into question the constructed boundaries of the nation-state and have raised normative questions for ethical and political relationships in an increasingly global age.

Issues of human rights and the decision-making and regulative capacities of supranational governance structures only generated further reflection. Cosmopolitans have responded to this context with a variety of claims. These claims can be roughly divided into moral and political categories. Moral claims examine what moral or ethical responsibilities result from our shared humanity as it is experienced in a global age. Political cosmopolitanism outlines proposals for legal or political solutions to global problems.

These claims can be broken down as follows:

- Moral
  - Global poverty requires a moral dedication to redistributive efforts across boundaries.
  - The pursuit of national-self interest or unilateral political action should be balanced by concerns for the effect of such actions on the broader global community.
  - Nations have a duty to uphold morally grounded human rights and a responsibility to protect violations of such human rights.
- Political
  - Processes of globalization have threatened the autonomy of nationally based decisionmaking and, in particular, the popular sovereignty of democratic states.
  - People have become subject to an increasing number of decision-making bodies beyond the state without any corresponding rights to participate in their decision-making processes.
  - A number of issues of global or regional concern have emerged that require action beyond the level of the nation-state.

Within the literature on cosmopolitanism, these claims are espoused and contested on both theoretical and empirical grounds. It is not my intention to outline the depths of these debates here, but only to explicate the claims made about the current era in which we live and their importance for understanding the cosmopolitan position.

These arguments are not always made in ways that are compatible with one another. Moral cosmopolitans frequently do not posit political solutions to moral problems, and sometimes argue against them. Some political cosmopolitans deliberately avoid making moral arguments, while others critique them as being metaphysical, imperialist, or incapable of being enforced without proper institutional support. The guiding principle for moral cosmopolitanism is a global moral order based on shared humanity.

For political cosmopolitanism, the guiding principle is a global political order based on shared subjection to political power. Despite their differences, both the moral and political cosmopolitans assume that such problems create certain obligations that are universally binding across national boundaries. The global era creates conditions whereby people exist in ethical and/or political relationships with one another on a global scale. The arguments of both moral and political cosmopolitans serve to posit a normative order that recognizes such a condition.

Constructing Cosmopolitanism: Cosmopoli-tanism in a Global Era

So what does such an investigation into the ancient Greek roots of the term "cosmopolitanism" offer us in terms of the contemporary global era? We no longer look up into the sky and base an understanding of our ethical-political world on imaginative intimations of cosmos. We now live in a post-metaphysical context where such speculations are viewed as irrelevant with respect to demystified, modern scientific worldviews.

And we no longer live in the tight community of the polis where ethics and politics are loath to be separated. The nation state, in many respects, was envisaged as an ethical-political relationship; however, in the contemporary world of pluralism and multiculturalism, ethics and politics are more easily separated and are often considered irrespective of one another. Also, theories of ethical-political relationships beyond the nation-state have come under criticism for being irreconcilable with the nation-state system. Despite their continued problems, the democratic nation-state has been the preeminent normative framework for ethical political order in the modern era. And the nation-state system has provided the foundations for adjudicating relationships between states under the normative order of sovereign equality.

Law and legalistic forms of justice are widely administered just as to such a framework. But it is my argument that cosmopolitanism, as it is articulated above, is even more salient today than when it was first articulated nearly twenty-five hundred years ago. The claims of moral and political cosmopolitans portray a global era in which the contemporary practices of people, groups, and institutions, have deepened human interactions on a global level. Such actions construct a global context where ethical and political concerns can no longer, if they ever did, be contained solely within the frame of the nation-state.

People's participation in such a context constructs a world in which individuals and groups are increasingly engaged in ethical and/or political relationships with others beyond their national boundaries. However, corresponding rights and duties have not emerged in order to meet these new conditions. It is within this context that we can apply the cosmopolitan principles articulated above. Many of us no longer share Timaeus or Diogenes' views of the kosmos. However, their discourses were articulated, not in the service of scientifically explaining the natural world, but as a means to investigate and provide normative principles for order in human ethical-political relationships.

Such principles are important for analysing the global era for four reasons:

1. For in a global era, cosmopolitanism suggests that it is necessary to view ethical-political life from a global standpoint. Interrelations on local, national, transnational, regional, and supranational levels require a global frame of analysis. Although globalization might affect different regions disproportionately, it constructs and intensifies human relations on a global scale. An analysis of people's ethical-political relations must take this into account.
2. The nation-state emerged in a distinctive historical context, and political actors of the time participated—often disproportionately—in forming ethical-political relations to realise state-bound national political orders. As such, in an era of shifting forms of governance on a global scale, it is necessary to assess principles of ethical-political relationships in terms of the contemporary exercise of social and political power.
3. As globalization brings people closer together beyond the frame of the nation-state, people from diverse backgrounds are being brought together in ever widening and deepening relationships. Today, incredibly diverse individuals are increasingly unified around the world. It is crucial now to analyse the ways in which such a unity is constituted and, normatively, how to preserve difference in the face of ever-closer unions.
4. And in a changing context of mounting exercises of power on a global scale, it has become important to evaluate the status and prospects of freedom, particularly the freedom to critically participate in public discourse around the exercise of power on a global scale, in terms of the global era.

The polis, or political association, is currently conceived in terms of the nation-state as it is realised in the international state system. Such a context creates a dualistic political and legal system where formal politics either occurs a) within the framework of the state, or b) between states as political actors themselves. Law is either a) internal to a polity, concerned with citizens, or b) formed through agreements and customs realised between states as the subjects of international law. Some have argued that this necessarily limits the field of political relations to the political within and between nation-states. In other words, because the formal political institutions are state-based, the normative frame for political action must be limited to national institutions.

In another respect, legalistic conceptions of justice based on national identity, have framed the scope of ethical responsibility either primarily within a national framework. Such an outlook reflects a particular interpretation of the concept of politês. Such positions begin from the context of established political institutions as they are distinct from their members. This means that political institutions—often, today, state bureaucracies—exist separately from their members. Politics occurs within these formal political channels by virtue of membership in them. And in that, for some, the membership boundaries of the politeia designate ethical-national relationships, ethical relationships should exist at their strongest within the national community.

Cosmopolitan perspectives would view the issue of the ethical-political association from a different perspective. As I have sought to demonstrate in my reflection of politês above, the polity is constructed by the actions of those who are a part of it. People come together to form political associations in order to engage in public opinion- and will-formation around governing their lives. This means that ethical-political membership need not be limited to the existing forms of political institutions but should reflect conditions of political action around the globe. Cosmopolitan perspectives suggest that new ethical and political standards might be required to meet the needs of ethical and/or political relationships in the global era where new modes of ethical and political associations are under formation. Such positions are based on the current distribution of governance structures around the globe, the rise of transnational social movements, and the increased intensity of relationships between people beyond formal political boundaries.

Rather than beginning from the given national framework for normatively assessing ethical responsibility and distributing political power, cosmopolitanism would seek to evaluate the current ethical and political practices of individuals, groups, and institutions in the global era.

From this perspective, it is:

- Necessary to reevaluate the current boundaries of ethical and political relationships and determine who are a part of such relationships and
- To articulate what rights, duties and responsibilities people owe one another based on such relationships. Such a position is based on the assumption that
- If people are subject to ethical and/or political relationships with others beyond the state, they should have ethical or political standing in that relationship. And thus, this position
- Presupposes the constitutive nature of ethical and political relationships beyond the frame of the nation- state in forming post-national ethical and political communities.

In sum, the cosmopolitan perspective takes the interrelations between people around the globe as the constitutive basis for a global ethical-political order of ethical.

Cosmopolitanism assumes that the actions of people across the globe in an increasingly globalized era constructs ethical and political relationships that can no longer be bound to the frame of the nation-state. There is, of course, no one articulation of cosmopolitanism today.

And the concerns articulated above generate a wide array of empirical analysis, theoretical reflection, and normative postulating. But it is not within the scope of this thesis for me to investigate different articulations of cosmopolitanism today. I have sought only to explicate the principles of cosmopolitanism through interpreting its origins in ancient Greek discourse and applying such an interpretation to the global era.

CULTURAL AREA

A cultural area or culture area is a region with one relatively homogeneous human activity or complex of activities. These areas are primarily geographical, not historical and they are not considered equivalent to Kulturkreis. A culture area is a concept in cultural anthropology where a geographic region and time sequence is characterized by substantially uniform environment and culture.

The concept of culture areas was originated by museum curators and ethnologists during the late 1800s as means of arranging exhibits. Clark Wissler and Alfred Kroeber further developed the concept on the premise that they represent long-standing cultural divisions.

The concept is criticized by some, who argue that the basis for classification is arbitrary. But other researchers disagree and the organization of human communities into cultural areas remains a common practice throughout the social sciences. The definition of culture areas is enjoying a resurgence of practical and theoretical interest as social scientists conduct more research on processes of cultural globalization.

AUTO-SEGREGATION

Auto-segregation is the separation of a religious or ethnic group from the rest of society in a state by the group itself. Through auto-segregation, the members of the separate group can establish their own services, and maintain their own traditions and customs. For example, some world tribes have preferred to stay in reservations and not to integrate with the rest of the state's population. By remaining in a reservation or on their original lands, they can preserve their language and beliefs. On the other hand, some supremacist groups self-segregate to avoid integrating with other groups that they consider inferior. Racists, radical Islamists, Orthodox Jews, ultranationalists, different Hindu castes and other supremacist or ethno-centric groups commonly segregate themselves from other communities through various practices like endogamy. The apartheid system in South Africa is an extreme example of this trend.

Endogamy as self-segregation

Endogamy encourages group affiliation and bonding. It is a common practice among displanted cultures attempting to make roots in new countries whilst still resisting complete integration, as it encourages group solidarity and ensures greater control over group resources. However endogamy can also serve as a form of self-segregation and helps a community to resist integrating with surrounding populations. It thus helps minorities to survive as separate communities over a long time, in societies with other practices and beliefs. Ethno-religious groups which have successfully resisted complete integration for the longest, for example the Romany gypsies, the Ashkenazi Jews of Europe and the white people of South Africa, practise a higher level of endogamy.

Islam typically enforces a limited form of endogamy, Muslim men can take wives from neighbouring non-muslim populations but Muslim women are normally forbidden to marry outside of the Muslim community. This may be to ensure that Islam spreads into surrounding populations and is not diluted through integration with them.

CULTURAL ASSIMILATION

Cultural assimilation is a socio-political response to demographic multi-ethnicity that supports or promotes the assimilation of ethnic minorities into the dominant culture. It is opposed to affirmative philosophy which recognizes and works to maintain differences.

The term assimilation is often used with regard to immigrants and various ethnic groups who have settled in a new land. New customs and attitudes are acquired through contact and communication.

The transfer of customs is not simply a one-way process. Each group of immigrants contributes some of its own cultural traits to its new society. Assimilation usually involves a gradual change and takes place in varying degrees; full assimilation occurs when new members of a society become indistinguishable from older members.

Cultural influence

A group can spontaneously adopt a different culture due to its political relevance, or to its perceived superiority. The first is the case of the Latin language and culture, that were gradually adopted by most of the subjugated people.

The second is the case of subjugated, but older and richer culture, which see itself imitated by the new masters, *e.g.* the victorious Roman Republic adopted more from the Hellenistic cultures than it imposed in most domains, except such Roman specialties as law and the military.

Assimilation of immigrants

Immigrant assimilation is a complex process in which an immigrant fully integrates themselves into a new country. Social scientists rely on four primary benchmarks to assess immigrant assimilation: socioeconomic status, geographic distribution, second language attainment, and intermarriage.William A.V. Clark defines immigrant assimilation "as a way of understanding the social dynamics of American society and that it is the process that occurs spontaneously and often unintended in the course of interaction between majority and minority groups".

It has been found that between 1880 and 1920, the United States took in roughly 24 million immigrants. This increase in immigration can be attributed to many historical changes. Later, during the cold war from the 1960s through the 1980s and the disintegration of the Soviet Union in the late 1980s, over 1.8 million Jews (including some non-Jewish family members) emigrated from the former Soviet Union.

The major destination countries were Israel (about 1.1 million), the United States (over 400,000), Germany (about 130,000), and Canada (about 30,000). The beginning of the twenty-first century has also marked a massive era of immigration, and sociologists are once again trying to make sense of the impact that immigration has on society and the impact it has on immigrants themselves.

Theoretical Explanations

Researchers have attempted to explain the assimilation rate for post 1965 immigrants in the United States with experiences of immigrants who entered the United States between 1880 and 1920. Many of the methods and theories that are used to assess immigrant assimilation today are derived from earlier immigrant studies.

One of the leading theories in understanding immigrant assimilation came from William I. Thomas and Florian Znaniecki whom published "The Polish Peasant in Europe and America". William I. Thomas and Florian Znaniecki's study on Polish immigrants (1880–1910) assessed how these immigrants built an institutional community in the United States during the Napoleonic War. Another influence on immigrant assimilation came from Robert Park, Ernest Burgess, and William I.

Thomas, in which they trained graduate students to study the experiences of immigrants in Chicago. Robert Park, Ernest Burgess, and William I. Thomas provided these graduate students with theoretical tools such as Park's theory on collective behaviour.

The third theory on immigrant assimilation comes from Gordon's book, Assimilation in American life. Gordon highlighted the generational change in immigrant groups, it states that the first generation or foreign born were less assimilated and less exposed to American life than their American-born children (the second generation), and their grandchildren (third-generation) were more like the American mainstream than their parents.

Theoretical Models to Immigrant Assimilation

The first, classic and new assimilation model sees immigrants and native-born people following a "straight-line" or a convergence. This theory sees immigrants becoming more similar over time in norms, values, behaviours, and characteristics. This theory also expects those immigrants residing the longest in the host population, as well as the members of later generations, to show greater similarities with the majority group than immigrants who have spent less time in the host society. The second, racial or ethnic disadvantage model states that immigrant's chances to assimilate are "blocked". An example of this model would be discrimination and institutional barriers to employment and other opportunities.

The third, the segmented assimilation model theorizes that structural barriers, such as poor urban schools, cut off access to employment and other opportunities—obstacles that often are particularly severe in the case of the most disadvantaged members of immigrant groups, and such impediments can lead to stagnant or downward mobility, even as the children of other immigrants follow divergent paths towards classic straight-line assimilation.

Core Measurements to Immigrant Assimilation

Researchers have assessed that assimilation exists among immigrants because we can measure assimilation on four primary benchmarks. These core measurable aspects of immigrant assimilation that were formulated to study European immigrants to the United States are still the starting points for understanding current immigrant assimilation. These measurable aspects of assimilation are socioeconomic status, spatial concentration, language attainment, and intermarriage.

- Socioeconomic Status is defined by educational attainment, occupation, and income. By measuring socioeconomic status researchers want to find out if immigrants eventually catch up to native-born people in terms of human capital characteristics.
- Spatial Concentration is defined by geography or residential patterns. The spatial residential model (based on theories of Park) proposed by

Massey states that increasing socioeconomic attainment, longer residence in the U.S, and higher generational status lead to decreasing residential concentration for a particular ethnic group.

- Language Attainment is defined as the ability to speak English and the loss of the individual's mother tongue. The three-generation model of language assimilation states that the first generation makes some progress in language assimilation but remains dominant in their native tongue, the second generation is bilingual, and the third-generation only speaks English.
- Intermarriage is defined by race or ethnicity and occasionally by generation. High rates of intermarriage are considered to be an indication of social integration because it reveals intimate and profound relations between people of different groups, intermarriage reduces the ability of families to pass on to their children a consistent ethnic culture and thus is an agent of assimilation.

Intermarriage came under particular scrutiny by the Jewish community in the early-mid 20th century as Jewish leaders more and more often turned to social scientists to explain why Judaism was a typically endogamic religion. Although intermarriage was viewed as a firm base from which to begin an argument for assimilation, it was also seen as a way to gradually ease the transition into their new culture. Julius Draschler, a graduate student at Columbia University, believed that as long as people are allowed to maintain some differences, such as the Jewish practice of only marrying another Jew, they will delay the inevitable while simultaneously enriching the nation in the process of their slow assimilation.

While Draschler acknowledged that assimilation was the ultimate endpoint for all American groups, he hoped to prove through his intermarriage studies that, the more gradual the process, the better. Such need to justify (or vilify) the intermarriage practice became increasingly important after the 1950s as Jews (as well as other typically endogamic cultures, such as African-Americans) began to engage in more exogamic relationships.

Immigrant Name Changing as a Form of Assimilation

While the changing of immigrant names is not one of the 4 measurable benchmarks for assimilation outlined by early sociologists, it nonetheless represents a clear abandonment of the old as new immigrants are absorbed into the fabric of society. It is often believed that, due to language barriers, or the lack of training and sensitivity by government officials, names were often changed, without consent, by inspectors on Ellis Island. This general misconstruction of the facts is refuted in an object released by the Immigration and Naturalization Service, claiming that inspectors did not personally take names, instead inventorying the passengers using manifestos created by the shipping companies themselves.

As a matter of fact, many immigrants changed their names willingly. It's suggested by the Immigration and Naturalization Service that most name blunders were likely the fault of the origin, and not the destination. Donna Przecha, a published and well-known expert in genealogy, suggests a number of alternative explanations for name changing, one of which was a need for employment. A huge surplus of labour began to immigrate to the United States, many of whom were unskilled, with names that were often difficult to pronounce. Employers were not bound by the same anti-discriminatory legislature that they are now, and tended to gravitate towards individuals with more American names.

Comfort and fitting in was also a heavy motivator behind the changing of names. Many, if not most, US immigrants in the mid 1900's planned to make the United States their new home, permanently. Given this fact, it should come as no surprise that many immigrants welcomed the impending assimilation brought on by their host country. Eager to begin their new lives, many did as much as they could to become "American" as quickly as possible, particularly children. Of course, simplicity was yet another factor in the abandonment of old titles. As immigrants poured in from various European countries, many found their names to be difficult to pronounce and/or spell for many Americans, such as those names with many syllables, or with a large number of Z's.

Policies on Immigrant Assimilation

When considering immigrant assimilation it is important to consider why immigrants migrate. One reason immigrants migrated was the 1986 Immigration Reform and Control Act (IRCA), which legalized 2.3 million formerly undocumented Mexican Immigrants. This Act freed these newly legalized immigrants from the fear of being apprehended, and many of these immigrants moved to states beyond the nearest U.S-Mexican border.

Modifications for Assessing Immigrant Assimilation

Studies on immigrant assimilation in the 19th century and 20th century conclude that immigrants had a hard time catching up to the same human capital characteristics as native-born people in the 19th century, but studies in the 20th century suggest that immigrants eventually catch up to native born people. Timothy J. Hatton explains this puzzle on immigrant assimilation in the 19th century and in the 20th century. He explores how recent studies have been producing misleading results between the two. Hatton focuses his research on the specification of the earnings function.Hatton argues that that specification of the earnings function should be improved in two ways.

First, immigrants who arrived as children should be treated separately from those who arrived as adults.

Second, specification of the earnings function should be better approximate to the true shape of age-earnings profiles. Hatton points out that with these modifications, the patterns of immigrant earnings which have emerged make more sense with those of the 20th century and with traditional views on immigrant assimilation in the 19th century.

Owning a Home and Immigrant Assimilation

Owning a home can be seen as a step into assimilation. William A.V. Clark explores this link in his book "Immigrants and the American Dream Remarking the Middle Class". Clark is aware that the process of assimilation is more than just being able to purchase a home. He argues that "homeownership" is one of the steps of assimilation, it is becoming part of the community and a neighbourhood, and being a part of the daily activities that take place in a community.

Naturalization and Immigrant Assimilation

Other than marriage, Citizenship is one of the most significant factors in assimilation. The immigration debate focuses not only the number of immigrants, who should be admitted, and who should be allowed to be admitted but also the processes of incorporation and, most importantly, how citizenship should be extended and to whom. For example, should it be extended to those who arrive illegally? Allowing for naturalization of immigrants can create tension in assimilation. On one hand, those who favour the admission of immigrants input that these new residents will help build and enrich the American democratic process. However, others argue that the nature and legitimacy of the nation may be challenged and perhaps even threatened.

New Immigrant Gateways and Immigrant Assimilation

Although it is changing, the overwhelming majority of immigrants still settle in traditional gateway states such as Florida, New York, California, Illinois, Texas, and Massachusetts. It has found that immigrants settle in traditional gateways where there are large populations of foreign-born people. Walters and Jimenez have illustrated the changes in the geographic distribution and the rates of growth of immigration in the United States.

They show the number of foreign-born individuals in states where the foreign-born population grew by a factor of two or more between 1990 and 2000. Walters and Jimenez found that the largest percentage growth in the foreign-born population, was found in either the Midwest or the South in additional none of the traditional gateways were included in this large percentage growth. Walters and Jimenez noted that a reason these traditional gateways did not have an increase at the same rate of the new gateways was because, new gateways did not have many immigrants to begin with. Walters and Jimenez have argued that this new change in geography could possibly change the way researchers assess immigrant assimilation. They argue that these new gateways are unique and they propose that immigrant assimilation may be different from the experiences of immigrants in more traditional gateways in at least three ways.

First, the long history of immigration in these established gateways means that the place of immigrants in terms of class, racial, and ethnic hierarchies in these traditional gateways are more structured or established on the other hand these new gateways do not have much immigration history therefore the place of immigrants in terms of class, racial, and ethnic hierarchies is less defined and immigrants may have more influence to define their position.

Second, the size of new gateways may influence immigrant assimilation. Having a smaller gateway may influence the level of segregation among immigrants and native-born people.

Third, the difference in institutional arrangements may influence immigrant assimilation. Traditional gateways unlike new gateways have many institutions set up to help immigrants which include legal-aid, bureaus, social organizations. Finally, Walters and Jimenez have only speculated that these differences may influence immigrant assimilation and the way researchers should assess immigrant assimilation.

CULTURAL IDENTITY

Culture refers to the customs, practices, languages, values and world views that define social groups such as those based on nationality, ethnicity, region or common interests. Cultural identity is important for people's sense of self and how they relate to others. A strong cultural identity can contribute to people's overall wellbeing. Cultural identity based on ethnicity is not necessarily exclusive. People may identify themselves as New Zealanders in some circumstances and as part of a particular culture in other circumstances.

They may also identify with more than one culture. The desired outcomes recognise the importance of a shared national identity and sense of belonging, and the value of cultural, social and ethnic diversity. They recognise New Zealand is a multicultural society, while also acknowledging that Mâori culture has a unique place. For example, under the Treaty of Waitangi, the Crown has an obligation to protect the Mâori language.

Defining a national identity is not simple. New Zealand is a diverse nation, made up of many cultural groups, with many different customs and traditions.

While people may describe themselves as "New Zealanders", how they define their "New Zealand-ness" will vary from person to person. For example, some people might see a New Zealand identity in aspects of New Zealand's history or in New Zealander's achievements in sporting, artistic or other endeavours, while others might see it through a sense of national characteristics or traits, or through national symbols and icons.

Mâori culture may form one aspect of national identity, since it is both unique to New Zealand and a part of our identity in the outside world. Cultural identity is an important contributor to people's wellbeing. Identifying with a particular culture helps people feel they belong and gives them a sense of security.

An established cultural identity has also been linked with positive outcomes in areas such as health and education. It provides access to social networks, which provide support and shared values and aspirations. Social networks can help to break down barriers and build a sense of trust between people, a phenomenon sometimes referred to as social capital. However, strong cultural identity expressed in the wrong way can contribute to barriers between groups. And members of smaller cultural groups can feel excluded from society if others obstruct, or are intolerant of, their cultural practices.

CULTURAL IMPERIALISM

Cultural imperialism is the act of a nation imposing it's cultural values onto another, usually weaker, nation. Cultural imperialism can take the form of an active, formal policy or a general attitude. A metaphor of colonialism is employed: the cultural products of the first world "invade" the third-world and "conquer" local culture. In the stronger variants of the term, world domination is the explicit goal of the nation-states or corporations that export the culture. The term is usually used in a pejorative sense, usually in conjunction with a call to reject foreign influence.

The term appears to have emerged in the 1960s. and has been a focus of research since at least the 1970s. Terms such as "media imperialism", "structural imperialism", "cultural dependency and domination", "cultural synchronization", "electronic colonialism", "ideological imperialism", and "economic imperialism" have all been used to describe the same basic notion of cultural imperialism. Various academics give various definitions of the term. American media critic Herbert Schiller wrote: "The concept of cultural imperialism today best describes the sum of the processes by which a society is brought into the modern world system and how its dominating stratum is attracted, pressured, forced, and sometimes bribed into shaping social institutions to correspond to, or even promote, the values and structures of the dominating centre of the system. The public media are the foremost example of operating enterprises that are used in the penetrative process. For penetration on a significant scale the media themselves must be captured by the dominating/ penetrating power. This occurs largely through the commercialization of broadcasting." Tom McPhail defined "Electronic colonialism as the dependency relationship established by the importation of communication hardware, foreign-produced software, along with engineers, technicians, and related information protocols, that vicariously establish a set of foreign norms, values, and expectations which, in varying degrees, may alter the domestic cultures and socialization processes." Sui-Nam Lee observed that "communication imperialism can be defined as the process in which the ownership and control over the hardware and software of mass media as well as other major forms of communication in one country are singly or together subjugated to the domination of another country with deleterious effects on the indigenous values, norms and culture."

Ogan saw "media imperialism often described as a process whereby the United States and Western Europe produce most of the media products, make the first profits from domestic sales, and then market the products in Third World countries at costs considerably lower than those the countries would have to bear to produce similar products at home."

Downing and Sreberny-Mohammadi state: "Imperialism is the conquest and control of one country by a more powerful one. Cultural imperialism signifies the dimensions of the process that go beyond economic exploitation or military force. In the history of colonialism, the educational and media systems of many Third World countries have been set up as replicas of those in Britain, France, or the United States and carry their values. Western advertising has made further inroads, as have architectural and fashion styles. Subtly but powerfully, the message has often been insinuated that Western cultures are superior to the cultures of the Third World."

The issue of cultural imperialism emerged largely from communication studies. However, cultural imperialism has been used as a framework by scholars to explain phenomena in the areas of international relations, anthropology, education, science, history, literature, and sports. It can refer to either the forced acculturation of a subject population, or to the voluntary embracing of a foreign culture by individuals who do so of their own free will. Since these are two very different referents, the validity of the term has been called into question. Cultural influence can be seen by the "receiving" culture as either a threat to or an enrichment of its cultural identity. It seems therefore useful to distinguish between cultural imperialism as an (active or passive) attitude of superiority, and the position of a culture or group that seeks to complement its own cultural production, considered partly deficient, with imported products. The imported products or services can themselves represent, or be associated with, certain values.

The "receiving" culture does not necessarily perceive this link, but instead absorbs the foreign culture passively through the use of the foreign goods and services. Due to its somewhat concealed, but very potent nature, this hypothetical idea is described by some experts as "banal imperialism." Some believe that the newly globalised economy of the late 20th and early 21st century has facilitated this process through the use of new information technology. This kind of cultural imperialism is derived from what is called "soft power". The theory of electronic colonialism extends the issue to global cultural issues and the impact of major multi-media conglomerates, ranging from Viacom, Time-Warner, Disney, News Corp, Sony, to Google and Microsoft with the focus on the hegemonic power of these mainly US-based communication giants.

One of the reasons often given for opposing any form of cultural imperialism, voluntary or otherwise, is the preservation of cultural diversity, a goal seen by some as analogous to the preservation of ecological diversity. Proponents of this idea argue either that such diversity is valuable in itself, or instrumentally valuable because it makes available more ways of solving problems and responding to catastrophes, natural or otherwise.Palestinian writer, philosopher, and literary theorist, Edward Said, who was one of the founders of the field of post-colonial study, wrote extensively on the subject of cultural imperialism.

His work attempts to highlight the inaccuracies of many assumptions about cultures and societies, and is largely informed by Michel Foucault's concepts of discourse and power. The relatively new academic field of post-colonial theory has been the source for most of the in-depth work on the idea of discursive and other non-military mechanisms of imperialism, and its validity is disputed by those who deny that these forms are genuinely imperialistic. David Rothkopf, managing director of Kissinger Associates and an adjunct professor of international affairs at Columbia University (who also served as a senior US Commerce Department official in the Clinton Administration), wrote about cultural imperialism in his provocatively titled In Praise of Cultural Imperialism? in the summer 1997 issue of Foreign Policy magazine.

Rothkopf says that the US should embrace "cultural imperialism" as in its self interest. But his definition of cultural imperialism stresses spreading the values of tolerance and openness to cultural change in order to avoid war and conflict between cultures as well as expanding accepted technological and legal standards to provide free traders with enough security to do business with more countries. Rothkopf's definition almost exclusively involves allowing individuals in other nations to accept or reject foreign cultural influences.

He also mentions, but only in passing, the use of the English language and consumption of news and popular music and film as cultural dominance that he supports. Rothkopf additionally makes the point that globalization and the Internet are accelerating the process of cultural influence. Culture is sometimes used by the organizers of society—politicians, theologians, academics, and families—to impose and ensure order, the rudiments of which change over time as need dictates. One need only look at the 20th century's genocides. In each one, leaders used culture as a political front to fuel the passions of their armies and other minions and to justify their actions among their people.

Rothkopf then cites genocide and massacres in Armenia, Russia, the Holocaust, Cambodia, Bosnia and Herzegovina, Rwanda and East Timor as examples of culture (in some cases expressed in the ideology of "political culture" or religion) being misused to justify violence. He also acknowledges that cultural imperialism in the past has been guilty of forcefully eliminating the cultures of natives in the Americas and in Africa, or through use of the Inquisition, "and during the expansion of virtually every empire." The most important way to deal with cultural influence in any nation, just as to Rothkopf, is to promote tolerance and allow, or even promote, cultural diversities that are compatible with tolerance and to eliminate those cultural differences that cause violent conflict:

- "Multicultural societies, be they nations, federations, or other conglomerations of closely interrelated states, discern those aspects of culture that do not threaten union, stability, or prosperity (such as food, holidays, rituals, and music) and allow them to flourish. But they counteract or eradicate the more subversive elements of culture (exclusionary aspects of religion, language, and political/ideological beliefs). History shows that bridging cultural gaps successfully and serving as a home to diverse peoples requires certain social structures, laws, and institutions that transcend culture. Furthermore, the history of a number of ongoing experiments in multiculturalism, such as in the European Union, India, South Africa, Canada and the United States, suggests that workable, if not perfected, integrative models exist. Each is built on the idea that tolerance is crucial to social well-being, and each at times has been threatened by both intolerance and a heightened emphasis on cultural distinctions. The greater public good warrants eliminating those cultural characteristics that promote conflict or prevent harmony, even as less-divisive, more personally observed cultural distinctions are celebrated and preserved."

6

Economic Geography

Economic geography is the study of the location, distribution and spatial organization of economic activities across the Earth. The subject matter investigated is strongly influenced by the researcher's methodological approach. Neoclassical location theorists, following in the tradition of Alfred Weber, tend to focus on industrial location and use quantitative methods. Since the 1970s, two broad reactions against neoclassical approaches have significantly changed the discipline: Marxist political economy, growing out of the work of David Harvey; and the new economic geography which takes into account social, cultural, and institutional factors in the spatial economy.

Economic geography is usually regarded as a subfield of the discipline of geography, although recently economists such as Paul Krugman and Jeffrey Sachs have pursued interests that can be considered part of economic geography.

Krugman has gone so far as to call his application of spatial thinking to international trade theory the "new economic geography", which directly competes with an approach within the discipline of geography that is also called "new economic geography". The name geographical economics has been suggested as an alternative.

Given the variety of approaches, economic geography has taken to many different subject matters, including: the location of industries, economies of agglomeration (also known as "linkages"), transportation, international trade and development, real estate, gentrification, ethnic economies, gendered economies, core-periphery theory, the economics of urban form, the relationship between the environment and the economy (tying into a long history of geographers studying culture-environment interaction), and globalization.

This stage will introduce economic geography as a sub-discipline of geography that uses a geographical approach to study the economy. The stage will stress that an economic-geographical approach to studying economies is very different from the approach used by mainstream economics. In this stage as suggested, explore some of the key differences between the approaches used by geographers and economists. The stage will suggest that the field of economic geography offers some unique insights and is well placed to analyse and understand the contemporary world economy in all its complexity. One of the key features and strengths of the economic-geographical approach is the use of the concepts of space, place and scale and these will be introduced in turn.

The stage will also point out that economic geography itself represents a dynamic, evolving and diverse body of knowledge. However, this diversity also allows economic geography to engage with a number of issues in contemporary societies and economies. Indeed, despite the claims that economic globalisation will inevitably bring about 'the end of geography', geography matters more than ever and economic geography provides us with useful tools to analyse and understand economic processes that shape our world.

WHAT IS ECONOMIC GEOGRAPHY?

Economic geography is a sub-discipline that uses a geographical approach to study the economy. It is a vibrant and exciting branch of geography. Its name would suggest that economic geography lies somewhere between, or at the overlap of, the disciplines of geography and economics. This is true to some extent. In fact, both geographers and economists use the term 'economic geography'. However, they mean different things by it. Indeed, it is important to stress from the outset that the approach that geographers are using to study the economy is very different from that used by most economists. A Contemporary Introduction written by Neil Coe and his colleagues, this subject guide uses the term economic geography and economic-geographical approach to describe the approach used by geographers.

On the other hand, the type of 'economic geography' that economists are using, can be best described as 'geographical economics' or 'spatial economics'. More generally, this distinction between 'economic geography' and 'geographical economics' reflects fundamental differences between the way the economy is treated by geographers on the one hand, and economists on the other. In other words, an economic-geographical approach to studying the economy is very different from the one used by mainstream economics.

HISTORY OF ECONOMIC GEOGRAPHY

In the history of economic geography there were many influences coming mainly from economics and geographical sciences. First traces of the study of spatial aspects of economic activities on Earth can be found in Strabo's *Geographika* written almost 2000 years ago. This has recently been challenged, however, by seven Chinese maps of the State of Qin dating to the 4th century

BC. During the period known in geography as environmental determinism notable (though later much criticized) influence came from Ellsworth Huntington and his theory of climatic determinism.

Valuable contributions came from location theorists such as Johann Heinrich von Thunen or Alfred Weber. Other influential theories were Walter Christaller's Central place theory, the theory of core and periphery.

Fred K. Schaefer's article *Exceptionalism in geography: A Methodological Examination* published in American journal Annals (Association of American Geographers) and his critique of regionalism had a big impact on economic geography. The article became a rallying point for the younger generation of economic geographers who were intent on reinventing the discipline as a science. Quantitative methods became prevailing in research. Well-known economic geographers of this period are William Garrison, Brian Berry, Waldo Tobler, Peter Haggett, William Bunge (Apurba Dutta, Ranibandh) Contemporary economic geographers tend to specialize in areas such as location theory and spatial analysis (with the help of geographic information systems), market research, geography of transportation, land or real estate price evaluation, regional and global development, planning, Internet geography, innovation, social networks and others.

Economics' Approaches

The key difference is that mainstream economists usually pay little attention to the geographical dimensions of economic processes while economic geographers consider geography as being essential for the understanding of the ways economies work. From this, two completely different views of the economy, and the way it operates, emerge. Most mainstream economists see the economy as a machine that works just as to certain principles and whose behaviour can be predicted using modelling techniques. Mathematics is therefore the main 'language' economists 'speak'. The body of thought that underpins such a conceptualisation of the economy can be referred to as 'economic orthodoxy'. Let us first explore the key components of economic orthodoxy before introducing the key concepts of an economic-geographical perspective.

EVOLUTIONARY/INSTITUTIONALIST APPROACHES AND NEW ECONOMIC GEOGRAPHY

Economic geography approaches that draw from heterodox economics and the evolutionary/institutionalist perspective represent a diverse and evolving group. However, some common features are discernible. The evolutionary/institutionalist perspective emphasises the importance of social, cultural and institutional factors for the understanding of the ways economies work. This is in contrast to both neo-classical views and the Marxist approach (that assumes that such factors are determined by, rather than being determinants of, the economy).

However, the evolutionary/institutionalist perspective sees the economy as always embedded in, and constituted by, social, cultural and institutional spheres. Economic geography approaches developed from this perspective thus see uneven development as inextricably linked to (or shaped by) institutional contexts. One of the key points that such economic geography approaches are making is that social, cultural and institutional contexts are placespecific. In other words, economic fortunes of regions (or whole countries) depend on the institutional arrangements that these regions (or countries) are able to create. At the regional level, for instance, the concept of 'institutional thickness' has been proposed to capture the strength of local/regional institutions, their ability to cooperate and to promote a coherent development strategy.

In line with the view that successful economies are increasingly knowledge-based or learning economies, successful regions have also been conceptualised as learning regions. The key feature of such regions is their ability to innovate, to learn and to accumulate knowledge in various forms, thanks to their institutional set-up. It is argued, for instance, that the capacity to innovate and to learn depends on various collaborative networks, which are sustained thanks to the institutions of trust, shared culture and social capital, all of which are dependent on particular regional settings. In this view then, regions are in fact seen as key engines of the knowledge economy and uneven development in such an economy is a result of differences in regional 'institutional thickness', innovation capacity, learning and knowledge accumulation.

Interestingly, there are two opposing views with regard to the prospect of achieving balanced development in the knowledge-based or learning economy. The first view is based on the assumption that economically lagging regions (or nations) can catch-up because favourable conditions for growth can be created locally by making appropriate institutional arrangements. This view is further supported by the assumption that thanks to information and communication technology (ICT), the key resource in the knowledge economy-knowledge-can move freely around the world. It should therefore be possible for previously underdeveloped regions to emulate the success of leading regions such as Silicon Valley.

The second, and opposing, view suggests that uneven development will continue to be a feature in the knowledge-based economy. This view is based on the assumption that the key sources of competitiveness and economic success is non-standardised tacit knowledge (as opposed to standardised, written, explicit knowledge). Tacit knowledge, the argument goes, is embedded in local/regional institutions, regional innovation cultures and clusters and these are apparently place-specific to the extent that they cannot be replicated by regions elsewhere.

One way or another, the interest in regional institutional settings has been associated with the emergence of so-called new economic geography. While the term 'new economic geography' is used by some economists to describe recent advances in economics in relation to space in geography the term is used to describe an economic geography approach which moves away from viewing economic processes as separate from social, cultural and political contexts and emphasises that these contexts are crucial for understanding economic dynamics. New economic geography therefore also enthusiastically embraces the notions of culture, social capital, ethnicity and gender in its study of the economy, reflecting a wider 'cultural turn' in social sciences.

How Does the Economy Work Over Space

The perspectives on the economy presented offer a good starting point to explore the question of what the economy is and how it works. However, the problem is that all views presented above could be seen as 'aspatial'. Indeed, they do not tell us much about how the economy or economies work over space. Economic and geographical considerations are, in other words, impossible to separate. The question of how the economy work(s) over space, across scales and in particular places, is the key question of economic geography. This is an important question economic processes are enfolding in space in a highly uneven way and are engaged in producing and reproducing inequalities at various spatial scales. How can we explain this uneven and unequal development? The three perspectives on the economy presented in the previous part provide three very different ways of approaching this question. In other words, different perspectives on 'the economy' have profound implications for the theoretical conceptualisation of economic geographies.

ALTERNATIVE APPROACHES

It is clear from the above two sub-sections that mainstream economic and Marxist perspectives differ dramatically in their analysis of the workings of the economy. However, despite the differences, these two perspectives also share one common feature-they both focus on formal market transactions. Indeed, as we have seen, mainstream economics is concerned with the relationship between the demand and supply of goods or services as expressed by a price fixed through the market mechanism.

The Marxist analysis, meanwhile, focuses on the difference between the price of labour (exchange value of labour power) and the exchange value of the commodities produced by the labour. However, what constitutes 'the economy' and 'the economic' is a contentious issue. Echoing these concerns, a number of alternative economic approaches have emerged. These approaches usually fall within a category of heterodox economics since they are providing a counterbalance to the established mainstream (orthodox) economic views. One of the leading heterodox approaches is associated with evolutionary and institutional economics.

Evolutionary and institutional economics is in itself a diverse set of approaches, but there are some key shared characteristics that clearly distinguish these approaches from both the mainstream economics and Marxist perspectives. The starting point of evolutionary/institutional and other alternative approaches is their insistence that the economy cannot be reduced to market transactions only.

Instead, they argue that wider social, cultural and institutional contexts need to be taken into consideration if one is to explain how economies work. Institutional contexts are defined broadly here and may include both formal institutions (*e.g.* laws, regulations, formal procedures) and informal institutions (*e.g.* habits, customs, conventions, cultural norms, etc.) at various scales-from the level of the firm to the institutional landscapes underpinning the whole economy. The inclusion of the wider social, cultural and institutional considerations has profound implications for the understanding of the ways economies work.

Importantly, such an inclusion challenges the neo-classical notion of the rational behaviour of 'economic man' guided by the 'invisible hand' of the market. Instead, it emphasises the way in which social institutions play an essential role in guiding the action of economic agents. (This also differs from the Marxist view that the role of economic agents is structured by the prevailing social relations of production). In the evolutionary/institutionalist view, firms, for instance, are not seen as atomistic units competing against each other on the free market. Rather, firms are perceived as being embedded within wider socio-economic relations and networks.

These networks may include various formal and informal links with suppliers, customers and competitors. Importantly, transactions within these networks are not simply guided by market competition. Rather they often involve valuable elements of coordination and cooperation. This is important because such cooperative networks are often crucial for fostering innovation which is seen as vital for economic development or economic evolution. In turn, this raises the question whether the 'pure market' is the best mechanism for ensuring economic progress.

Evolutionary and institutionalist economists would argue that successful economies are neither pure markets nor pure hierarchies. Instead, successful economies are 'mixed economies' with important roles for the public sector and for different kinds of policy. Mixed economic systems are also seen as capable of producing a diversity of economic forms which contributes to the adaptability and longterm survival of economic systems. Another line of argument advanced by alternative approaches relates to the claim that successful economies are increasingly knowledge-intensive or knowledge-based. The knowledge-based economy can be simply defined as an economy in which knowledge becomes the key economic resource. While all economies can be seen as knowledge-based, there is a perception that we witness a major shift in the relative importance of land, physical capital and knowledge capital, in favour of the latter. For some observers, the shift towards the knowledge-based economy represents an epochal transformation.

As Burton-Jones vividly put it: 'Since ancient times, wealth and power have been associated with the ownership of physical resources. The traditional factors of production, materials, labour, and money, have been largely physical in nature. Historically the need for knowledge has been limited, and access to it largely controlled by those owning the means of production. Steam power, physical labour, and money capital largely facilitated the Industrial Revolution... In contrast, future wealth and power will be derived mainly from intangible, intellectual resources: knowledge capital. This transformation from a world largely dominated by physical resources, to a world dominated by knowledge, implies a shift in the locus of economic power as profound as that which occurred at the time of the Industrial Revolution. We are in the early stages of a "Knowledge Revolution."'

The notion that the economy is moving towards a post-industrial, knowledge-intensive phase, in turn, opens up a whole set of questions. Both mainstream economics and Marxist approaches have been devised in the context of an industrial era. But will the same principles apply to the new knowledge economy? Evolutionary and institutionalist economists have devised their own approaches to account for the ways knowledge economies work.

One of the most influential concepts is that of the 'learning economy' introduced by Lundvall and Johnson. The starting point of the 'learning economy' concept is the argument that if knowledge is the most fundamental resource in our contemporary economy, then learning is 'the most important process'. Although Lundvall and Johnson admit that knowledge always has been a 'crucial resource' for the economy, and was in the past 'layered in traditions and routines', they argue that knowledge and learning have more recently become much more fundamental resources than before. They argue that the economy is now characterised by 'new constellations of knowledge and learning in the economy' mainly through the development of ICTs, flexible specialisation and, finally, changes in the process of innovation.

These changes are bringing challenges that firms have responded to by changing organisational forms and by building alliances in order to gain access to a more diversified knowledge base. This implies 'broader participation in learning processes' to include all layers within the firm, the development of 'multiskilling and networking skills' and enhancing the 'capacity to learn and to apply learning to the processes of production and sales'. This is why Lundvall and Johnson 'regard... capitalist economies not only as knowledge-based economies but also as "learning economies"'.

They offer the following definition of the 'learning economy': The learning economy is a dynamic concept; it involves the capacity to learn and to expand the knowledge base. It refers not only to the importance of the science and technology systems-universities, research organisations, in-house RandD departments and so on-but also to the learning implications of the economic structure, the organisational forms and the institutional set-up.'

At the core of the 'learning economy' are apparently firms that 'start to learn how to learn' and which are able to handle various types of knowledge. Lundvall and Johnson distinguish at least four categories of knowledge: know-what, know-why, know-who and know-how. The first category, know-what, represents knowledge about 'facts'. The meaning of this is probably close to that of 'information'. The, second category, know-why, refers to scientific knowledge of principles and laws of motion in nature and in society. This kind of knowledge, Lundvall and Johnson argue, is extremely important for technological development. The third term, know-who, is already a more complex construction that reaches a sphere of specific social relations and time-space dimension. A simple example of know-who can be a situation when, for a successful innovation, it is more important to know key persons than to know basic scientific principles. Know-when and know-where refers to economically useful knowledge about markets with their temporal and spatial dimensions, for instance. Finally, knowhow refers to practical skills in production or other spheres of economic activity. Lundvall and Johnson also address different aspects of learning. Importantly, they do not understand learning as a simple absorption of science and technical knowledge. Rather, they define it more broadly as learning changes in economic structures, organisational and institutional forms. Learning is presented as a dynamic and interactive process aimed at the accumulation of knowledge at the level of the firm and the economy as a whole.

Learning is present in both production and consumption processes and is expressed through 'learning by doing' and 'learning by using'. From the point of view of permanent renewal and adaptation of economic and organisational structures, Lundvall and Johnson have also introduced an innovative term 'forgetting'. They argue that the 'learning economy' should not only preserve and store its pool of knowledge, but also should be able to 'forget'. 'Forgetting' at the level of individual workers refers to their ability to abandon obsolete skills and professional expertise. An example of 'forgetting' at the level of the firm or economy includes closing down ailing branches or whole sectors.

Thus, the 'learning economy' is supposed to intelligently manage continuous self-organised learning. The work of Lundvall and Johnson and other evolutionary/institutionalists has proved highly influential in framing the discussion on contemporary economic geographies, despite the fact that there remain questions about the precise nature of the supposed transformation of the economy towards the 'knowledge-based economy' or 'learning economy'. One contentious issue relates to the question of whether the transformation beyond an old industrial economy also signifies a move beyond a capitalist economy. Geoffrey Hodgson-one of the prominent evolutionary/institutionalist economists-contributed to the debate by offering his own definitions of the 'knowledge-intensive economy' and 'learning economy'.

Hodgson has argued that the 'knowledge-intensive economy' would still be a capitalist one, but it would be an economy in which an 'enlightened group of business leaders' is 'aware of the kind of democratic culture and participatory industrial relations that facilitate productivity'. Alongside 'collaborative and co-operative relationships between firms... against the neo-liberal insistence on fierce, price driven, market competition', Hodgson suggests that:'Such a progressive movement of business people could find valuable allies among trade unionists and the population as a whole'. However, for Hodgson, the 'learning economy' or 'market cognitism', in contrast, is a scenario clearly 'beyond capitalism' where the 'degree of control by the employer over the employee is minimal'. Hodgson has argued that such an economy, 'would not be socialist, in any common sense of the word', but nevertheless, 'it is not capitalism' presumably because the means of production are effectively controlled by the workers themselves, not by the employers. Such a benign view of the emerging new 'knowledge era' thus implies that the contradictions identified by Marx as inherent to the capitalist economy may be waning. This point is hotly debated but if proven true, it can have potentially important implications for the way we conceptualise economic geographies of the 'new era'.

ECONOMIC GEOGRAPHY, BY THE NUMBERS

Quantification in Context

A common perception among contemporary economic geographers is that quantification is either dead or dying: an approach that is a historical curiosity a remnant of a misguided attempt to replicate the methodological norms and practices of science. As a social construction, an 'ideal' set of methodological norms and practices that we label 'quantification' is supposed to be derived from a failed and discredited social ontology and epistemology grounded, as it is, in the modernist project of positivism/empiricism.

Following the publication of Andrew Sayer's (1984) highly influential *Method in Social Science,* someone practising quantitative economic geography is supposed to engage in 'extensive' research, employing large-scale survey and statistical analysis to search for regularities among map patterns, thereby producing descriptive accounts lacking in explanatory power. In contrast, the preferred suite of qualitative methodologies are characterized as 'intensive' case studies, examining individual agents and their understandings in their causal contexts in an attempt to uncover the processes generating observed outcomes. We find this characterization of competing research designs deeply frustrating, bearing little relation to the way in which I, and others, engage in quantitative economic geography. This stereotype is promulgated through an unsustainable dualism between quantitative and qualitative ways of knowing. Equally troubling is the fact that this dualism appears to be widening the gulf that separates competing economic geographies, creating unnecessary and mutual antagonisms.

Published in the 1980s at a time of intense intellectual ferment about the foundation of economic geography, Sayer's critical-realist manifesto represents a watershed in debates about methodology in economic geography. Looked at through the eyes of many contemporary economic geographers, critical realism may have been superseded by variants on a post-modern methodology, nonetheless the dualism between 'extensive' and 'intensive' research strategies has remained hugely influential in shaping contemporary discourse and research training, at least in the UK.

At best, quantification seems to be tolerated in so far as it is capable of providing background information as a prelude to the real, and preferred, business of 'intensive' research. At worst, faced with the apparent inadequacies of superficial 'extensive' methodologies, many economic geographers have simply abandoned quantification completely, in favour of a suite of supposedly 'deeper' causal explanations provided by qualitative methodologies. It is but a short step from critique based upon such stereotypes to outright dismissal and institutional marginalization. The construction of quantitative geography and geographers as somehow not on the 'cutting edge' of research in economic geography is likely to produce an acute sense of paranoia among the 'old' and an increasing sense of insecurity among the 'young'. Who would want to participate in a failed enterprise, something that we used to do, and that is of limited relevance in answering questions about those aspects of social reality that the 'great and good' think call for an explanation?

Where to begin? Reports of the death of quantitative economic geography are much exaggerated. Certainly, there are still plenty of economic geographers who continue to practice quantitative methodologies. With the recent resurgence of geographical economics, some have once again sought to appeal to the strictures of 'scientific' methodology to justify their research practices. However, it is possible to reject positivist/empiricist philosophies without abandoning quantification and empirical modelling in economic geography. Given the onslaught on the rigour and relevance of quantitative economic geography over the past two decades, what is clear is that there is a need to defend quantitative research practices in economic geography. My view is that there is something worth saving: the positivist 'ideal' may be neither attainable nor desirable, nonetheless quantitative methodologies can provide us with critical understanding and explanation of social reality which can both inform policy debate and allow us to evaluate empirically our theoretical claims.

Rather than rehearse these methodological debates here, I want to move the discourse forward by engaging with the theory and practice of quantitative economic geography in the context of its own application. In particular, I want to foreground the status of 'truth' claims that are associated with employing empirical models to bridge the gap between 'theory' and 'data'. We focus on the question: what, if anything, is the value added by quantitative economic geography? What we expect to achieve in practice raises some non-trivial epistemological questions regarding the potentials and limitations of empirical modelling. Should we aim for 'true' models of the mechanisms and processes operating in the geographical world? Alternatively, are we limited to building empirically adequate models that are, perhaps, approximately accurate and precise representations of the empirical data? More broadly, should we judge empirical models by their correspondence with the 'facts', their coherence with accepted belief systems, or their usefulness in solving problems?

These are fundamental questions that deserve attention by all economic geographers regardless of their methodological commitments. We will confront these questions directly by critically examining my own methodological practices through the lens of collaborative research that we have been conducting into the dynamics of uneven development across Australian local labour markets. This entails the use of spatial econometric models and methods to empirically test popular 'institutional' theories of local economic growth.Typically, such theories are constructed and empirically validated using 'intensive' research designs and qualitative methodologies, rather than empirical modelling methodologies. This research puts into sharp focus questions of ontological commitment and epistemological standards of success when employing empirical models in economic geography.

NEO-CLASSICAL APPROACH, LOCATION THEORY AND BEYOND

Let us start with the neo-classical approach. The application of the neoclassical model for the understanding of the ways in which the economy works over space looks straightforward enough. Echoing the view that the 'invisible hand' of the market will ensure equilibrium between demand and supply, neo-classical theory of spatial development implies that any uneven development is temporary, because market forces will ensure that some sort of spatial equilibrium or balanced development will be achieved in the long run.

This view is based on the assumption that, following the logic of the rational economic man, both producers (firms) and consumers (workers) will move between regions in search of the most profitable location.

Simply put, labour will move from poorer to richer regions (in search of higher wages) and capital will move in the opposite direction (in search of cheaper labour and land). Even more complex neo-classical models that involve other factors of production (*e.g.* technology) are all built around the assumption that some sort of spatial equilibrium will be achieved in the long run, because such factors of production will inevitably spread or disperse over space. The processes of spatial dispersal can indeed be observed in reality. However, the examples of spatial equilibrium that the neo-classical theory envisages, are hard to find. One way of accounting for this discrepancy is to acknowledge that, in real life, factors of production cannot move 'freely' over space. Indeed, there are various constraints involved. One of the obvious obstacles is the friction of distance.

The calculation of the cost associated with moving people, machinery, materials or goods across space and the implication of this for location in space forms the basis of the neo-classical location theory. Key concepts that build upon the location theory include the central place theory, urban hierarchy, market potential and accessibility. These concepts help us to understand how the friction of distance influences the location of economic activities in space.

Further insights into why economic activities simply do not disperse in space are, among others, offered by the concepts of agglomeration economies, increasing returns and cumulative causation. These latter concepts identify additional market advantages arising from the spatial concentration of economic activities. In essence, these concepts show that rather than having a self-correcting dispersal effect, market forces can in fact reinforce existing inequalities in space. The kind of spatial equilibrium envisaged by the neo-classical theory is therefore hard to achieve. It could be argued that these latter concepts 'use the approach and language of neo-classical economics to reach contrary conclusions'.

AN ECONOMIC-GEOGRAPHICAL PERSPECTIVE

In contrast to a rather limited appreciation of geography by most economists, geographers emphasise the fact that no economy can function at the head of a pin. In other words, 'all economies must take place'. Geography, therefore, is always intrinsically present in all economic processes. One could therefore argue that, in fact, there are 'no economies, only economic geographies'. It follows then, that the kind of universalism that mainstream economics assumes is somewhat problematic.

Indeed, if all economic processes have a geographical dimension, then it is difficult to imagine that economic rules can apply equally to all places. Another major difference between an economic-geographical perspective and the assumptions of economic orthodoxy concerns the notion of a 'rational man'—homo economicus.

Mainstream economists assume that people are always behaving as rational, profitmaximising individuals responding to market signals. However, life is more complex than that and people's behaviour is not always the outcome of rational decision-making. Rather, it can be influenced and conditioned by their gender, race, age, class, religion, culture, health or disability. Geographers are keen to take these aspects on board when studying economies. A 'geographical man/woman'–or what we will call here homo geographicus–can behave very differently from the way they are supposed to behave just as to economic orthodoxy. This has important implications for the remaining assumptions of economic orthodoxy. Indeed, if people are not behaving in a predictable way, than it is hard to expect that the entire economy will behave just as to some predictable laws and principles.

However sophisticated, mathematical models may not be able to capture all the complexity of economic processes happening in the real world. Worse still, mathematical models are not very helpful in elucidating the ways people relate to each other within societies and economies. In other words, 'the language of mathematics limits the ways in which economists can think about questions of power and social relations'. However, the questions of power and social relations are crucial in understanding economies because people do not live and work in isolation.

We are connected to each other in complex ways and economic geography helps us to explore these connections and relations. This exploration becomes more important in the age of globalisation. Further to this, it could be argued that these connections and relations are not limited to market exchanges and transactions.

Indeed, there is a wide range of economic processes happening outside the scope of the market. The diversity of forms of economic processes, both within and outside the scope of the market, means that many economic geographers are not talking about 'the economy' but about 'economies'. In recent years, the notion of 'diverse' or 'alternative' economies attracted much interest among geographers. The notion of 'diverse economies' further undermines the universalism of economic orthodoxy and paves the way for alternative explanations of what the economy is and how it works. Thus, one way or another, geographers in general, and economic geographers in particular, help to build a much richer, and perhaps more accurate, picture of the contemporary globalising economy. Coe and his colleagues go as far as to suggest that 'the set of approaches offered by the field of economic geography is best placed to help us appreciate and understand the modern economic world in all its complexity'. They identify the following key concepts that form part of the economic-geographical approach: space, place and scale.

Mainstream Economics

Key components of economic orthodoxy could be simply summarised as follows.

- One of the key assumptions of the economic orthodoxy is that all people are behaving in a rational, self-interested and economising, profit-maximising manner. This type of rational individual is sometimes referred to as 'economic man' or homo economicus.
- Economic orthodoxy assumes that these rational individuals are competing against each other on the market. Mainstream economists believe that the market is the best mechanism to ensure economic efficiency since, they believe, perfect competition on the market guarantees that supply will meet demand at a particular price and the economy will be in equilibrium. The notion of equilibrium is one of the central assumptions of mainstream economic thought and shapes the way in which economists see the world around them.
- Mainstream economists believe that the market economy operates just as to certain laws and principles that could be studied as a 'science'. One of the main concerns of this economic 'science' is to predict the behaviour of the economy using mathematical models and equations. The achievement of the aforementioned equilibrium is one of the key concerns of such modelling.
- Mainstream economists believe that these laws and principles work everywhere and therefore economic models are applicable to them in every context. In other words, economic orthodoxy believes in certain universalism.

Some would argue that such a portrayal of economic orthodoxy is somewhat simplistic, a caricature of an increasingly diverse body of economics.

However, a tendency among economists to assume some sort of universal applicability of basic economic 'laws' is rather pervasive. Within this world of universal laws there is a little room for local differences and geography in general. Indeed, geography rarely enters economists' equations. The use of geography by economists is somewhat limited. There are some important exceptions, however. Among them is Paul Krugman, US economist and the Nobel Prize winner for economics in 2008. Over the years, Krugman has made an important contribution in terms of bringing geography into economics and is seen as a leading figure of the so-called 'New Economic Geography'. However, his notion of geography is still somewhat limited and narrow, especially when compared with the conceptualisation of geography used by the economic geographical perspective. Indeed, there are stark differences between the 'New Economic Geography' used by economists and the 'new economic geography' used by geographers.

Key Concepts of Economic Geography

An economic-geographical approach puts spatial concepts such as space, place and scale at the centre of the analysis. These concepts form part of the common language that is shared among professional geographers.

It is therefore essential that you familiarise yourself with these concepts right at the start:

- *Space*: The concept of space refers to physical distance and area. The concept of space allows us to ask simple questions such as where a particular process is happening.

  Four interrelated elements of the concept of space can be identified:

  1. Territoriality and form
  2. Location
  3. Flows across space
  4. The concept of uneven space as a necessary condition of a capitalist system.
- *Place*: The concept of place aims to capture the specificity or uniqueness of particular places that are carved out of space. Through the notion of place, geographers are able to explore the richness and complexity of particular places and economic processes which are always embedded in environmental, social, cultural, institutional and political contexts. The idea of being embedded is very important because environmental, social, cultural, institutional and political contexts influence economic processes. Many Western values, for instance, may be alien to many other cultures, societies or nations. Therefore, the way economies are constructed and performed may be very different in different places.

Despite its importance for geographical research, the notion of place is somewhat vague because it can take various shapes and sizes.

- *Scale*: The concept of scale therefore helps us to organise places through a typology of spatial scales.

  Spatial scales that are commonly used by economic geographers include:
  - Global scale
  - Macro-regional scale
  - National scale
  - Regional scale
  - Local scale
  - Lived places.

It is worth noting that the precise typology is sometimes problematic. The terms 'local' and 'regional', for instance, are often used rather loosely.

In some cases, it is difficult to establish whether we are looking at a national, regional or local scale. When reading economic geography literature, you should always pay attention to what definition of scale a particular author is using.

Further to this, it is important to realise that the above three key concepts are not simply neutral tools for describing the world–they can also be seen as representations of the world. Indeed, the way these concepts are used by academics, the media or politicians influences the way we look at the world and how we understand its problems.

Major Theoretical Perspectives

While most geographers would recognise and use the concepts of space, place and scale, it is important to realise that concepts of space, place and scale are themselves subject to debate and alternative interpretations in geography.

For instance, some geographers use the term space to describe absolute geographical space, while others are using the term to describe relative space or relational space.

You need to keep this in mind when reading some geography texts. More generally, you need to be aware of the fact that economic geography is a vibrant, dynamic and continuously evolving sub-discipline composed of a diverse set of approaches and concepts. This subject guide will help you to learn about the key approaches and concepts that contemporary economic geography has to offer.

These approaches and concepts will be explained in some detail in subsequent stages. However, already at this point, it is useful to highlight the various intellectual traditions within which these approaches and concepts are anchored.

Four main theoretical perspectives in economic geography are:

- *Neo-classical location theory*: Location theory flourished in the 1950s and the 1960s and was primarily interested in establishing and explaining patterns in the distribution of economic activities across space. This type of economic geography was firmly anchored in a neoclassical economics theory and used a model-based approach to study the location of economic activities in space. This period in the development of economic geography is often called a 'quantitative revolution' which provided foundations for 'regional science', 'geographical economics' and 'spatial economics'. However, many economic geographers became dissatisfied with this approach and started exploring alternatives. More recently, the interest in regional science and geographical economics has been revived through the work of economist Paul Krugman and his 'New Economic Geography'.
- *Behavioural approach*: A behavioural approach emerged in the late 1960s as one of the reactions to the 'quantitative revolution'. It moved away from a simple neo-classical assumption of homo economicus and explored a wider range of factors that influence economic decisionmaking of human actors in various situations. The problem with this approach, however, is that it fails to explore fully the relationships between individuals and society.
- *Structuralist approach/Marxist political economy*: By contrast, a Marxist political economy approach, places social relations at the centre of its analysis, with an emphasis on class. Since the 1970s Marxist views started to influence geography and still have a significant influence on economic geography today. Importantly, Marxist-inspired economic geography moved the attention from spatial patterns and locational issues to questions of social relations and economic structures of capitalist economies.
- *Post-structuralist approaches/New economic geography/Cultural turn*: However, since the mid-1990s, a new type of economic geography has started to emerge from post-structuralist ideas. An important contribution of the new economic geography is its insistence that economic process cannot be seen in isolation from social, cultural and political contexts. In fact, new economic geography argues that social, cultural and/or institutional factors are central to the functioning of the economy/economies. Thus the emphasis on the notion of class has been replaced by the interest in categories such as gender, race, age, religion and culture. This change of emphasis is often referred to as the 'cultural turn'. This emphasis on cultural factors also represents one of the key differences between the 'new economic geography' used by geographers

and the one used by economists. Furthermore, the cultural turn brought with it a change of focus away from structural features towards more particular features of societies and economies.

You will familiarise yourself with these major theoretical perspectives step by step of this subject guide. The important thing to remember is that economic geographers do not always agree which approach is best and concepts they are working with are continually tested and contested. None of the theoretical perspectives is perfect; each of them has its strengths and weaknesses. However, collectively, they provide critical insights into the ways in which societies and economies work. The importance of economic geography for understanding the economic world around us will be explored in the subsequent part. However, before moving on to the next part, let me reiterate the difference between the 'new economic geography' described by geographers and the 'New Economic Geography' described by economists.

The difference between the two reflects a fundamental difference of understanding concerning what economic geography is about. Paul Krugman, the key proponent of NEG, economic geography is about 'the location of production in space'; in other words, it is a 'branch of economics that worries about where things happen in relation to one another'.

In investigating the patterns of location of production in space, Krugman uses complex economic models in which geography is inserted as an important factor. In this way, Krugman's NEG has much in common with neo-classical location theory. This subject guide will not explore Krugman's theory in any detail. However, by learning about neoclassical location theory you will gain a good understanding of the basic principles on which Krugman's theory builds. This, in turn, will help you to study Krugman's work in the future should you choose to do so. In contrast to NEG, the 'new economic geography' described by geographers as part of the 'cultural turn' is not represented by one single theory. Rather it is very much a diverse set of approaches. More importantly, the new economic geography of the cultural turn represents a dramatically different view of economies and their geographies. While there have been attempts to foster a dialogue between geographers and economists the gap between the two types of new economic geographies is rather noticeable.

IMPORTANCE OF ECONOMIC GEOGRAPHY

Powerful arguments have been put forward about the impact of globalisation in general, and the effects of the ICT revolution in particular, on economic activities. Some observers have come to the conclusion that electronic communications have 'space-shrinking' effects and will bring about the 'death of distance' and thus, ultimately, the 'end of geography'.

The 'death of distance' thesis has been expressed by Cairncross as follows:

- 'Distance will no longer determine the cost of communicating electronically. Companies will organize certain types of work in three shifts just as to the world's three main time zones: the Americas, East Asia/Australia, and Europe...No longer will location be key to most business decisions. Companies will locate any screen-based activity anywhere on earth, wherever they can find the best bargain of skills and productivity.'

A similar argument has been put forward by O'Brien who argued that ICTs will allow money to be moved around the globe without constraints, thus spelling the 'end of geography':

- 'The end of geography, as a concept applied to international financial relationships, refers to a state of economic development where geographical location no longer matters, or matters less than hitherto. In this state, financial market regulators no longer hold sway over their regulatory territory; that is rules no longer apply to specific geographical frameworks, such as the nation-state or other typical regulatory/ jurisdictional territories. For financial firms, this means that the choice of geographical location can be greatly widened... Stock exchanges can no longer expect to monopolize trading in the shares of companies in their country or region... For the consumer of financial services, the end of geography means a wider range of services will be offered, outside the traditional services offered by local banks.'

Both the authors of these statements attempt to convince their readers that, thanks to ICTs, space and place no longer matter or at least they matter much less than before. Indeed, they both seem to suggest that location in space is no longer an issue for firms as they can locate 'anywhere on earth'. Also, the role of place is apparently greatly diminished. Cairncross, for instance, suggests that the only place characteristics that firms may be interested in can be reduced to 'the best bargain of skills and productivity'.

O'Brien, in the meantime, does not seem to recognise any role that places may play in the globalised financial markets. But, interestingly, both Cairncross and O'Brien seem to imply that the national scale is increasingly irrelevant in the global economy. Indeed, O'Brien specifically points out that financial market regulators 'no longer hold sway' and that rules no longer apply to nation-states, because financial flows are spilling over traditional national boundaries.

Similarly, Cairncross seems to suggest that the time zone is the only geographical scale that holds any relevance in the new era of global electronic communications. What is interesting about the above statements of Cairncross and O'Brien is that they both see globalisation as something positive.

Note, for instance, Cairncross's suggestion that companies will benefit from the new locational freedom by allowing them to find and exploit 'the best bargain of skills and productivity'. O'Brien, meanwhile, suggests that the 'end of geography' will be beneficial for both financial firms and their customers.

Views such as these can be labelled as 'hyperglobalist'. Some of them go as far as to suggest that freeing economic activities from their traditional geographical constraints will bring benefits to all people in all corners of the globe. However, this, manifestly, does not seem to be the case. Today's world is ridden with sharp inequalities both within and between countries and geography plays an important role in understanding economic and social processes and their uneven manifestations in the age of globalisation.

Importance of Economic Geography in the Era of Globalization

Despite the hyperglobalist views, the role of space, place and scale do not diminish in the globalising world. Quite the opposite perhaps. Indeed, as economic activities are increasingly internationalised, interconnections between various places increase, competition between them intensifies and inequalities are on the rise, so geography becomes more important than ever. And as we have pointed out earlier, an economic-geographical approach is perhaps 'best placed to help us appreciate and understand the modern economic world in all its complexity'.

This conviction is based on the knowledge that economic geography offers powerful tools for analysing and understanding contemporary economies and societies. Economic geography, for instance, can help us to understand that, despite years and decades of economic globalisation, the pattern of investment, production, trade and consumption is highly uneven. Economic geography can also help us to understand that even footloose multi-national corporations have to be 'grounded' in specific locations and often 'embedded' in places and their socio-political, institutional and cultural contexts.

Economic geography also helps to elucidate the ways in which MNCs and other economic activities are 'governed' at various geographical scales from local and regional to national, macro-regional and global levels. Economic geography also helps us to understand that despite the widespread use of ICTs, trading places for global financial capital remain stubbornly located in a small number of global cities and these global cities, in turn, influence economic processes around the world.

Thanks to these and other insights, economic geography can thus contribute to our understanding of inequalities at various geographical scales from poverty in urban areas to global uneven development. No other discipline can claim such a wide scope of interest and relevance to today's rapidly changing world. By following this subject guide, you will gain solid foundations in economic geography approaches, concepts and theories and their applicability to the contemporary world and policy-making.

Issues for Economic Geography

We highlighted the fact that economic geography can be seen as a diverse set of approaches and concepts that economic geographers use to study economic processes. In turn, this diversity of economic geography approaches allows economic geographers to engage with a diverse set of questions about the economy and society. Concrete questions often depend on a theoretical standpoint.

Peter Dicken and Peter Lloyd in their textbook Location in Space argue that:

- 'Fundamentally, the economic geographer is concerned with the spatial organisation of economic systems: with where the various elements of the system are located, how they are connected together in space, and the spatial impact of economic processes.'

On the basis of this, they argue that economic geographers are interested in three interconnected questions.

- In what ways are economic activities organised spatially on the earth's surface, and how do such spatial forms or patterns change over time?
- Why are economic activities organised spatially in particular ways; that is, what are the underlying processes at work?
- How does the spatial organisation of economic activities itself influence economic and other social processes?

On the other hand, Roger Lee suggests that economic geography is 'a geography of people's struggle to make a living' and should therefore concern itself with 'the sustainable and humane production, use and reproduction of the social, natural and material conditions of human existence'.

On the basis of this, Lee argues that an 'inclusive economic geography' should include the study of:

- The cultural and environmental origins of economic activity, articulated through socially constructed gender and kinship relations; and the struggle to establish a particular set of social relations of production and their geographical extent
- The conceptualisation of nature
- The forms of calculation and measurement of value
- The processes and forms of production and consumption generated by such relations and value systems
- The division of labour
- The conditions of development within a particular set of social relations
- The forms of state and politics which support and legitimise particular social relations and processes of production and consumption

- The construction of cultural and ideological forms which shape the basis of discourse within a particular value system
- The structuring of relationships within and between different sets of social relations
- The conditions of transformation from one set of social relations of production to another.

This is a long list indeed–it reflects the view discussed earlier that there are 'no economies, only economic geographies'. Put differently, given that all economic processes are inherently spatial, economic geographers should be concerned about all the processes related to the people's struggle to make a living. However, an important question arises about whether such an approach is still needed in the era of globalisation in which space is apparently being dissolved by modern information and communication technologies.

APPROACHES IN ECONOMIC GEOGRAPHY

We introduced economic geography as a subdiscipline of geography which uses a geographical approach to study economies. We have highlighted the fact that the economic-geographical approach of studying economies is very different from the one used by mainstream economics. We have also noted that economic geographers see the economy through the prism of space, place and scale.

What we have not done is to explore the question of what 'the economy' actually is. However, this is a fundamental question. Indeed, the way in which we define what 'the economy' is influences our understanding of how 'the economy' works and what can be done about it. Importantly, the definition of 'the economy' and 'the economic' has an important bearing on our understanding of the way economic processes work over space, across scales and in particular places.

In other words, the way in which we define 'the economy' has profound implications for our understanding of economic geographies. This stage thus aims to address this issue by exploring the different theoretical perspectives on 'the economy' and their geographical implications. The point here is not to provide a detailed description of the various economic geography concepts.

Rather the aim here is to allow the reader to grasp and recognise the key differences in the theoretical foundations on which various economic geography concepts have been developed. Economic geography is not a monolithic sub-discipline. Rather it is a sub-discipline which draws on various intellectual traditions.

This stage will consider three broad perspectives on the economy:

- The mainstream economic perspective.

- The Marxist perspective.
- Alternative approaches.

These three perspectives represent contrasting views on how the economy works and in turn offer three quite different ways of approaching economic geographies. But first, let us explore the question of what the economy is.

Defining the Economy

Let us start with a definition of 'the economy'. The term is used in everyday life with such frequency that we rarely pause to think what the economy actually is. Most people take the notion of the economy for granted. In fact, many economics dictionaries and textbooks take it for granted too and do not even bother defining it. The term 'economy' had not featured in the original version of Raymond Williams' Keywords either. So what is 'the economy'?

The Concise Oxford English Dictionary suggests that the word 'economy' is in fact of Greek origin. The Greek term 'oikonomia' basically means 'household management'–from oikos 'house' and nomos 'managing' from nemein 'manage'. The hint of this original meaning still survives today and 'economy' can mean 'careful management of available resources'. In travel this can mean that you buy the cheapest air or rail ticket and travel 'economy class'. However, since about the eighteenth century the term economy also began to gain a new meaning and now can refer to economic affairs at a much larger geographical scale, namely that of a nation.

Nowadays, the notion of 'the economy' is perhaps still most commonly used to describe the economic processes of a country. The Concise Oxford English Dictionary defines the economy as 'the state of a country or area in terms of the production and consumption of goods and services and the supply of money'. However, as it will become apparent below, even this latter definition is somewhat problematic.

Problematising and Re-defining the Economy

GDP represents a fairly standard way of measuring the economy. It captures three key economic agents–namely households, firms and the government–all of which play important roles in the economy. Yet measuring the economy in this way can be highly problematic. One of the key problems is that GDP measurement is derived from a definition of the economy that is rather narrow–it includes certain things and processes but excludes others.

Coe offer a very good example of this problem. If you have taken a bus or drive a car to your place of work or study then you have engaged in an economic act. Your bus fare or your fuel bills and parking costs would be included in your individual consumption and therefore included in the conventional definition of the economy. But if you decide to cycle or walk instead, no money will change hands and, therefore, oddly, you have not engaged in an economic act! Another good example is unpaid work. Since no wages are paid, unpaid work occurs outside the formal monetary economy and therefore is not included in the consideration of the state of the economy.

This way, not only is the economy miscounted, but also the work of certain people is discounted. A similar problem arises with the 'black economy'. In the 'black economy', money can indeed change hands, but because these monetary transactions are not recorded by the government, they are not included in what counts as 'the economy'. Yet, the livelihoods of millions of people around the world may be dependent on such transactions. Thinking about what constitutes an economic act or process is crucial for our understanding of the economy and is, therefore, a point of contention. The way in which cultural, social, political and environmental processes are related to the economic processes is another contentious issue. A conventional definition of the economy supports the impression that the economy is somewhat separated from other dimensions of our lives. This in turn helps to create the impression that the economy is something 'out there', which affects our lives, but which we, as individuals, cannot control.

This impression is often reinforced by the way the economy is represented in everyday use and policy documents. Indeed, the economy is often represented by metaphors such as a 'machine', an 'organism' or a 'body'; that presumably has a life of its own. However, it could be argued that the economy is inseparable from cultural, social, political and environmental processes.

Ray Hudson, for instance, understands 'the economy' as referring to:

- those simultaneously discursive and material processes and practices of production, distribution and consumption, through which people seek to create wealth, prosperity and wellbeing and so construct economies; to circuits of production, circulation, realisation, appropriation and distribution of value.

However, he is quick to add that value is 'always culturally constituted and defined' and that '[w]hat counts as "the economy" is, therefore, always cultural, constituted in and distributed over space, linked by flows of values, monies, things and people that conjoin a diverse heterogeneity of people and things'. He further argues that '[e]qually importantly, the social processes that constitute the economy always involve biological, chemical or physical transformation via human labour of elements of the natural world'.

This also means that thinking about 'the economy' in terms of evergrowing GDP, for instance, may not be a universally shared, nor necessarily desirable, concept. Indeed as Hodder and Lee have argued several decades ago, that it is 'all too easy, for instance, to assume that the dream of each less-developed country is to become developed'. Indeed, 'such a view can easily disregard highly developed local cultures'. They add that 'self-respect is at least as important a measure of social and economic progress as are increases in... material wealth'. Similarly, studying 'the economy' without considering the environmental dimension of economic processes is problematic, not least because 'economic activities are taking an increasing toll of balanced interactions within the life-giving ecosystem'. Another way to approach a definition of 'the economy' is to remind ourselves of the notion introduced in that there are 'no economies, only economic geographies'. In turn, economic geographies can be defined as 'geographies of people's struggle to make a living'. Importantly, this struggle to make a living is framed in both material and social processes. In other words, 'all economies and economic geographies are both material and social constructs'. What is more, in the construction of economic geographies the relations between the material and the social are 'inseparable and mutually formative'. The recognition of this further undermines the notion of the economy as simply being 'the state of production and consumption of goods and service and the supply of money' or as being measurable by GDP.

How does the Economy Work

We have attempted to answer the question 'what is the economy?' The process of defining the economy can be problematic. What should and should not be included in the notion of 'the economy' remains a contentious issue. In this part as suggested, attempt to address an issue which is even more contentious: 'How does the economy work?' As already pointed out in the introductory part, the answer to this question is in part influenced by the way we define the economy. However, even people who would share the view about what the economy is can disagree profoundly on the question of how it works. Large numbers of economists and social scientists work on this question every day and we have no space here to review all of their theories. Instead, what as suggested, attempt to do in this is to identify three basic theoretical perspectives on the economy. First, as suggested, examine the mainstream economic perspective, which sees the functioning of the economy through the lens of market forces and which maintains that individual self-interest mediated by the 'invisible hand' of the market leads to equilibrium and prosperity. Second, as suggested, introduce the Marxist perspective which, in contrast, argues that the capitalist market economy is ridden by internal contradictions and produces both inequality and instability. Finally, as suggested, have a look at the alternative approaches, especially those associated with evolutionary and institutionalist economics, which try to go beyond the boundaries of market-based processes and which pay attention to wider social, cultural and institutional contexts in order to explain how economies function.

Measuring the Economy

Perhaps the most common way of measuring 'the state in which a country is in terms of the production and consumption of goods and services' is an indicator called Gross Domestic Product. GDP measures, in money terms, the total market value of production in a particular economy in a given year. It is usually calculated as a sum of expenditures by households, firms and the government plus net exports.

By household expenditure we mean the total amount spent by individuals in a given year including their expenditure on food, fuel, housing, clothing, household appliances, leisure, etc. Expenditure by firms is measured as investment expenditure by which we mean the amount invested by businesses in future productive capacity. Government expenditure is the amount spent by the government to build infrastructure or provide services. Finally, net exports represent the value of goods and services sold to other countries minus the value of goods and services imported from abroad.

The Marxist Approach

The Marxist perspective on the economy is derived from the work of Karl Marx and Friedrich Engels, two German philosophers of the late nineteenth-century. Like Adam Smith, Karl Marx was interested in the question of how wealth is created in the economy and how wealth is distributed among members of society.

However, in stark contrast to the win–win situation alluded to by Smith, Marx pointed out that wealth will increasingly concentrate in the hands of the few. How so? To answer this question, Marx devised his labour theory of value. In order to explain the basics of the labour theory of value as devised by Marx, let us go back to the pin-making factory described earlier. As we have seen, the productivity gains from organising pin production in the pin factory were substantial. But who reaps the benefits? If the factory was jointly owned by the 10 workers who work there, it is possible to imagine a situation in which they could split the benefits of their production between themselves. However, in the capitalist market economy, the factory is likely to be privately owned. The owner, the capitalist, would own the land on which the factory is built, the factory building itself, the raw materials needed to produce the pins and all the machinery and tools used by the workers. In other words, he or she would own the means of production. Workers, on the other hand, do not own the means of production and the only way they can sustain themselves is to sell their own work to capitalists. Thus, in the capitalist market economy, labour itself becomes a commodity–labour power can be bought and sold like any other commodity. So, workers sell their labour and receive wages in exchange for their work and that looks fine on the surface. However, the question arises as to what capitalists do to sustain themselves? They have to engage in the circuit of capital and make profit.

The way Marx described how the circuit of capital works. Imagine a capitalist who has capital in the form of money–money capital (M)–to invest. He or she can turn this money capital into productive capital (P) by purchasing two commodities–the labour power (LP; *e.g.* labour of 10 workers) and the means of production (MP; *e.g.* pin-making factory, raw materials, machinery, tools, etc., needed to produce pins). The labour power and the means of production are then combined in the process of production to produce 48,000 pins a day–representing another form of capital–commodity capital (C).

Commodity capital can be turned back into money capital when the factory owner sells pins on the market at a certain price (and this price represents what Marxists call exchange value). For the capitalist to survive, he or she has to make a profit. This means that the money he or she receives in exchange for the commodities produced must be greater than the money originally invested in the enterprise (M′ > M). The search for profit is the motivating force of the capitalist economy. The crucial point in the Marxist analysis is a recognition that, ultimately, all value comes from human labour and the only way for a capitalist to make profit is to appropriate surplus value (s).

Surplus value is the difference between the wages the factory owner pays workers for their labour and the value these workers produce for him or her in the factory while making pins. To frame it differently, workers add value to the commodities they produce by applying their labour, and this value is greater than the reward they get in exchange for their efforts in the form of wages.

This is the basis of exploitation in the capitalist economy. However, capitalists have to engage in it, if they are to survive the cut-throat competition from other capitalists, who have to do exactly the same. Those capitalists who fail to generate profit (or enough profit) go out of business. The effort to maximise profit is therefore an imperative of the capitalist economy. All capitalists, individually, have to act in a profit-maximising manner, which echoes the self-interested behaviour described by Adam Smith. Such behaviour, in turn, further exacerbates competition and so it could be argued that one of the key features of capitalism is that it is inherently competitive. However, Marx argued that such individual action will not lead to the equilibrium and win–win situation envisaged by Smith–far from it.

Marx argued that capitalism (the system based on capital) is both unequal and unstable. He argued that inequalities within society will increase as capitalists try to increase their profits and squeeze workers' wages, by introducing machines, intensifying labour processes or simply by forcing workers to work longer hours, for example. Capitalists can also endeavour to replace workers by machines and by doing so, they create a growing pool of the unemployed, which in turn will push wages down further still. The result of this process will be an increasing concentration of wealth in the hands of a few (the capitalist class) and the impoverishment of the working class masses (proletariat). Simply put, the capitalist system will ensure that the rich will become richer and the poor will become poorer. Ethical issues aside, Marx argued that such a system is unlikely to reach an equilibrium of the kind envisaged by Adam Smith, because sooner or later the fundamental economic contradiction arises: too many commodities (*e.g.* pins) will be produced, but there will be too few people able to buy them.

Marxists call this situation an overaccumulation. Overaccumulation can take various forms, but overaccumulation of capital in the form of unsold commodities is one of the most striking symptoms. Ian Craib offers a very good illustration of how such a crisis of overaccumulation can happen, using a crucial distinction in Marxist theory between use value and exchange value:

- 'If I am a worker and I produce £50 worth of goods in a day (the use value of my labour to my employer), and I receive £10 a day in wages (the exchange value of my labour power), then I do not receive in wages sufficient to buy back the value of goods I have produced. This applies right across the system, so that if stocks of unsold goods build up, workers have to be laid off, and the economy enters a crisis, a depression, or slump, until the stock of goods are used up and firms go back into production. There is a cycle of growth and slump, something that capitalist economies have been trying to deal with for over a century and a half.'

This is then one of the possible causes of the familiar boom-and-bust cycle. Each boom is followed by a crisis in which devaluation must take place to kickstart the accumulation process all over again. For Marx then, the capitalist economy is neither equal nor stable–it is inherently unequal and crisisprone. The profit-making imperative that drives the capitalist economy and makes it dynamic, is also a source of its fundamental contradiction. Marxist conceptualisation of the economy therefore represents a stark contrast to the equilibrium-prone and win–win expectations of mainstream economics. Importantly, Marx also argued that in the long run, the capitalist system is unsustainable, because the increasing contradictions will reach a tipping point at which the system will eventually collapse.

This, Just as to Marx will happen in the most advanced capitalist countries, where the contradictions between labour and capital will be the greatest. The collapse of capitalism will pave a way (via a socialist revolution led by the working class) for a new social and economic order (communism). Marx said very little about how such a new system would operate. However, for a system to be freed from exploitation, both private property and class relations based on property rights would have to be abolished. While Marxism provides a powerful analysis of the way the economy works, it also leaves us with a number of important issues. Indeed, the economy does not always work as predicted by Marx and, so far, the socialist revolution has failed to materialise in the most advanced capitalist countries. One of the key questions therefore is how can we account for the fact that the capitalist system manages to survive despite its contradictions? Economic geographers have made an important contribution to the debate on this question. But for now, let's turn to the alternative approaches.

Mainstream Economic Views

The mainstream economic perspective is mainly associated with neoclassical economic theory. The neo-classical school of thought has been developing since the late nineteenth-century and currently represents the dominant way of looking at the economy. Neo-classical economics is rooted in the belief that the market is the most efficient mechanism for the allocation of resources and hence the creation of prosperity.

The neo-classical school of economic thought has been built on the foundations laid down by Adam Smith, a Scottish economist and the founder of the classical political economy. Back in the eighteenth century, Smith devised an economic theory, the features of which remain with us today. This includes his concepts of rational self-interest and the 'invisible hand' of the market, concepts that underpin much of contemporary mainstream economic thinking. In seeking to identify how wealth is created, Adam Smith argued that the main cause of prosperity is the division of labour.

Smith expressed his arguments in his famous work titled An Inquiry into the Nature and Causes of the Wealth of Nations published in 1776. In it, Smith used an example of a factory making pins to explain the power of the division of labour and the productivity that can be achieved from this. He argued that a single worker working alone at home would be lucky to produce even one pin per day and certainly not 20. However, he observed that in a pin-making factory 10 workers can engage in the production of pins by dividing 18 specialised pin-making tasks between them: One man draws out the wire, another straights it, a third cuts it, a fourth points it, a fifth grinds it at the top for receiving the head; to make the head requires two or three distinct operations; to put it on, is a peculiar business, to whiten the pins is another; it is even a trade by itself to put them into the paper; and the important business of making a pin is, in this manner, divided into about eighteen distinct operations, which, in some manufactories, are all performed by distinct hands, though in others the same man will sometimes perform two or three of them... Smith.

By dividing the work between them in this way, Smith argued, 10 workers can together produce about 48,000 pins per day. That is 4,800 pins per worker per day, representing a massive improvement of productivity when compared to the output achievable without the division of labour. The above improvement of productivity in the pin-making factory is impressive indeed.

But how does the pin-making factory know how many pins to produce and at what price to sell them? The mainstream economists, this problem will be solved by what Smith called the 'invisible hand' of the market. The market will determine both the quantity of goods produced and the price at which these goods will be sold, by matching supply with demand. This is how it works. From a producer's point of view, the higher the price customers are prepared to pay for a product the more the producer will be prepared to produce.

However, the higher the price, the less the goods will be in demand by the customers. Under perfect market conditions, supply and demand curves will intersect in the middle, thus fixing both the quantity of goods to be produced and the price under which they will be sold. In other words, the markets will achieve equilibrium. However, is based on the expectation that both producers and consumers are acting in a rational, economising or profit-maximising way.

In other words, they are behaving as homo economicus. Adam Smith argued that such behaviour is motivated by 'self-interest'. He further argued that by pursuing their own self-interests, individuals, led by the 'invisible hand' of the market, are unintentionally contributing to a greater societal good, a win–win situation, from which everybody will benefit. If pin-makers, shoe-makers, butchers and bakers all pursue their individual self-interest, the market will ensure that everybody will be better off. Since the times of Adam Smith, economic theory has developed a lot, but the key principles he introduced are still with us. The analysis of the workings of the economy through the lens of rational profit-making agents and the belief that markets are capable of delivering both equilibrium and efficiency, is central to neo-classical economic theory. However, such an understanding of the economy has been challenged by Marxist and other alternative approaches which as suggested, examine in turn.

ART OF ECONOMIC GEOGRAPHY

How do you turn economic geography into art? The Mexican painter, writer, and long-time communist Diego Rivera did it between 1932 and 1933 in painting the 25 panels of the mural "Detroit: Man and Machine" at the Detroit Institute of Arts. The panels tell a rich and complex economic geographical story: extracting resources from the ground, bringing together "hands" of workers from across the world, using various kinds of machinery -furnaces, stamping machines, drills, hoists, conveyor belts -in conjunction with the brawn of labor to manufacture and assemble, and finally produce, the finished product, in this case a car.

The mural was paid for by Edsel Ford, son of Henry, and modeled on perhaps the most famous factory of the twentieth century -the Rouge complex, the Ford automobile manufacturing plant located at Dearborn, Michigan, just outside Detroit. The complex was first used to produce automobiles from 1913. Twenty years later, by the time Rivera came to paint it, it was already a symbol of the modern machine age, and more generally of the energy and might of industrial capitalism. Operations at the Rouge complex were vertically integrated, that is, all the different component processes of manufacture were contained within a single site, and as a result the workforce requirements were immense. At one point 75,000 employees worked there. The "B" building alone was a quarter of a mile long, containing the entire assembly-line operation on a single level (and much of the focus of Rivera's artistic attention).

The assembly-line technique used in the "B" building was one of Henry Ford's most significant innovations, and was first introduced to the plant in 1927. Workers stood in place, and the work came to them on a conveyor belt. Once the work task was completed, the belt moved on, making the worker, as one Ford assembly-line employee put it, "nothing more or less than a robot". There is a clear sense of that in Rivera's mural. The workers do not simply tend the machines, but are fully integrated with them, their bodies synchronized with the swirling, ceaseless movement of industrial manufacture at the plant.

In many ways the Ford family were an unlikely patron of Rivera. Ford senior was vehemently anti-left, and anti-union. He once said, "people are never so likely to be wrong as when they are organized." What Rivera and Ford shared, however, was a fascination with machines, and the idea that the combination of "human and mechanical action" could produce a "creative power unparalleled in history". To capture that power in paint, Rivera spent his first three months in Detroit meticulously preparing before even picking up a paintbrush. He toured the plant, spoke to workers and engineers, and had hundreds of photographs taken of the different parts of the production process. What emerges, in spite of Rivera's communist sympathies, is a relatively uncritical portrait of industrial capitalism at the Rouge. True, one of the workers is carrying a partially obscured placard with the words "We want." But the full placard would have read "We want beer," a popular anti-prohibition slogan at the time. In contrast, Rivera's next mural commission, which was for another industrial mogul, John D. Rockefeller, was more overtly political, and included Lenin as one of the onlookers. In this case Rockefeller balked, and ordered the finished mural to be chipped off the wall of the Rockefeller Center, New York

City, where it had been painted.

For Rivera, the Rouge complex and its production of automobiles was an illustration of a broader phenomenon that he labeled a "wave-like movement" and found in "water currents, electric waves, stratifications of different layers under the surface of the earth, and in a general way throughout the continuous development of life". Economic geography as it emerges from the contributions to this volume is a bit like this, too. The kinds of phenomena that economic geographers study - natural resources, manufacturing, information, money - are always on the move, continually undergoing transformation, morphing into new forms and identities. Of course, capturing that flux and movement is difficult. Diego Rivera did it by painting larger-than-life stories on walls. His 25 panels are a synchronic depiction of the economic geographical processes that produced and maintained the industrial behemoth of 1930s Detroit. But there are clearly other means to make that same depiction, some of which, we would argue, are found in the essays collected here. Of course, they are not couched in a visual idiom, relying on vivid colors or daring brush strokes, but in their own way, we contend, they are just as striking.

Although economic geographers are not in the business of daubing paint, at least in their professional lives, there is an art to what they do. For economic geographers of whatever stripe face the same difficulty as Diego Rivera - to represent on a flat surface economic geographical events that exist "out there." Rivera's medium was paint, and his flat surface was a wall, whereas the medium of economic geographers is writing, and their flat surface is a sheet of A4 or eight-and-a-half by eleven inch paper. In both cases, there is a need for appropriate techniques, sensitive interpretation, enthusiasm, dedication, adequate preparation, and prior training. One of the primary aims of this volume is to introduce you to the art of economic geography.

The first is that since the 1970s there have been some enormous changes affecting the economy, and society more generally: deindustrialization, industrial restructuring, the rise of information technology (IT) and computerization, the feminization of the labor market, and globalization. Such changes beg understanding, and indeed are already subject to much scrutiny. What emerges from that work is that in many cases these changes are inextricably bound up with issues of space and place. We don't mean merely that, like many processes, they take on particular geographical forms (although there is nothing mere about that), but that space and place are integral to the evolution of the processes themselves. In this sense, economic geographers are in exactly the right time and place to practice their art.

Consider again globalization. Arguably globalization has existed since the very first economic geographers were writing in the late nineteenth century, and likely well before then (certainly it is recognizable in Andree's ruminations).

One aspect of globalization that has changed, though, is the means by which it is effected.

Whereas in Andree's time it was bound up with Western European colonial policy and bureaucracy, now its prime bearers are multinational and transnational corporations (MNCs and TNCs). MNCs and TNCs are fundamentally economically geographical institutions. Their very definition and rationale is based on the idea of geographical differentiation: that different parts of their operations are located in different places. As such, they are ripe for economic geographical study. Others can and should study MNCs and TNCs, but the sensibility of economic geography is especially suited to the task and, given the role that they play in the globalization process, is ever more germane.

To take another example, the Fordist-style manufacture that Rivera depicted in his murals was increasingly abandoned from the 1970s onwards, and replaced by what was called post-Fordism, or flexible specialization. That move was not only about transforming a particular method of production - from assembly line and Taylorism to batch production and work teams - but also about transforming geography. Flexible specialization implied a set of new spatial arrangements that were part of its very definition. Greater physical interaction and closer proximity between firms became necessary by comparison to the more arm's-length relationship that had characterized Fordism in order to realize the benefits of flexible specialization. Subcontractors needed to be close to the production plant in order to respond quickly to changed demands; R&D staff were brought in from their research facilities, sometimes thousands of kilometers away, to work more centrally in the factory in order to consult with production staff; and workers were no longer spatially segmented along the assembly line, but enjoyed greater interaction and collaboration in work teams. Whatever else it was, the move from Fordism to flexible specialization entailed an economically geographical shift.

These are only a couple of examples, but we hope that they illustrate the broader argument. The recent changes in the economy, which have affected so many people in so many different ways, are not only economic but also fundamentally geographical. Economic geography is relevant not just as background atmospherics, to add ambience and color, but for understanding why economic change occurs at all. It enters into its very frame, its skeletal structure. And what is bred in the bone, comes out in the marrow.

The second reason for the renewed attention to economic geography is that it continues to undergo potent intellectual shifts, making it an arena of discursive ferment and vibrancy. Economic geography, in fact, has long been an important forum for trying out new ideas. Much of human geography's quantitative revolution of the 1960s, for example, was discussed within the context of economic geography. Since the late 1970s and early 1980s, the discipline has propelled discussions around political economy. As an approach, political economy is pervasive: it is how economic geography is now done. That said, political economy is no single, staid, monolithic tradition, but is multiple, dynamic, and differentiated. Debate is not always friendly, but through it new approaches, new theories, and new possibilities emerge, and constantly invigorate the field.

Political economy as a tradition began in the eighteenth century, but it is perhaps most closely associated with Marx's nineteenth-century writings about capitalism. In both cases, there was the insistence that the political and the economic are irrevocably bound; that the economy cannot be treated as sovereign and isolated, but must be understood as part of a set of wider social processes. While sharing these views, political economists and economic geographers have continued to debate two central questions: the definition of the social, and the nature of the connection between the social and the economic.

For Marx, the answers to those contentious questions were clear-cut. The social meant class relations, which under capitalism primarily consists of an antagonistic relationship between the working class and the capitalist class. Social classes, in turn, are connected to the economy by a functional relationship. This means that the form of the relationship among social classes is set by what contributes best to the development of the economy. Such a functional relationship is certainly not always smooth and unproblematic, but ultimately the economy prevails and produces those social relationships that are most appropriate for its development. If capitalism can best develop by a set of class relations consisting of workers and capitalists, that is what happens. The best, and the most well-known, economic geographical translation of Marx's views about social processes and their connection to the economy was carried out by David Harvey (1982), particularly in his writings during the 1970s and 1980s on the geography of accumulation.

Subsequently, other economic geographers, drawing upon other traditions of political economy, have developed alternative approaches, ones providing quite different answers to the two questions about the definition of the social, and its relation to the economy. This is not the place to provide a full-blown review, but those alternatives include:

- Doreen Massey's (1984) work on spatial divisions of labor. This is much more catholic than Harvey's in its definition of the social, and in the relationship it posits between the social and the economic. (Importantly, place itself partly determines the development of the economy.)
- Regulationist theory. This partly defines the social in terms of institutional and regulatory frameworks, and also attempts to move away from crude functional-ism.

- The analytical approach. This uses both mathematical reasoning and rigorous, formal statistical testing to determine logically how space and place make a difference both to the definition of social processes and to their relation to the economy.

This review is necessarily very brief. Sustained examples of such political economic approaches can be found in the ensuing chapters. Our point, like the one we made about economic change, is that contemporary discussions around political economy make economic geography stimulating and provocative. There is a Chinese saying: "May you live in interesting times." Our argument is that they are here now in economic geography.

Purpose and Organization

Our broad purpose in commissioning the essays that make up this volume is to provide advanced undergraduate and graduate students, and faculty colleagues both inside and outside economic geography, with a sense of the state of the art of economic geography. We chose to focus on the ideas, concepts, and theories current within the discipline, rather than on empirical findings, because a discipline is characterized primarily by the questions it asks.

We identified individuals who we thought characterized both the unity and diversity of economic geography, and we asked them to provide their own accounts. We asked only geographers to contribute because, as we argue above, economic geography is quite different from geographical economics. Certainly, exchanges of views between geographers and economists about economic geography are an important part of the evolution of the identity of the discipline, but we leave that task to others.

Geography has always been a synthetic discipline, taking seriously the relationships between things studied separately in other disciplines (such as nature, and society). The essays synthesize across the human sciences, treating economic processes as part of other social processes, rather than separable from, superior to, or more fundamental than the rest of society. The themes addressed include: consumption and the family, social class, labor organizations (unions), questions of political governance, organization of producers (corporations), and social and ethnic networks. Each chapter seeks to show the importance of a geographical perspective in understanding the intersection of the economic with the social.

Last, but certainly not least, geography is not just about place but also about space: about how the distinctive economic characteristics of places, and the conditions of economic possibility that they face, depend on their economically geographical interdependencies with other places. We turn attention to the geographical flows of commodities, money, and people, and to the transportation and communications systems produced to facilitate them.

These essays suggest that even though the world is becoming smaller, one of the core metaphors for globalization, it is also an increasingly differentiated world, in part precisely because the interdependencies between places are increasing. The final essay links geographical thinking about globalization to similar work in international political economy.

In sum, we hope that these essays provide useful resources for further reading in economic geography, and also that some of you will join in this endeavor. We also hope that you are provoked to be critical: that you will reflexively re-examine your current thinking, and ask new questions about the adequacy of economic geography's representations and approaches highlighted here. If so, our goals in compiling this volume will have been achieved.

ECONOMISTS AND ECONOMIC GEOGRAPHERS

Economists and economic geographers differ in their methods in approaching similar economic problems in several ways. To generalize, an economic geographer will take a more holistic approach in the analysis of economic phenomena, which is to conceptualize a problem in terms of space, place and scale as well as the overt economic problem that is being examined. The economist approach, according to economic geographers, has four main drawbacks or manifestations of "economic orthodoxy that tends to homogenize the economic world in way that economic geographers try to avoid

Location Theory

Location theory is concerned with the geographic location of economic activity; it has become an integral part of economic geography, regional science, and spatial economics. Location theory addresses the questions of what economic activities are located where and why. Location theory rests — like Micro-economic theory generally — on the assumption that agents act in their own self interest. Thus firms choose locations that maximize their profits and individuals choose locations that maximize their utility.

Origins

While others should get some credit for even earlier work (e.g., Richard Cantillon, Etienne Bonnot de Condillac, David Hume, Sir James D. Steuart, and David Ricardo), it was not until Johann Heinrich von Thunen's first volume of *Der Isolierte Staat* in 1826 that location theory can be said to have really gotten underway. Indeed, the prominent regional scientist Walter Isard has called von Thunen "the father of location theorists." In *Der Isolierte Staat*, von Thunen notes that the costs of transporting goods consumes some of Ricardo's economic rent. He notes that because these transportation costs and, of course, economic rents, vary across goods, different land uses and use intensities will result with distance from the marketplace. A German hegemony of sorts seems to have taken hold in location theory from the time of von Thunen through to Walter Christaller's 1933 book *Die Zentralen Orte in Suddeutschland*, which formulated much of what is now understood as central place theory. An especially notable contribution was one by Alfred Weber, who published *Uber den Standort der Industrien* in 1909.

Working from a model akin to a physical frame adapted from some ideas by Pierre Varignon (a Varignon frame), Weber applies freight rates of resources and the finished goods along with the finished good's production function to develop an algorithm that identifies the optimal location for manufacturing plant. He also introduces distortions induced by labour and both agglomerative and deglomerative forces. Weber then moves on to discuss groupings of production units, anticipating Losch's market areas.

Carl Wilhelm Friedrich Launhardt conceived much of that for which Alfred Weber received credit, prior to Weber's work. Moreover, his contributions are surprisingly more modern in their analytical content than Weber's. This suggests that Launhardt was ahead of his time and simply was not readily understood by many of his contemporaries. Whether Weber was familiar with Launhardt's publications remains unclear. Weber was most certainly influenced by others, most notably Wilhelm Roscher and Albert Schaffle, who seem likely to have read Launhardt's work. Regardless, location theoretic thought blossomed only after Weber's book was published.

Resources and Development

Humans through technology and institutions transform things available with nature.

- Resources are of two types natural and human.
- Resources can be classified in the following ways –
  - (a) On the basis of origin – biotic and abiotic
  - (b) On the basis of exhaustibility – renewable and non-renewable
  - (c) On the basis of ownership – individual, community, national and international
  - (d) On the basis of status of development – potential, developed stock and reserves.
- The oceanic area up to 12 nautical miles from the coast line is called *territorial waters* of a country.
- The area up to 200 km from the coast line in which the country has the exclusive rights to exploit the natural resources is the *exclusive economic zone*. It includes territorial waters in it.
- Resource planning is the technique or strategy for the judicious use of resources in a country.

- *Sustainable economic development* means 'development should take place without damaging the environment, and development in the present should not compromise with the needs of the future generations.'
- *Agenda 21* is the declaration signed in 1992 at the UNCED, Rio de Janeiro, Brazil. It aims at achieving global sustainable development. It is an agenda to combat environmental damage, poverty, disease through global co-operation.
- Land supports natural vegetation, wild life, human life, economic activities, transport, and communication systems.
- About 43 per cent of the land area is plain, which provides facilities for agriculture and industry.
- Mountains account for 30 per cent of the total surface area of the country. They ensure perennial flow of some rivers; provide facilities for tourism and ecological aspects.
- About 27 per cent of the area of the country is the plateau region. It possesses rich reserves of minerals, fossil fuels and forests.
- Islands are less than 1 per cent of the area of the country. They provide opportunities for sea trade, tourism, and fish catch.
- Net sown area is over 80 per cent of the total area in Punjab and Haryana. Due to gentle sloping lands covered with fertile alluvial soils and black soils, climate favours cereal cultivation, good irrigation facilities, high population pressure.
- Net sown area is less than 10 per cent in Arunachal Pradesh, Mizoram, Manipur and Andaman Nicobar Islands because of mountainous areas, lack of irrigational facilities, infertile soils, low density of population, etc.
- The use of land is determined both by physical factors such as topography, climate, and soil types as well as human factors such as population density, technological capability and culture and traditions etc.
- If a land is left uncultivated for more than 5 agricultural years it is called Culturable waste land.
- If a land is left uncultivated for the past 1 to 5 agricultural years it is called Other than current fallow.
- If a land is left without cultivation for one or less than one agricultural year it is called Current fallow.
- Net sown area is the total area sown with crops and orchards. Area sown more than once in the same year is counted only once.
- Area sown more than once in an agricultural year plus net sown area is known as gross cropped area.

- Barren Land: This includes all land covered by mountains, deserts, etc.
- Land which cannot be brought under cultivation except at an huge cost is classified as unculturable land.
- The top most layer of the earth crust which is composed of organic and non-organic matter is called soil. Soil is renewable natural resource. The soil is a living system.
- 33 % of geographical area should be under Forest in the country according to the National Forest Policy 1952.
- Alluvial soils are the most widely spread and important soil of our country.
- Alluvial soils are found in the entire northern plains, Rajasthan and Gujarat, eastern coastal plains, deltas of the Mahanadi, Godavari, Krishna and Kaveri rivers.
- Duars, Chos and Terai are the Piedmont plains where alluvial soils are coarse.
- According to their age alluvial soils are of two types: old alluvial (Bangar) and new alluvial (Khadar).
- Black soils are also known as *regur* soils or cotton soils.
- Black soils develops on Basaltic lava rocks.
- Black soils are found in the Deccan trap (*Basalt*) region of Deccan plateau, the plateaus of Maharashtra, Madhya Pradesh and Chhattisgarh.
- Red soil develops on crystalline igneous rocks.
- Red and yellow soils are found in the eastern and southern parts of the Deccan plateau, the Western Ghats.
- The laterite soil develops due to intense leaching in areas with high temperature and heavy rainfall.
- Laterite soils are found in Karnataka, Kerala, Tamil Nadu, Madhya Pradesh, and the hilly areas of Orissa and Assam.
- The denudation of the soil cover and subsequent washing down is described as soil erosion.
- When the running water cuts through the clayey soils and makes deep channels it is called gullies.
- The land becomes unfit for cultivation and is known as bad land.
- In the Chambal basin such lands are called ravines.
- Sometimes water flows as a sheet over large areas down a slope. In such cases the top soil is washed away. This is known as sheet erosion.
- Wind blows loose soil off flat or sloping land known as wind erosion.

7

Environmental Geography

NATURAL ENVIRONMENT

The natural environment comprises all living and non-living things that occur naturally on Earth. In its purest sense, it is thus an environment that is not the result of human activity or intervention. The natural environment may be contrasted to "the built environment", and is also in contrast to the concept of cultural landscape.

For some, there is a difficulty with the term "natural environment" in that nearly all environments have been directly or indirectly influenced by humans at some point in time. In order to address this concern, some level of human influence is thus allowable without the status of any particular landscape ceasing to be "natural."

The term's meaning, however, is usually dependent more on context than a set definition. Many natural environments are the product of the interaction between nature and humans. For this reason, the term ecosystem has been used to describe an environment that contains nature, and includes people. It follows then that environmental problems are human or social problems. Some also consider it dangerously misleading to regard "environment" as separate from "people."

Challenges

It is the common understanding of natural environment that underlies environmentalism-a broad political, social, and philosophical movement that advocates various actions and policies in the interest of protecting what nature remains in the natural environment, or restoring or expanding the role of nature in this environment. While wilderness is increasingly rare, wild nature (e.g., unmanaged forests, uncultivated grasslands, wildlife, wildflowers) can be found in many locations previously inhabited by humans. Goals commonly expressed by the environmentalists include: reduction and clean up of manmade pollution, with future goals of zero pollution; reducing societal consumption of non-renewable fuels, development of alternative, green, low carbon or renewable energy sources; conservation and sustainable use of scarce resources such as water, land and air; protection of representative or unique or pristine ecosystems; preservation and expansion of threatened or endangered species or ecosystems from extinction; the establishment of nature and biosphere reserves under various types of protection, and, most generally, the protection of biodiversity and ecosystems upon which all human and other life on earth depends.

More recently, there has been a strong concern about climatic changes caused by anthroprogenic releases of greenhouse gases, most notably carbon dioxide, and their interactions with human uses and the natural environment.

Efforts here have focused on the mitigation of greenhouse gases that are causing climatic changes (i.e., through the Climate Change Convention and the Kyoto Protocol), and on developing adaptative strategies to assist species, ecosystems, humans, regions and nations in adjusting to these climatic changes. A more profound challenge however, is to identify the natural environmental dynamics in contrast to environmental changes not within natural variances. A common solution is to adapt a static view neglecting natural variances to exist.

Methodologically this view could be defended when looking at processes which changes slowly and short time series, while the problem arrives when fast processes turns essential in the object of the study.

BUILT ENVIRONMENT

The phrase built environment refers to the manmade surroundings that provide the setting for human activity, ranging from the large-scale civic surroundings to the personal places.

In architecture and environmental psychology, the phrase is a useful acknowledgment that a small fraction of buildings constructed annually, even in the industrialized world, are designed by architects, and that users of the built environment encounter issues that cross the traditional professional boundaries between urban planners, traffic engineers, zoning authorities, architects, interior designers, industrial designers, etc.

Historically, much of the built environment has taken the form of vernacular architecture, and this is still the case in large parts of the world. In the industrialized world, many buildings are produced by large scale development remote from its eventual users.

In landscape architecture, the built environment is identified as opposed to the natural environment, with the recognition that places like Central Park may have the look, feel, and nourishing quality of natural surroundings while being completely artificial and "built", thus blurring the line between the two.

In urban planning, the phrase connotes the idea that a large percentage of the human environment is manmade, and these artificial surroundings are so extensive and cohesive that they function as organisms in the consumption of resources, disposal of wastes, and facilitation of productive enterprise within its bounds. Recently there has also been considerable dialogue and research into the impact of the built environment's impact on population health.

CULTURAL LANDSCAPE

The Dresden Elbe Valley World Heritage Site is according to the UNESCO "an outstanding example of land use, representing an exceptional development of a major Central-European city" having almost half a million inhabitants.

Cultural landscape is defined as the human-modified environment, including fields, houses, churches, highways, planted forests, and mines, as well as weeds and pollution. A cultural landscape defined as: "A geographic area, including both cultural and natural resources and the wildlife or domestic animals therein, associated with an historic event, activity, or person or exhibiting other cultural or aesthetic values."

In the USA, there are four general types of cultural landscapes, not mutually exclusive: historic sites, historic designed landscapes, historic vernacular landscapes, and ethnographic landscapes.

"The cultural landscape is fashioned from a natural landscape by a cultural group. Culture is the agent, the natural are the medium, the cultural landscape is the result.

Under the influence of a given culture, itself changing through time, the landscape undergoes development, passing through phases and probably reaching ultimately the end of its cycle of development. With the introduction of a different, alien culture, a rejuvenation of the cultural landscape sets in, or a new landscape is superimposed on remnants of the old one" (Sauer's, 1925).

Sauer was explicitly concerned to counter an environmental determinism which had dominated the American geography of the previous generation, within which human agency was given scant autonomy in the shaping of the visible landscape. Sauer believed, and was determined to stress the agency of culture as a force in shaping the visible features of the Earth's surface in delimited areas. Within his definition, the physical environment retains a central significance, as the medium with and through which human cultures act.

Interestingly this results in elements of the physical environment, such as topography, soils, plants and animals needing to be incorporated into studies of the cultural landscape; so far as they provoke human responses and adaptations, or have themselves been altered by human activity (e.g. forest clearing and dams). Cronon (1995) believes that Sauer's definition cannot be upheld today since it is clear that there is no clear distinction between nature and culture, since both interlink and should be regarded together as co-productions.

The Myth of the Pristine Landscape

With the arrival of Europeans to North and South America and their subsequent forays into the hearts of these continents, explorers frequently encountered sparsely inhabited landscapes they thought was untouched wilderness, a belief which has persisted into contemporary time.

In a 1992 journal article, William M. Denevan closely examines this idea of "a world of barely perceptible human disturbance" and instead argues for the alternative hypothesis in which the state of American landscapes as they were in early post-contact times were largely shaped by anthropogenic processes such as deforestation and agricultural burning.

These extensive modifications done on the part of pre-contact peoples to their local ecosystems effectively transformed them into cultural and humanized landscapes. That indigenous peoples were capable of altering the landscapes in which they lived assigns much more agency to them than was previously credited to them for the past several centuries. It also refutes the notion of the 'noble savage' who lived in immaculate harmony with nature and left little to no impact on his landscape.

ECOLOGY

Ecology, œcology or ecological science, is the scientific study of the distribution and abundance of living organisms and how the distribution and abundance are affected by interactions between the organisms and their environment. The environment of an organism includes both physical properties, which can be described as the sum of local abiotic factors such as insolation (sunlight), climate, and geology, as well as the other organisms that share its habitat. The term oekologie was coined in 1866 by the German biologist Ernst Haeckel the word is derived from the Greek and therefore "ecology" means the "study of the household [of nature]".

The word "ecology" is often used in common parlance as a synonym for the natural environment or environmentalism. Likewise "ecologic" or "ecological" is often taken in the sense of environmentally friendly.

Scope

Ecology is usually considered a branch of biology, the general science that studies living organisms. Organisms can be studied at many different levels, from proteins and nucleic acids (in biochemistry and molecular biology), to cells (in cellular biology), to individuals (in botany, zoology, and other similar disciplines), and finally at the level of populations, communities, and ecosystems, to the biosphere as a whole; these latter strata are the primary subjects of ecological inquiries. Ecology is a multi-disciplinary science.

Because of its focus on the higher levels of the organization of life on earth and on the interrelations between organisms and their environment, ecology draws heavily on many other branches of science, especially geology and geography, meteorology, pedology, genetics, chemistry, and physics.

Thus, ecology is considered by some to be a holistic science, one that overarches older disciplines such as biology which in this view become sub-disciplines contributing to ecological knowledge.

Agriculture, fisheries, forestry, medicine and urban development are among human activities that would fall within Krebs' (1972: 4) explanation of his definition of ecology: "where organisms are found, how many occur there, and why".

As a scientific discipline, ecology does not dictate what is "right" or "wrong". However, ecological knowledge such as the quantification of biodiversity and population dynamics have provided a scientific basis for expressing the aims of environmentalism and evaluating its goals and policies. Additionally, a holistic view of nature is stressed in both ecology and environmentalism. Consider the ways an ecologist might approach studying the life of honeybees:

- The behavioral relationship between individuals of a species is behavioral ecology-for example, the study of the queen bee, and how she relates to the worker bees and the drones.
- The organized activity of a species is community ecology; for example, the activity of bees assures the pollination of flowering plants. Bee hives additionally produce honey which is consumed by still other species, such as bears.
- The relationship between the environment and a species is environmental ecology-for example, the consequences of environmental change on bee activity. Bees may die out due to environmental changes. The environment simultaneously affects and is a consequence of this activity and is thus intertwined with the survival of the species.

Disciplines of Ecology

Ecology is a broad discipline comprised of many sub-disciplines. A common, broad classification, moving from lowest to highest complexity, where complexity is defined as the number of entities and processes in the system under study, is:

- Ecophysiology and Behavioral ecology examine adaptations of the individual to its environment.
- Autecology studies the dynamics of populations of a single species.
- Community ecology (or synecology) focuses on the interactions between species within an ecological community.
- Ecosystem ecology studies the flows of energy and matter through the biotic and abiotic components of ecosystems.
- Landscape ecology examines processes and relationship across multiple ecosystems or very large geographic areas.

Ecology can also be sub-divided according to the species of interest into fields such as animal ecology, plant ecology, insect ecology, and so on. Another frequent method of subdivision is by biome studied, e.g., Arctic ecology (or polar ecology), tropical ecology, desert ecology, etc. The primary technique used for investigation is often used to subdivide the discipline into groups such as chemical ecology, genetic ecology, field ecology, statistical ecology, theoretical ecology, and so forth. Note that these different systems are unrelated and often applied at the same time; one could be a theoretical plant community ecologist, or a polar ecologist interested in animal genetics.

ENVIRONMENTAL DETERMINISM

Environmental determinism is the theory that a people's physical, mental and moral habits are directly due to the influence of their natural environment. Prominent environmental determinists included Carl Ritter, Ellen Churchill Semple, and Ellsworth Huntington. Popular hypotheses included "heat makes inhabitants of the tropics lazy" and "frequent changes in barometric pressure make inhabitants of temperate latitudes more intellectually agile."

Environmental determinist geographers attempted to make the study of such influences scientific. Around the 1930s, this school of thought was widely repudiated as lacking any basis and being prone to (often bigoted) generalizations. Environmental determinism remains an embarrassment to many contemporary geographers, and leads to skepticism among many of them of claims of environmental influence on culture (such as the theories of Jared Diamond).

Regional Geography

Regional geography was coined by a group of geographers known as possibilists and represented a reaffirmation that the proper topic of geography was study of places (regions). Regional geographers focused on the collection of descriptive information about places, as well as the proper methods for dividing the earth up into regions. Well-known names from these period are Alfred Hettner in Germany and Paul Vidal de la Blache in France. The philosophical basis of this field in United States was laid out by Richard Hartshorne, who defined geography as a study of areal differentiation, which later led to criticism of this approach as overly descriptive and unscientific.

The Quantitative Revolution

The quantitative revolution in geography began in the 1950s. Geographers formulated geographical theories and subjected the theories to empirical tests, usually using statistical methods (especially hypothesis testing). This quantitative revolution laid the groundwork for the development of geographic information systems. Well-known geographers from this period are Fred K. Schaefer, Waldo Tobler, William Garrison, Peter Haggett, Richard J. Chorley, William Bunge, and Torsten Hagerstrand.

Critical Geography

Though positivist approaches remain important in geography, critical geography arose as a critique of positivism. The first strain of critical geography to emerge was humanistic geography. Drawing on the philosophies of existentialism and phenomenology, humanistic geographers (such as Yi-Fu Tuan) focused on people's sense of, and relationship with, places.

More influential was Marxist geography, which applied the social theories of Karl Marx and his followers to geographic phenomena. David Harvey and Richard Peet are well-known Marxist geographers. Feminist geography is, as the name suggests, the use of ideas from feminism in geographic contexts. The most recent strain of critical geography is postmodernist geography, which employs the ideas of postmodernist and poststructuralist theorists to explore the social construction of spatial relations.

GEOGRAPHICAL IDEAS

Frames of the World

The Idea of the Map: "Of all the ideas explored and developed by geographers over the last several thousand years, the map has become the most central to Western civilization. Once the privilege instrument of monarchs and prelates, it is now the everyday tool of magazine readers, weather watchers, mall users, museum visitors, and the dwellers of labyrinthine modern office buildings.... "All maps are not born equal. The placemat map and the topographic map play radically different social roles, depending not only on their intrinsic nature but also on the context of their production and use.... Central to many of our most astonishing discoveries, from continents to the earth's history, the map is also a testament to our overweening desire to control and dominate others, nature, and even our past."

The Weather Map: Exploiting Electronic Telecommunications to Forecast the Geography of the Atmosphere: "Weather is the soap opera we all watch.... An ongoing drama that affects our lives, the weather story is common ground for casual conversations and new acquaintances. What we rarely talk about, though, is the way the story reaches us.

Instead of going outside to sniff the breeze, we merely turn on the television or check the daily paper for a wealth of information about today's weather, tomorrow's weather, and weather across the country. Weather maps have well-established slots on morning and evening TV newscasts and are the starring attraction on their own cable channel, available 24 hours a day.... Snapshot views of the state of the weather are so readily available, we easily forget they are one of the great inventions of modern geography."

Geographic Information Systems: "Over the past three decades [now closer to four], as part of a more general trend toward the use of digital technology for information handling, a significant change has occurred in the nature of geographic information and its role in society. Unlike numbers and text, maps and images have created major problems for digital storage and processing because of their relative complexity and high density of information.

The so-called 'geographic information technologies' that have appeared over the past twenty [or more] years and grown to form a major new area of application in electronic data processing are the result of significant research developments in hardware and software. The new technologies are likely to be every bit as the map has been on our thinking about the world. They broaden our perspective by offering new capabilities that are less constrained, but at the same time they impose new filters that may be just as subtle as the ones associated with paper maps."

The World as a Human Home

Human Adjustment: "The concept of human adjustment, applied fifty years ago to floodplains and now to global [climate] change, has served as a practical guide to action, as research paradigm, and as aspiration for humane coexistence with the natural world. The concept is rooted in antiquity as 'art in partnership with nature,' but it was first given its modern expression by Gilbert F. White.

Based on research in which he identified eight specific forms of human adjustment to floods, White identified four principles to ensure the optimal use of floodplains. "First, public policy should take into account all possible adjustments. Second, it should recognize that adjustments are not neutral but rather can favour one form of floodplain use over others. Therefore, third, society should consider carefully the various uses of the floodplains made possible by such adjustments, recognizing the differential need for floodplain use and location. And fourth, society should weigh the full range of social costs and benefits it incurs in employing these adjustments, not merely the costs and benefits that are easy to measure."

Kates goes on to describe how White's paradigm shift — sometimes called (archaically) the Man-Land tradition — has influenced public policy related to a wide variety of environmental hazards and constraints.

Water Budget Climatology: "Many knowledgeable individuals believe that water will be the next real environmental crisis for the world. Many regions of the word face difficult water problems, including quality and quantity of supply, ownership of water rights, the loss of fresh water sources through misuse, and even the need to create new supplies to meet growign demands. Comprehensive plans based on quantitative knowledge of our water resources are necessary if rational development of these resources is to occur. "The concept of a climatic water budget is fundamental to any evaluation of what might happen as societies, either willfully or inadvertently, undertake both small-or large-scale modifications of their environments. Such a water budget results from a daily, weekly, or monthly comparison of the supply of water from precipitation with the climatic demand for water as given by evapotranspiration...." These budgets are influenced both by "natural" factors and by changes in either precipitation, temperature, or land use invoked by humans. Land use matters greatly, because different surfaces can store dramatically different amounts of water in the soil, and can likewise evaporate dramatically different amounts of water from plant or inert surfaces.

Human Transformation of the Earth: "In the phrase 'human transformation of the eart,' the adjective is not superflous. For billions of years, the earth has been transforming itself, changing both ephemerally and irreversibly at scales from the local to the global. The recognition of natural environmental transformation is an idea with a long and interesting history of its own. Recognition of such change has often gone along with the idea that we should do what we can to stop it.... But as the twentieth century draws to a close, human action has become unmistakeably the principle force altering the earth's surface, and in the minds of many, it has become far more threatening than any natural force of change."

The World as a Linked Mosaic

Spatial Organization and Interdependence: "Evidence for the many ways in which spatial organization links individuals, cities, regions, and nations is around us every day. Driving through the countryside from Milwakee to Chicago, for instance, we notice that television antennas be in to change from north-pointing to south-pointing, and that the mailbox logos shift from Milwaukee newspapers to Chicago newspapers. The network television programs we watch in either city will usually emanate from New York,

Washington, or Los Angeless — and will often focus on events in far-off places such as London, Moscow, or Sarajevo. Understanding the spatial organization that links cities, regions, and nations is increasingly essential as improved transport and communications speed up the daily flows of people, goods, and information. As these linkages accelerate and strengthen, the *interdependence* of places at all geographic scales becomes increasingly clear.... The geographer's concern with spatial organization is reflected at all scales, within and among neighbourhoods, cities, regions, and nations."

Nested Hexagons: Central Place Theory: "As Labour Day approaches, we travel with our children to a regional mall to buy back-to-school clothing, but for a pair of socks a small neighbourhood store will usually suffice. We do our weekly grocery shopping at a neighbourhood supermarket or discount warehouse, but when all we need is a half-gallon of milk or a bag of Doritos, we go to the nearest convenience store or gas station food mart. For a routine medical checkup we go to a nearby doctor's office or clinic, but for major surgery we travel to a large regional hospital.

> *"Similar patterns can be found in the largest metropolitan areas and smallest rural towns."*
>
> *"Central place theory provides a comprehensive approach to understanding the spatial organization of human settlements, specifically the location of consumer goods and services. Its wide influence lies in recognizing predictable relationships among consumers, firms, and urban places."*

Megalopolis: The Future is Now: "The idea of megalopolis was popularized by the French geographer, Jean Gottmann, around 1960. The term can be used in two ways: as the proper name for Gottmann's original study area — the urbanized Northeast of the United States — and as a generic term for the coalescence of metropolitan areas into a continuous network of urban development. Megalopolis symbolized an enlarged scale of urban life, new forms of spatial organization, changing modes of economic behaviour, and the advent of information as the raw material of urban economic life. Gottmann went so far as to argue that megalopolis signaled a turning ponit in the history of human settlement. "This chapter explores how and why did megalopolis become such an important idea, how it was used to explain the momentous geographic, economic, political, and social changes in American cities, what effects it had on the discipline of geography, how it entered the popular lexicon, and what it says about the future of urbanization worldwide."

CASTE AND ENVIRONMENT

The question has troubled sociologists for years: How has India's caste system, so elaboration estimated 40,000 castes rigid, hereditarily determined, hierarchical and oppressive a social structure, lasted for so many centuries? Madhav Gadgil, an ecologist, and anthropologist Kailash Malhotra feel that the answer probably lies in the discipline that the caste system brought to the use of natural resources. It was a system which, on the one hand, forced its members to share natural resources and on the other, created the right social milieu in which sustainable patterns of resource use were encouraged to emerge. In other words, it was a social system which both forced and cajoled the social being right from birth to adopt sustainable cultural mores.

Within the caste system, birth determined a human being's occupation. An "ecological space" and its natural resources could only be used by a definite occupational group. This "resource partitioning" helped to reduce competition and, hence, conflict among human beings over scarce natural resources, and to create the right psychological environment: the allottees of an ecological space developed sustainable patterns because they had no worry that their resources would be snatched away from them and probably also because they knew that if they exhausted the resources in their own space, they would not be allow to use any other.

Malhotra and Gadgil are quick to point out that even though the caste system lasts till today, it has stopped "resource partitioning." The growing monetarization of the Indian economy, first encouraged by the invading British then by independent Indian in the name of development, has destroyed the ancient sustainable and shared patterns of resource use evolved over centuries. Social tensions are increasing as people fight over scarce natural resources, and because the caste system continues even after losing it *raison d'etre,* it has become a source of social power and oppression.

These conclusions emerge from 12-year study of rural society in western Maharashtra. Here the Western Ghats rise abruptly, some 50 km inland from the Arabian Sea, to an altitude of 1,000 metres to 1,500 metres. Their 15 km to 20 km wide crestline is marked with heavy rainfall, more than 3,000 mm a year and it supports low but stable agricultural and pastoral productivity. The simple society here, mostly marked by single clan settlements, consists of few sedentary castes of cultivators, pastoralists and huntergatherers, which include Gavils who are mainly cultivators and Kunbis who are buffalo herders and shifting cultivators.

Further eastward, the Western Ghats merge with the Deccan plateau through a series of broken hills, and the rainfall in this tract falls to about 1,500 mm to 1,000 mm near the edge of the plateau. This tract supports rich agriculture and neighbours a complex rural society with a number of artisan and service castes. Still further east, the rainfall decreases further, to less than 600 mm in a semiarid tract of 100 km width. Agriculture here is practised only in the river valleys. Pastoralists and huntergatherers use large tracts of uncultivated land.

Because the terrain favours sedentary existence during the four monsoon months, and uncultivated lands are available for grazing, several pastoral as well as nonpastoral nomadic castes have established their base villages in this semi-arid tract. They migrate to the higher rainfull tracts, both to the east and west of the semi-arid tract, for the eight months of the year. Among those who have their base villages in this tract are Hatkars, Tirumal Nandiwallas, Fulmali Nandiwallas, Vaidus and Phasapardis.

NICHE DIVERSIFICATION

The first example of "ecological niche diversification" is exhibited by the Kunbis and Gavli Dhangaras living on the crestline of the Western Ghats. The Kunbis cultivate paddy in the river valleys, practise shifting cultivation on the lower hill slopes and hunt extensively, they barter their cereals for butter produced by the Gavlis and other goods. The only cattle they keep are for draught purposes.

The Gavlis on the other hand, live on the upper hill terraces. Although they practise some shifting cultivation, their main occupation is keeping buffaloes and cattle. They curdle the milk, consume the butter milk locally and barter the butter for cereals from the Kunbis. As they get their protein supply from butter milk, they do not need to hunt. Thus, the cultivation of valleys and lower hill slopes is restricted to the Kunbis and of hill terraces to the Gavlis. Maintenance of domesticated animal and exploitation of all fodder and grazing is restricted to the Gavlis and the hunting of wild animals to the Kunbis.

Another instance of niche diversification is provided by the three nomadic hunting communities of the semi-arid tracts of western Maharashtra: Tirumal Nandiwallas, Phasepardis and Vaidus. The primary occupation of the Nadiwallas is entertainment and fortune telling, that of the Vaidus dispensation of herbal medicines, while the Phasepardis are specialist hunter-gatherers. Unlike the settle castes the Tirumal Nandiwallas and Vaidus also hunt in addition to their primary occupation. But the three castes use distinctly different hunting techniques and specialize in different prey species.

The Tirumal Nandiwallas use dogs to hunt wild pigs, large carnivorous mammals (leopard cat, hyena, fox and aquatic animals (fish, crab, turtle), Vaidus use baited traps for smaller carnivorous (mongoose, civet, jackal and cat), monitor lizards and aquatic animals. The Phasepardis—specialize in black buck, wild pig and birds such as doves, quails, partidges and peafowl.

Wild meat means a lot to these castes. Gadgil and Malhotra studied the Tirumal Nandiwallas in greater detail and found that the median annual biomass of hunted animal is 2,180 kg. per family or Tirumal Nandiwallas who are thorough in their use of the hunted animals. They even eat portions like the brain and the viscera, normally rejected by other people. Almost two-thirds of the live weight of the prey is consumed. In terms of per capita daily consumption the median works out to 57 gm of protein and 850 calories from hunted wild meat. For the Tirumal Nandiwallas, the hunted meat provides a more than adequate level of protein and over one-third of the calorific requirements of an average person.

What is striking is that while the hunting techniques used by the three groups are significantly different, none of them are sophisticated that they cannot be adopted by another.

WOMEN AND ENVIRONMENT

It is difficult to define quite where "environment" begins or ends for women in developing countries. As childbearers, family caretakers and consumers; as food-products, fuel and water gatherers and users; as field, forest, factory and office workers, women are primary managers, and often preservers of natural resources. As activists and leaders women are involved in campaigns to promote environmental awareness and protection.

Women's work is generally undervalued. As a result, women constitute a disproportionate number of the poorest groups of people and are victims of hunger, illiteracy, poor health, scarce social and technical services, inadequate population policies, and other consequences of poverty. In addition, women's participation and influence is inadequately represented in decision-making spheres concerning environment and development issues affecting the quality of their lives.

Because of their daily tasks in the care of the family and community, women in developing countries effect and are affected by their environment. Poverty requires women to exploit natural resources in their daily tasks, rather than conserving them. Similarly, environmental degradation restricts the ability of women to overcome poverty. Given this relationship between poverty and resources degradation, actions to further the interests of both will be mutually reinforcing. The following overview is intended to illustrate the nature of the relationship between women and environment, how development activities have compromised this relationship, and how activities designed to address both women and environment are mutually reinforcing. Women play multiple roles in the family, the community and economy. Women may produce food and income. In many cultures women are the holders and teachers of family values and traditions. Because of their special responsibilities in family and community, women have the potential to influence community attitudes and activities towards the environment.

There are natural linkages between the daily tasks involved in carrying out these roles and the natural and human resource environments. Women are the major producers of food for domestic consumption. They are the main drawers and carriers of water. They procure almost all the fuelwood for domestic use. In urban areas, shelter, sanitation, potable water, and a host of other social services are critical activities for women.

Women and men differ in their perceptions of their environment and its appropriate or potential use. For example, women may perceive a local forest as a source of food, fuel and medicine for household use while men may perceive the value of the local forest as the sale of the cut trees in the market. Additionally, because women are often dependent on free goods such as water, fuel wood and fodder, they have a special interest in environmental protection and rehabilitation. Women are often key agents in maintaining and enhancing the quality and stock of communal natural resources.

The environmental knowledge acquired by many women is both useful and detailed. Close daily contact makes women, more than men, familiar with properties and uses of the natural environment, for example, disease and drought resistant crops and three varieties, efficient fuel, wood, and medicinal plants. A survey in Sierra Leone revealed that women could identify thirty-one different forest products while men were only able to identify eight. Women are often very aware of the ecological relationships that affect their everyday lives, for instances, trees and soil stability, trees and water regulation, plants and microclimates, etc. Women thus represent a valuable information source on the local environment.

Women are not only resource managers. They are also the victims of environmental mismanagement and contribute to environment degradation. Where the resource base is declining or degraded, it is women who must search further and longer for fuel and water. It is women who are most easily marginalized onto unproductive lands. Increased time and labour burdens are often manifested by stress, ill-health and malnutrition. The consequent entrenched impoverishment in turn forces women to further exploit the resource base, often violating their own knowledge and the well-being of the community.

Women's local environmental interests have been affected by inappropriate development. For example, macro economic policies (increased cash cropping, timber production, higher food prices, reduced social spending) set up complex interactions which marginalize women by, for example, removing resources from their management and control and/or affecting women's ability to respond to a disturbed or changed resource base.

Projects and programmes have also failed to address the specific needs of women. Although women's role in productive sectors such as agriculture, water, forestry, energy, and human settlements is well documented, their concerns, needs and special knowledge are often underestimated if not totally ignored. For example, as primary food producers or labourers in agriculture they are often denied land, remuneration, credit, training and other supports which would improve their health, income and status in an ecologically sustainable path.

Even environmental protection and repair projects with specific social objectives often fail to recognize the differing needs of women and men; consequently, projects are planned with unequal benefits accruing to both. While it is evident that women in developing countries are often the victims and agents of environmental degradation, it is important to balance this view with the recognition that women are central to resource management and are participating in, and leading, ecology movements in many countries. One example of women's grassroots environmental activity is the Chipko Movement in India. This movement began as a response to the deforestation of the natural forest with reforestation by a single commercial species, eucalyptus. Indigenous forests provided food, fuel, fodder, household utensils, dyes, medicines, and income-generating products, Replacement by a single species had drastically affected rural women's ability to maintain a subsistence household. In order to protect the trees, women embraced the trees as a human shield against the tree cutters, have been challenged in the courts and have defied their own families. The movement has subsequently spread to other parts of India and to other issues.

As well as women's grassroots activity, there are some examples of donor-sponsored resource projects which have been enhanced by women's participation in the planning, design and implementation. For example, the Andhra Pradesh Social Forestry Project in India indicates that initiative to address women's needs and aspirations have accrued direct benefits to women and their communities and enhanced overall project success.

The process of women's participation, both as agents and beneficiaries, brings many benefits. Such benefits include raising the status and self-esteem of women. Economic gains may accrue from new income earning opportunities such as small scale local enterprises (soil, fuel and water conservation, seed selection, waste recycling, local exchanges of indigenous knowledge). Material benefits extend to the well-being of the family and community such as increased food security, child nutrition, health and education. Women's participation in resource decision-making contri-butes directly to the protection and rehabilitation of the environment. Furthermore, increasing the capacity of women to overcome their own poverty has associated social benefits. As women's income rises, there is a corresponding decrease in fertility rates. Rapid population growth-strongly correlated to conditions of poverty, compounds the relationship between poverty and environmental degradation. Therefore, improving the status of women is fundamental to bringing about changes in population growth and its associated effects on the environment.

In sum: what happens to the environment is central to women's lives. Women have important contributions to make in the search for solutions to the environmental crisis. Limiting women from environmental decision-making will ultimately affect the sustainability of social and economic gains. Similarly, Pursuing inherently unsustainable development paths will eventually undermine any long-term change in women's position.

Current wisdom is to see women not just as victims, but as major local assets to be incorporated in the interests of better environmental management. Supporting women's role as environmental decision-makers requires recognition and validation of women's role in the development process.

ENVIRONMENTALISM FOR THE 21ST CENTURY

As we begin the 21st century, environmental thinkers are divided along a sharp fault line. There are the doomsayers who predict the collapse of the global ecosystem. There are the technological optimists who believe that we can feed 12 billion people and solve all our problems with science and technology. I do not believe that either of these extremes makes sense. There is a middle road based on science and logic, the combination of which is sometimes referred to as common sense. There are real problems and there is much we can do to improve the state of the environment.

I was born and raised in the tiny fishing and logging village of Winter Harbour on the northwest tip of Vancouver Island, in the rainforest by the Pacific. I didn't realize what a blessed childhood I'd had, playing on the tidal flats by the salmon spawning streams in the rainforest, until I was shipped away to boarding school in Vancouver at age fourteen. I eventually attended the University of BC studying the life sciences: biology, forestry, genetics; but it was when I discovered ecology that I realized that through science I could gain an insight into the mystery of the rainforest I had known as a child. I became a born-again ecologist, and in the late 1960's, was soon transformed into a radical environmental activist.

I found myself in a church basement in Vancouver with a like-minded group of people, planning a protest campaign against US hydrogen bomb testing in Alaska. We proved that a somewhat ragtag looking group of activists could sail a leaky old halibut boat across the North Pacific Ocean and change the course of history. By creating a focal point for opposition to the tests we got on national news and helped build a ground-swell of opposition to nuclear testing in the US and Canada. When that bomb went off in November 1971 it was the last hydrogen bomb ever detonated on planet Earth. Even though there were four more tests planned in the series, President Nixon cancelled them due to public opposition. This was the birth of Greenpeace. Flushed with victory and knowing we could bring about change by getting up and doing something, we were welcomed into the longhouse of the Kwakiutl Nation at Alert Bay near the north end of Vancouver Island. We were made brothers of the tribe because they believed in what we were doing. This began the tradition of the Warriors of the Rainbow, after a Cree legend that predicted one day when the skies are black and the birds fall dead to the ground and the rivers are poisoned, people of all races, colours and creeds will join together to form the Warriors of the Rainbow to save the Earth from environmental destruction. We named our ship the Rainbow Warrior and I spent fifteen years on the front lines of the eco-movement as we evolved from that church basement into the world's largest environmental activist organization.

Next we took on French atmospheric nuclear testing in the South Pacific. They proved a bit more difficult than the US Atomic Energy Administration. But after many years of protest voyages and campaigning, involving loss of life on our side, they were first driven underground and eventually stopped testing altogether.

In 1975 we set sail deep-sea into the North Pacific against the Soviet Union's factory whaling fleets that were slaughtering the last of the sperm whales off California. We put ourselves in front of the harpoons in little rubber boats and made Walter Cronkite's evening news. That really put Greenpeace on the map. In 1979 the International Whaling Commission banned factory whaling in the North Pacific and soon it was banned in all the world's oceans. In 1978 I was arrested off Newfoundland for sitting on a baby seal, trying to shield it from the Hunter's club. I was convicted; under the draconianly named Seal Protection Regulations that made it illegal to protect seals. In 1984 baby sealskins were banned from European markets, effectively ending the slaughter

Can you believe that in the early 1980's, the countries of Western Europe were pooling their low and medium level nuclear wastes, putting them in thousands of oil drums, loading them on ships and dumping them in the Atlantic ocean as a way of "disposing" of the wastes. In 1984 a combined effort by Greenpeace and the UK Seafarer's Union put an end to that practice for good.

By the mid-1980's Greenpeace had grown from that church basement into an organization with an income of over US$100 million per year, offices in 21 countries and over 100 campaigns around the world, now tackling toxic waste, acid rain, uranium mining and drift net fishing as well as the original issues. We had won over a majority of the public in the industrialized democracies. Presidents and prime ministers were talking about the environment on a daily basis.

For me it was time to make a change. I had been against at least three or four things every day of my life for 15 years; I decided I'd like to be in favour of something for a change. I made the transition from the politics of confrontation to the politics of building consensus. After all, when a majority of people decide they agree with you it is probably time to stop hitting them over the head with a stick and sit down and talk to them about finding solutions to our environmental problems.

All social movements evolve from an earlier period of polarization and confrontation during which a minority struggles to convince society that its cause it is true and just, eventually followed by a time of reconciliation if a majority of the population accepts the values of the new movement. For the environmental movement this transition began to occur in the mid-1980s. The term sustainable development was adopted to describe the challenge of taking the new environmental values we had popularized, and incorporating them into the traditional social and economic values that have always governed public policy and our daily behaviour. We cannot simply switch to basing all our actions on purely environmental values. Every day 6 billion people wake up with real needs for food, energy and materials. The challenge for sustainability is to provide for those needs in ways that reduce negative impact on the environment. But any changes made must also be socially acceptable and technically and economically feasible. It is not always easy to balance environmental, social, and economic priorities. Compromise and co-operation with the involvement of government, industry, academia and the environmental movement is required to achieve sustainability. It is this effort to find consensus among competing interests that has occupied my time for the past 15 years.

Not all my former colleagues saw things that way. They rejected consensus politics and sustainable development in favour of continued confrontation and ever-increasing extremism. They ushered in an era of zero tolerance and left-wing politics. Some of the features of this environmental extremism are:

Environmental extremists are anti-human. Humans are characterized as a cancer on the Earth. To quote eco-extremist Herb Hammond, "of all the components of the ecosystem, humans are the only ones we know to be completely optional". Isn't that a lovely thought? They are anti-science and technology. All large machines are seen as inherently destructive and unnatural. Science is invoked to justify positions that have nothing to do with science. Unfounded opinion is accepted over demonstrated fact.

Environmental extremists are anti-trade, not just free trade but anti-trade in general. In the name of bioregionalism they would bring in an age of ultra-nationalist xenophobia. The original "Whole Earth" vision of one world family is lost in a hysterical campaign against globalization and free trade.

They are anti-business. All large corporations are depicted as inherently driven by greed and corruption. Profits are definitely not politically correct. The liberal democratic, market-based model is rejected even though no viable alternative is proposed to provide for the material needs of 6 billion people. As expressed by the Native Forest Network, "it is necessary to adopt a global phase out strategy of consumer based industrial capitalism." I think they mean civilization.

And they are just plain anti-civilization. In the final analysis, eco-extremists project a naive vision of returning to the supposedly utopian existence in the garden of Eden, conveniently forgetting that in the old days people lived to an average age of 35, and there were no dentists. In their Brave New World there will be no more chemicals, no more airplanes, and certainly no more polyester suits.

Let me give you some specific examples that highlight the movement's tendency to abandon science and logic and to get the priorities completely mixed up through the use of sensationalism, misinformation and downright lies.

The Brent Spar Oil Rig

In 1995, Shell Oil was granted permission by the British Environment Ministry to dispose of the North Sea oil rig "Brent Spar" in deep water in the North Atlantic Ocean. Greenpeace immediately accused Shell of using the sea as a "dustbin". Greenpeace campaigners maintained that there were hundreds of tonnes of petroleum wastes on board the Brent Spar and that some of these were radioactive. They organized a consumer boycott of Shell and service stations were fire bombed in Germany. The boycott cost the company millions in sales. German Chancellor Helmut Kohl denounced the British government's decision to allow the dumping. Caught completely off guard, Shell ordered the tug that was already towing the rig to its burial site to turn back. They then announced they had abandoned the plan for deep-sea disposal. This embarrassed British Prime Minister, John Major.

Independent investigation revealed that the rig had been properly cleaned and did not contain the toxic and radioactive waste claimed by Greenpeace. Greenpeace wrote to Shell apologizing for the factual error. But they did not change their position on deep-sea disposal despite the fact that on-land disposal would cause far greater environmental impact.

During all the public outrage directed against Shell for daring to sink a large piece of steel and concrete it was never noted that Greenpeace had purposely sunk its own ship off the coast of New Zealand in 1986. When the French government bombed and sunk the Rainbow Warrior in Auckland Harbour in 1985, the vessel was permanently disabled. It was later re-floated, patched up, cleaned and towed to a marine park where it was sunk in shallow water as a dive site. Greenpeace said the ship would be an artificial reef and would support increased marine life.

The Brent Spar and the Rainbow Warrior are in no way fundamentally different from one another. The sinking of the Brent Spar could also be rationalized as providing habitat for marine creatures. It's just that the public relations people at Shell are not as clever as those at Greenpeace. And in this case Greenpeace got away with using misinformation even though they had to admit their error after the fact. After spending tens of millions of dollars on studies Shell recently announced that it had abandoned any plan for deep-sea disposal and will support a proposal to re-use the rig as pylons in a dock extension project in Norway. Tens of millions of dollars and much precious time wasted over an issue that had nothing to do with the environment and everything to do with misinformation and fundraising hysteria.

To make matters worse, in 1998 Greenpeace successfully campaigned for a ban on all marine disposal of disused oil installations. This will result in hundreds of millions, even billions of dollars in unnecessary costs. One obvious solution would be to designate an area in the North Sea for the creation of a large artificial reef and to sink oil rigs there after cleaning them. This would provide a breeding area for fish and other marine life, enhancing the biological and economic productivity of the sea. But Greenpeace isn't looking for solutions, only conflicts and bad guys.

Exotic Species

There has been a recent flurry of sensationalist warnings about the threat of exotic species. Zealous cadres of conservation biologists descend on wetlands to rip foreign weeds from the bog, declaring that "a rapidly spreading invasion of exotic plants and animals is destroying our nation's biological diversity." It's amazing how a word that was so good, as in "exotic paradise" and "exotic pleasure" is now used to describe an alleged biological Holocaust. I was inspired to write about exotic species when I heard a news story from Washington D.C. in the spring of 1999. The citizens of the Capitol were distressed to find that a family of beavers had taken up residence there and were busy felling the Japanese cherry trees that adorned the banks of the Potomac River. It became a national emergency of sorts and a great effort was made to trap every last beaver; only then were the townspeople put at ease. There was no mention made of the fact that the beaver is a native North American species whereas the cherry trees are exotics, imported from Japan. Yet there was no question which species the public favoured. In fact, the reason we dislike certain species and like others has nothing to do with whether or not they are exotic. By playing on people's natural suspicion of all things foreign, environmentalists confuse the issue and give the public a misleading picture.

There are actually thousands of exotic species that are not only beneficial, they are the mainstays of our daily lives. Food crops like wheat, rice, and cabbage are all exotics when grown in North America. Vegetables that originated in the Americas such as beans, corn and potatoes are exotics when they are grown in Europe. All around the world, agriculture is largely based on species that originated somewhere else. This is also the case for domestic animals, garden plants and street trees.

There are also hundreds of native species of plants and animals that we consider undesirable. For centuries we have referred to them as weeds, pests, vermin and disease. There are also many exotic species that fall into this category. And, of course, there are many native species that are considered extremely beneficial, especially those that provide food for a growing population.

The point is, both exotic and native species can be desirable or undesirable from a human perspective, depending on how they effect our lives. Our almost innate dislike of rats and spiders has nothing to do with whether or not they are native or exotic, it is due to the possibility of deadly disease or a fatal bite. And even though dandelions in the lawn are hardly a life-and-death issue, millions are spent each year to rid lawns of these "weeds".

Certain exotic species have resulted in severe negative impacts. The most notorious case involved the introduction of European species of animals to Australia, New Zealand, and the Pacific Islands when Europeans colonized these regions beginning about 225 years ago. Many native species, flightless birds and ground-dwelling marsupials in particular, were not able to survive the introduction of predators such as rats, cats and foxes. As a result, hundreds of native species were eliminated. Another well known exotic is Dutch elm disease, a fungus that actually originated in Asia, came through Europe and on to North America where it has resulted in the death of many native elms in the US and Canada.

There can be no doubt that we should always be careful when considering the introduction of a new species, and that regulations are needed to prevent undesirable accidental introductions. At the same time we must not lose sight of the fact that introduced species play a vital, indeed essential, role in modern society.

Each species must be evaluated on its own merits. The introduction of some species may be desirable in one region and yet undesirable in others. Islands are particularly susceptible to introductions because they are isolated and their native species are not subjected to as wide a variety of predators and diseases. When rats are introduced to islands that support large bird rookeries there is often a precipitous decline in bird populations due to predation on eggs and nestlings.

There is really no difference when considering the use of an exotic species of tree for managed forests. The main reason we tend to use native species of trees for forestry in North America is because they are the best available in terms of productivity and wood quality. In other regions this is not the case. Radiata pine from California has been very successful in New Zealand, Australia, and Chile. Eucalyptus from Australia is the forestry species of choice in many parts of Brazil, Portugal and South Africa. Douglas-fir from Oregon has become the number two species of softwood produced in France. And Chinese larch is a favourite for reforestation in Scotland where forest cover was lost centuries ago to sheep farming.

CLIMATE CHANGE

Global climate change is another area where extreme statements are made, in this case on both sides of the debate, when there is little in science to defend them. Some things are quite certain. Carbon dioxide levels are rising and our consumption of fossil fuels and deforestation in the tropics are probably the main causes. There is a lot of evidence that the earth's climate is warming: the glaciers in Alaska are retreating and great egrets are visiting northern Lake Huron. But here the consensus ends.

Climate change is a wonderful example to demonstrate the limitations of science. There are two fundamental characteristics of climate change that make it very difficult to use the empirical (scientific) method to predict the future. First there are simply too many uncontrollable variables — the empirical method works best when you can control all the variables except the one you are studying. Second, and even more significant, is the fact that we have only one planet to observe.

If we had 50 planet Earths and increased the carbon dioxide levels on 25 of them, leaving the other 25 alone, we might be able to determine a statistical difference between the two samples. With only one Earth, we are reduced to complex computer models of questionable value, and a lot of guesswork. Climate change is not about scientific certainty; it is about the evaluation and management of risk. I think it is fair to say that climate change poses a real risk, however small or large. When faced with the risk the logical thing to do is to buy and insurance policy.

Unfortunately we have no actuarial science on which to base the size of the insurance premium; this is where the guesswork comes in. Is it worth reducing fossil fuel consumption by 60 percent to avoid global warming? Should we add the risk of massive nuclear energy construction to offset carbon dioxide emissions? What does "worth doing away" really mean? Is it possible that global warming might have more positive effects than negative ones?

Climate change is a change in the statistical distribution of weather over periods of time that range from decades to millions of years. It can be a change in the average weather or a change in the distribution of weather events around an average (for example, greater or fewer extreme weather events). Climate change may be limited to a specific region, or may occur across the whole Earth.In recent usage, especially in the context of environmental policy, climate change usually refers to changes in modern climate. It may be qualified as anthropogenic climate change, more generally known as "global warming" or "anthropogenic global warming" (AGW).

Terminology

The most general definition of *climate change* is a change in the statistical properties of the climate system when considered over periods of decades or longer, regardless of cause. Accordingly, fluctuations on periods shorter than a few decades, such as El Nino, do not represent climate change.

The term sometimes is used to refer specifically to climate change caused by human activity; for example, the United Nations Framework Convention on Climate Change defines climate change as "a change of climate which is attributed directly or indirectly to human activity that alters the composition of the global atmosphere and which is in addition to natural climate variability observed over comparable time periods." In the latter sense climate change is synonymous with global warming.

Causes

Factors that can shape climate are climate forcings. These include such processes as variations in solar radiation, deviations in the Earth's orbit, mountain-building and continental drift, and changes in greenhouse gas concentrations. There are a variety of climate change feedbacks that can either amplify or diminish the initial forcing. Some parts of the climate system, such as the oceans and ice caps, respond slowly in reaction to climate forcing because of their large mass. Therefore, the climate system can take centuries or longer to fully respond to new external forcings.

Plate Tectonics

Over the course of millions of years, the motion of tectonic plates re-configures global land and ocean areas and generates topography. This can affect both global and local patterns of climate and atmosphere-ocean circulation.

The position of the continents determines the geometry of the oceans and therefore influences patterns of ocean circulation. The locations of the seas are important in controlling the transfer of heat and moisture across the globe, and therefore, in determining global climate. A recent example of tectonic control on ocean circulation is the formation of the Isthmus of Panama about 5 million years ago, which shut off direct mixing between the Atlantic and Pacific Oceans. This strongly affected the ocean dynamics of what is now the Gulf Stream and may have led to Northern Hemisphere ice cover.

During the Carboniferous period, about 300 to 360 million years ago, plate tectonics may have triggered large-scale storage of carbon and increased glaciation. Geologic evidence points to a "megamonsoonal" circulation pattern during the time of the supercontinent Pangaea, and climate modelling suggests that the existence of the supercontinent was conducive to the establishment of monsoons.

The size of continents is also important. Because of the stabilizing effect of the oceans on temperature, yearly temperature variations are generally lower in coastal areas than they are inland. A larger supercontinent will therefore have more area in which climate is strongly seasonal than will several smaller continents or islands.

Solar Output

The sun is the predominant source for energy input to the Earth. Both long-and short-term variations in solar intensity are known to affect global climate.

Three to four billion years ago the sun emitted only 70% as much power as it does today. If the atmospheric composition had been the same as today, liquid water should not have existed on Earth. However, there is evidence for the presence of water on the early Earth, in the Hadean and Archean eons, leading to what is known as the faint young sun paradox.

Hypothesized solutions to this paradox include a vastly different atmosphere, with much higher concentrations of greenhouse gases than currently exist Over the following approximately 4 billion years, the energy output of the sun increased and atmospheric composition changed, with the oxygenation of the atmosphere around 2.4 billion years ago being the most notable alteration. These changes in luminosity, and the sun's ultimate death as it becomes a red giant and then a white dwarf, will have large effects on climate, with the red giant phase possibly ending life on Earth. Solar output also varies on shorter time scales, including the 11-year solar cycle and longer-term modulations.

Solar intensity variations are considered to have been influential in triggering the Little Ice Age, and some of the warming observed from 1900 to 1950. The cyclical nature of the sun's energy output is not yet fully understood; it differs from the very slow change that is happening within the sun as it ages and evolves. While most research indicates solar variability has induced a small cooling effect from 1750 to the present, a few studies point toward solar radiation increases from cyclical sunspot activity affecting global warming.

Orbital Variations

Slight variations in Earth's orbit lead to changes in the seasonal distribution of sunlight reaching the Earth's surface and how it is distributed across the globe. There is very little change to the area-averaged annually averaged sunshine; but there can be strong changes in the geographical and seasonal distribution. The three types of orbital variations are variations in Earth's eccentricity, changes in the tilt angle of Earth's axis of rotation, and precession of Earth's axis. Combined together, these produce Milankovitch cycles which have a large impact on climate and are notable for their correlation to glacial and interglacial periods, their correlation with the advance and retreat of the Sahara, and for their appearance in the stratigraphic record.

Gradual Push, Sudden Shift

During a gradual push, things sometimes tip, slip, and break. Had the 1997 El Nioo lasted twice as long, the rain forests of the Amazon basin and Southeast Asia could have quickly added much additional carbon dioxide to the air from burning and rotting, with heat waves and extreme weather quickly felt around the world (The "Burn locally, crash globally" scenario).

Most abrupt climate shifts, however, are likely due to sudden circulation shifts. The best-known examples are the several dozen shutdowns of the North Atlantic Ocean's Meridional Overturning Circulation during the last ice age, affecting climate worldwide. But there have been a series of less dramatic abrupt climate shifts since 1976, along with some near misses. The circulation shift in the western Pacific in the winter of 1976-1977 proved to have much wider impacts. Since 1950, El Nioos had been weak and short, but La Nioas were often big and long, This pattern reversed after 1977. Land temperatures had remained relatively trendless from 1950 to 1976, despite the CO_2 rising from 310 to 332 ppm as fossil fuel emissions tripled. Then in 1977 there was a marked shift in observed global-mean surface temperature to a rising fever on land at about 2°C/century. The expansion of the tropics from overheating is usually thought to be gradual, but the percentage of the land surface in the two most extreme classifications of drought suddenly doubled in 1982 and stayed there until 1997 when it jumped to triple (after six years, it stepped down to double). While their inception correlates with the particularly large El Ninos of 1982 and 1997, the global drought steps far outlast the 13-month durations of those El Ninos.

In addition to near-misses for Burn Locally, Crash Globally in 1998, 2005, and 2007, there have also been two occasions when the Atlantic's Meridional Overturning Circulation lost a crucial safety factor. The Greenland Sea flushing at 75 °N shut down in 1978, recovering over the next decade. While shutdowns overlapping in time have not been seen during the fifty years of observation, previous total shutdowns had severe worldwide climate consequences.This makes abrupt climate shifts more like a heart attack than like a chronic disease whose course can be extrapolated. Some abrupt climate shifts are minor, some are catastrophic—and one cannot predict which or when. In the recent past, there have been at least several sudden shifts and several near-misses per decade.

Volcanism

Volcanism is a process of conveying material from the crust and mantle of the Earth to its surface. Volcanic eruptions, geysers, and hot springs, are examples of volcanic processes which release gases and/or particulates into the atmosphere.

Eruptions large enough to affect climate occur on average several times percentury, and cause cooling (by partially blocking the transmission of solar radiation to the Earth's surface) for a period of a few years. The eruption of Mount Pinatubo in 1991, the second largest terrestrial eruption of the 20th century (after the 1912 eruption of Novarupta) affected the climate substantially. Global temperatures decreased by about 0.5 °C (0.9 °F). The eruption of Mount Tambora in 1815 caused the Year Without a Summer. Much larger eruptions, known as large igneous provinces, occur only a few times every hundred million years, but may cause global warming and mass extinctions.

Volcanoes are also part of the extended carbon cycle. Over very long (geological) time periods, they release carbon dioxide from the Earth's crust and mantle, counteracting the uptake by sedimentary rocks and other geological carbon dioxide sinks. According to the US Geological Survey, however, estimates are that human activities generate more than 130 times the amount of carbon dioxide emitted by volcanoes.

Ocean Variability

The ocean is a fundamental part of the climate system. Short-term fluctuations (years to a few decades) such as the El Nino–Southern Oscillation, the Pacific decadal oscillation, the North Atlantic oscillation, and the Arctic oscillation, represent climate variability rather than climate change. On longer time scales, alterations to ocean processes such as thermohaline circulation play a key role in redistributing heat by carrying out a very slow and extremely deep movement of water, and the long-term redistribution of heat in the world's oceans.

Human Influences

Anthropogenic factors are human activities that change the environment. In some cases the chain of causality of human influence on the climate is direct and unambiguous (for example, the effects of irrigation on local humidity), while in other instances it is less clear. Various hypotheses for human-induced climate change have been argued for many years. Presently the scientific consensus on climate change is that human activity is very likely the cause for the rapid increase in global average temperatures over the past several decades. Consequently, the debate has largely shifted onto ways to reduce further human impact and to find ways to adapt to change that has already occurred.

Of most concern in these anthropogenic factors is the increase in CO_2 levels due to emissions from fossil fuel combustion, followed by aerosols (particulate matter in the atmosphere) and cement manufacture. Other factors, including land use, ozone depletion, animal agriculture and deforestation, are also of concern in the roles they play-both separately and in conjunction with other factors-in affecting climate, microclimate, and measures of climate variables.

8

Population Geography

INTRODUCTION

Human beings evolved under conditions of high mortality due to famines, accidents, illnesses, infections and war and therefore the relatively high fertility rates were essential for species survival.

In spite of the relatively high fertility rates it took all the time from evolution of mankind to the middle of the 19th century for the global population to reach one billion. The twentieth century witnessed an unprecedented rapid improvement in health care technologies and access to health care all over the world; as a result there was a steep fall in the mortality and steep increase in longevity.

The population realised these changes and took steps to reduce their fertility but the decline in fertility was not so steep. As a result the global population has undergone a fourfold increase in a hundred years and has reached 6 billion.

POPULATION, SPATIAL DISTRIBUTION

Bangladesh has the third largest and most homogeneous population in south and southeast Asia and the eighth largest population in the world. About three-fourths of its population are rural, about two-thirds are agricultural, and more than 85% are Muslims. About 99% of the population speak the Bangla. The age structure is youthful (45% are in the age group of below 15 years), and the population density is very high.

Patterns of population distribution and size before the Buddhist period (until 10th century AD) are not known. During this period there were two main regions of highest population concentration: the Tista-Karatoya interfluves of East Bengal, covering what is now northern Bangladesh and part of northern West Bengal (India); and the lower Meghna valley covering eastern and central Bengal plain.

The southern and northeastern parts of East Bengal (now covering Khulna division and parts of Dhaka and Sylhet divisions) were either sparsely populated or uninhabited due to large covers of tidal forests, swamps and shifting river channels.

In mid-12th century when the Buddhist Pala dynasty was overthrown by the Sena kings, who were orthodox Hindus, and followed a policy of persecution of Buddhists, the dominant population group in that time, many Buddhists took refuge in Burma, Thailand, Sri Lanka, and even as far as Cambodia and Laos in fear of possible persecution.

Subsequently, the population of this part of Bengal declined significantly as the three major centres of Buddhist culture (Mahasthan, Paharpur and Mainamati) in East Bengal were destroyed.

The advent of Muslims coincided with the persecution of Buddhists in Bengal and north India by Hindus, and many oppressed Buddhists and untouchable Hindus embraced ISLAM during the 11th and 13th centuries. Buddhists were also attracted to Islam mostly by the cult of SUFISM, which has spiritual parallel with Buddhist philosophy. By 1211, Muslims in Bengal numbered between 2 and 3 million and the population of East Bengal during this time reached a total of about 6 million.

After the fall of the Brahminic Hindu rule by the invading Turks in the early 13th century, various parts of Bengal were consolidated and brought under a semi-independent Sultanate with capital first at GAUR and then at SONARGAON. From this period the region received a continuous flow of Muslim immigrants from various parts of India.

These immigrants led the great land reclamation schemes of southern Bengal and a few other non-settled areas, which continued for several centuries. Probably because of the late influx of Muslims in this part (southern Bengal/ delta area) their proportion has remained lower in later centuries.

During the period between the 13th and 15th centuries, however, the estimated population of Bengal fluctuated between 5 and 10 million owing to repeated visits of various natural disasters and epidemics.

During these two stages of population evolution, the pattern was of gradual growth over a short period followed by an abrupt decline in response to various disasters such as epidemics, natural hazards (FLOODs, EARTHQUAKEs, tropical CYCLONEs, river bank erosion, etc.) often followed by FAMINEs. The long-term change was more or less static.

During the British period the population distribution was taking a definite pattern in most parts of East Bengal and was assuming a highly settled rural pattern. The exact figures of birth or death rates were not known for this period, but considering the overall demographic situation of the 18th and 19th centuries, it may be thought that both were very high leading to a very low rate of population growth. During the 19th century, the population of East Bengal grew very slowly because of repeated occurrences of famines and epidemics.

The extent of population concentration in East Bengal during the present century is to be understood in its geopolitical context. The creation of a Muslim political unit in Bengal under the framework of Pakistan was not necessarily viewed as the result of direct Hindu-Muslim cleavage since in Bengal, Islam has always been accommodating and tolerant.

With the Partition of Bengal in 1947, East Bengal within the framework of Pakistan with a population of 42 million, was separated from relatively less densely populated area of high economic potentials (some having overall Muslim predominance), such as the BRAHMAPUTRA valley, the northern TEA plantation areas and part of the Calcutta-Hughli industrial complex.

The post-partition political antagonism between India and Pakistan affected East Pakistan both demographically and economically much more than the less populated and industrially developed West Pakistan.

Accompanying the partition was a wave of religious rioting, murder and arson together with mass displacement of population across the newly established borders of India and the two wings of Pakistan (West and East Pakistan) separated from each other by about 2000 km.

Order was not restored until spring, 1948. Consequently, a demographically significant population shift affecting regional population distribution by religion took place on the basis of religion-communal criteria.

Shortly after partition, the concentration of population by religious beliefs became more exclusive and distinctive as a result of selective population exchange based on religion. According to the Indian census sources, India received 2.55 million Hindu refugees from East Bengal. In exchange, East Bengal received 0.70 million from West Bengal and Bihar. Within less than a decade this culminated into what may be termed as the 'demographic divide' coupled with demographic immaturity, immobility and a lack of extraterritorial population expansion. With high birth and declining death rates, the population has been showing an accelerated increase during last several decades.

Table : Evolution of population, 1881-2001

Year	Population (miln)	increase in %	Exponential growth	density (persons per km^2)
1881	25.09	-	-	180
1901	28.92	-	-	206
1921	33.25	-	-	240
1941	41.99	-	-	300
1951	44.16	5.17	0.50	315

1961	55.22	25.16	2.26	325
1974	76.39	28.35	2.48	535
1981	89.91	17.69	2.32	625
1991	111.46	22.20	2.03	720
2001	129.25	15.96	1.53	832

The War of Liberation took place in 1971 and to thwart it, the Pakistani military junta embarked upon a military action that led to one of the greatest human tragedies of this century. It has been estimated that more than 1.6 million people died as a result of the Pakistani military persecution. Millions of Bengalis fled from their homes into neighbouring India. Over a nine-month period, 10 million REFUGEEs from Bangladesh poured into the Indian states of West Bengal, Assam, Meghalaya and Tripura. The average daily influx was approximately 36,000 persons and during the peak flow months of May and June, the refugee influx often exceeded 100,000 a day. In May 1971 alone, there were nearly 3 million new arrivals. Nearly all of those who arrived after mid-May (over 6 million) were sheltered in hastily constructed camps, but some moved in with relatives as well. By December 1971, about 1,200 camps were operating along the 2,160-km India-Bangladesh border.

This important geopolitical event, however, had virtually no demographic effect on the distribution of population in Bangladesh, since after the liberation of the country, almost all refugees returned home voluntarily. This was probably the most successful voluntary return of refugees in the world. But, at the same time, a sizeable well-to-do non-Bengali population left Bangladesh for Pakistan and some for India in exchange of the Bengalis stranded in Pakistan. Besides, about 125,000 non-Bengalis, popularly known as the Biharis, who collaborated with the Pakistanis, were repatriated with the POWs by the initiatives of the ICRC and the Indian government.

The growth of population in the present century has been the result of an excess of births over deaths as there has been no large-scale immigration. And since the last century, two stages of acceleration in the pattern of population change in Bangladesh have taken place: (a) the slow rate population growth until 1921; and (b) the accelerating increase of population since 1921 and a fresh momentum to it after 1951.

In 1901, Bangladesh had a population of 28.9 million. It increased by 9.1 percent by 1911. In the period 1911-21, the rate of increase was very slow at 5.4 percent due to high mortality from the influenza epidemic of 1918-19. After that the growth rate started to recover until 1931.

In view of the over estimation in the 1941 census, it is not possible to examine the exact rate of increase of population for the decade 1931-41. It is, however, observed that this decade was a normal one regarding the fertility and mortality conditions and the population increase might have been higher than 18 percent. In the next decade, the rate of increase was low at 5.2 percent due to the Bengal famine in 1943, which took away about 2.8 million lives, and to subsequent movement of population during the Partition of Bengal in 1947.

The decade 1951-61 showed a relatively higher rate of population increase, owing to somewhat stable socio-political conditions, the combined effect of the efforts of improved health condition adopted in post-famine years and a successful check on famines. To a great extent, this rise has been the result of an unprecedented acceleration of the rate of growth of Muslim population (26.9 percent) in the country.

The increase in population during 1951-61 and the subsequent period reflects the impact of the post-partition 'demographic divide', the eradication of several killer diseases, such as malaria, smallpox and cholera, particularly, in 1971-81, and an improvement in child and maternal mortality situation as a result of the Extended Programme on Immunisation (EPI) during 1981-91.

Various estimates confirm that the increase in the pre-partition period was not very rapid and the CBR and CDR were estimated at 50 to 55 and 41 to 47 respectively, although sometimes, especially during epidemics or famines the death rate reached as high as 60. This gave an annual rate of population increase of less than one percent during the early twentieth century.

After 1931, the growth of population became a little faster as a result of the consequences of measures undertaken to check the intensity of epidemics and local diseases as well as improvement in health and sanitary situations. This effected a drop in death rate to about 42 in the 1930s, while the birth rate remained more or less stable and high.

The mortality and fertility conditions were offset during 1941-51 by famine and the unsettled socio-political situation, resulting in a low annual increase in population (less than one percent). During 1951-61, the population increased by about 2.2 percent a year.

Table : Vital rates, 1881-1991

Year	CBR	CDR	IMR
1881	na	41.0	na
1901	na	44.4	na
1921	52.9	47.3	198
1941	54.7	37.8	200
1951	49.4	40.7	168
1961	48.1	29.7	144
1971	51.7	35.0	200
1981	42.0	14.0	122
1991	32.0	11.0	91

The first census of independent Bangladesh was held on 1 March 1974. Three major calamities-natural and man-made took place during the 1961-74 inter-census period contributing substantially to the total death rate. The tropical cyclone and tidal surge of November 1970 cost between 200,000 to 600,000 human lives, mostly in the coastal region. During the war of liberation, there were indiscriminate killings and torching of villages by the Pakistan army as they swept out from the towns into the rural areas in pursuit of the freedom fighters. An estimate by the UN put 16.6 million displaced from their homes within Bangladesh for at least one month. About 3 million people were killed. This raised the CDR from a normal level of 16 to 21 during the war. In 1974 (the census year), there was a famine in Bangladesh. The number of deaths during this famine was officially estimated at 30,000. Despite these catastrophes, the population count in 1974 reached 71.4 million. The above incidents also depressed the CBR to some extent although the overall trend in the fertility pattern was not affected.

During 1974 to 1991, a downward trend in CBR has been observed with a marked decline in the CDR. The decline in CBR and CDR was the result of the successful control of communicable diseases and food shortages/famines, improvement of medical facilities, and to some extent, the impact of the family planning activities.

The regional pattern of population density In 1901, there were 526 persons per sq. mile in Bangladesh. The respective figures for 1961 and 1991 were 1,004 and 1,998. Despite the change in the overall population density in the country, its regional patterns in the present decades have shown little change, particularly in the pre-independence decades. An exception was Dhaka, which had an abnormally high density of population (more than 7,000 persons per sq mile). Three generalised density zones can be identified for 1961 and 1974. These are: less densely populated zones in western and eastern Bangladesh; medium density zone in the central part extending from north to south; and very high density zone in and around Dhaka division.

In 1981 and 1991, the spatial pattern of population density showed a skewed distribution. The distribution fell into-2 to +5 (x = 1918 = 1005.4) with Dhaka remaining as a highly densely populated district in 1981. In 1991, the skewness further sharpened, ranging from-2 to +6 (x = 2313 = 1344.5), again with Dhaka as an exceptional district.

This presents Bangladesh as one of the most densely populated areas of the world, but unlike other densely populated areas in western Europe which have intensive agricultural and a high degree of industrial and urban development, Bangladesh is primarily a rural oriented agricultural country. The greater the amount of cropland, the larger is the population in the districts and the higher is the density of population per unit area. Bangladesh shows a significantly positive coefficient of correlation (r = + 0.923) between total cropland and population of different districts. Also, the influence of rivers on the human habitat is reflected in the greater concentration of population and economic institutions along their banks.

The differences in the spatial pattern of population in recent times were caused primarily by the regional differences in mortality and regional migration under a situation of post-partition demographic divide. With few exceptions, the decades of 1950s and 1980s experienced some movement of population within the country but there had been no uniformity in population change amongst the different regions. The patterns of population change during 1961-74 and 1974-81 periods were more consistent in the country. The most likely causes were the success in eradicating some of the communicable diseases and epidemic, and improvements in management of situations of local food shortage and famines.

Some areas in the western part of the country recorded a marked variation in the patterns of population change mainly because of forced population movements during the War of Liberation. People dislocated from these areas in 1971 returned after the War and along with them also returned many others, who migrated to India earlier from these areas. Many also moved to Dhaka and thereby abnormally increasing its population in 1974.

COMPONENTS OF POPULATION GROWTH

The age and sex composition of a population affects its social life in many ways.

Changes in age composition are due mainly to changes in birthrates and are presently increasing the proportion of aged and reducing the proportion of children in many countries. Migration is affected by the push given to people by unsatisfactory conditions at home by the pull of attractive opportunities elsewhere and by the channels or means through which they are able to migrate.

Sex Composition: The small family norm together with a desire for a male child has further distorted a sex ratio against the girl-child. The sex ratio has steadily declined: From 972 (for every 1000 boys) in 1901 to 927 in 1991. The latest census shows a slight overall improvement in the sex ratio to 933. Unfortunately, this is offset by a worsening of the sex ratio of children up to the age of six.

The sex ratio for children up to the age of six has gone down from 962 girls per 1000 boys in 1981, to 945 in 1991, to 927 in 2001. The sharpest declines in sex ratio for the child population are reported from Himachal Pradesh, Punjab, Haryana, Gujarat, Uttaranchal, Maharashtra and Chandigarh, where abortions of female fetuses are known to be widely practised.

Population Density: Defined as the number of persons per sq km the population density of India in 2001 was 324 per sq km. West Bengal is still the most thickly populated state with a population density of 903 in 2001. Bihar (880) is now the second highest densely populated state pushing Kerala to the third place.

Age Composition: The current age distribution of Indian population is little more than 31. 7 percent are under the age of 15 years (male 173, 869, 856; female 164, 003, 915); 63. 5 percent are between 15 and 64 (male 349, 785, 804; female 326, 289, 402), and 4. 8 percent are over the age of 60 (male 25, 885, 725; female 25, 235, 905).

The Indian Planning Commission's Technical Group on Population Projections predicted in the National Population Policy (2000) that India's population would be 1. 012 billion in March 2001, going up to 1. 179 billion and 1. 264 billion in March 2011 and 2016 respectively.

Morality: According to 2001 census Seventy-two out of every 1, 000 babies born die before their first birthday. Seven percent (72/1, 000) of newborn infants perish within a year of birth, because of low birth weight, pre-maturity, malnutrition, diarrhea diseases, acute respiratory infections and malnutrition. Compare this to the IMRs in Sri Lanka (18/1, 000) and China (41/1, 000 Moreover, in India, there are more female deaths (rural or urban areas) in the age group of 0-14 than elsewhere. Although the IMR has decreased from 146 per 1000 births in 1951 to 72 per 1000 births (1997) and the sex differentials are narrowing, there are wide inter-state differences.

Measurements of Mortality

" Crude Death Rate " Birth Rate " Infant Mortality Rate.

Factors for the Low Death Rate

" Health-care services " Vaccinations and control of epidemics " Reduction in the occurrence of famines and droughts.

Theories of Demography

Malthus: The essay on the principle of population an important work of Malthus is a landmark in the history of population studies. The theme of the Essay was mainly to argue that the tendency of the population to grow faster in relation to its means of subsistence has led to human misery and placed several obstacles in the path of human progress. In 1803, Malthus published the second edition of his essay, a much expanded and changed edition which can't really be called a re print of the 1797 essay, for in the new edition the emphasis was more on arguments against the poor laws than on country arguments against the opinions of Condorcet and Godwin.

Neo-Maltusian theory: Neo-Malthusians maintain that although the gloomy predictions of Malthus may have been pre-mature they are basically correct.

According to Anti Malthusians' world's resources are adequate for a much larger population. Exploitation not over population is the basic cause of world hunger.

Demographic Transition Theory

Two different interpretations have been given for this theory. One by Frank Notestein says that every country passes through three stages of population growth; 1. High birth rate and high death rate ii. High birth rate and low death rate (population explosion) iii. Low birth rate and low death rate. In western nations the desire for high standard of living led to the reductions in the birthrate. These nations are approaching a new equilibrium with both birthrates and death rates quite low and little population growth.

This is explained by the theory of demographic transition-the theory that industrial and commercial development first cuts the death rate but creates a desire for smaller families and eventually cuts the birthrate. The other theory is given by C. P Blacker. There are five phrases in this theory.

i. High stationary phase marked by high fertility and mortality rate.
ii. Early expanding phase marked by high fertility and high but declining mortality.
iii. Late Expanding phase with declining fertility but mortality declining more rapidly.
iv. Low stationary phase with low fertility and equally low mortality.
v. Declining phase with low mortality, low fertility and an excess of deaths over births.

Optimum Population Theory

According to Canan the propounder of this theory population must grow upto certain desired level after which further growth is harmful. The two important principles of this theory are:

1. When there is an increase in population than the ratio between the total population and the working population remains almost constant.
2. When at a point of time the population of a country increases the natural resources capital and technical know how do not change with the result that after sometime the law of diminishing returns begins to operate. This law provides that for maximum production all the sources of production should be combined in that proper ratio than it shall not be possible to have maximum production.

Population Policy

A policy is a plan of action, statement of aims and ideals especially one made by a government, a political party, a business company etc. Population policy is an effort to affect the size, structure and distribution or characteristics of population. In its broader range it includes efforts to regulate economic and social conditions which are likely to have demographic consequences.

National Population Policy

The immediate objective of this new policy is to address the unmet needs of contraception, health infrastructure, health personnel and to provide integrated service delivery for basic reproductive and child health care. The medium term objective is to bring the total fertility rated to replacement level by 2010. The long term objective is to achieve a stable population by 2045. In pursuance of these objectives 14 National Socio-Demogragraphic goals are formulated to be achieved by 2010. The important goals are:

1. Making school education compulsory and to reduce the drop-outs.
2. Reduce infant-mortality rate to 30 per 1000 live births.
3. Reduce maternal mortality rate to below 100 per 100000 live births.
4. Promote delayed marriage.
5. Achieve 80% institutional deliveries.
6. Prevent and control communicable diseases.
7. Promote vigorously the small family norm to achieve replacement levels of Total Fertility Rate.

The policy speaks about the formation of National Commission of Population under the chairmanship of the Prime-Minister to monitor and implement population policy and to guide planning implementations. The policy also suggests some promotional and motivational measures to promote adoption of the small family norm. The main features of the policy are

1. Reward panchayats and Zila Parishads for promoting small family norms.
2. Incentives to adopt two child norms.
3. Couples below poverty line, having sterilization with not more than two living children will be eligible for health insurance plan.
4. Strengthening abortion facility scheme.

POPULATION DYNAMICS

Structure and Dynamics

Population of India. Although India occupies only 2. 4% of the world's land area, it supports over 15% of the world's population. Only China has a larger population. Almost 40% of Indians are younger than 15 years of age. About 70% of the people live in more than 550, 000 villages, and the remainder in more than 200 towns and cities. Over thousands of years of its history, India has been invaded from the Iranian plateau, Central Asia, Arabia, Afghanistan, and the West; Indian people and culture have absorbed and changed these influences to produce a remarkable racial and cultural synthesis. Religion, caste, and language are major determinants of social and political organization in India today. The government has recognized 18 languages as official; Hindi is the most widely spoken.

Although 83% of the people are Hindu, India also is the home of more than 120 million Muslims—one of the world's largest Muslim populations. The population also includes Christians, Sikhs, Jains, Buddhists, and Parsis. The caste system reflects Indian occupational and religiously defined hierarchies. Traditionally, there are four broad categories of castes (varnas), including a category of outcastes, earlier called "untouchables" but now commonly referred to as "dalits."

Within these broad categories there are thousands of castes and subcastes, whose relative status varies from region to region.

Despite economic modernization and laws countering discrimination against the lower end of the class structure, the caste system remains an important source of social identification for most Hindus and a potent factor in the political life of the country.

India Population: The 1991 final census count gave India a total population of 846, 302, 688. However, estimates of India's population vary widely. According to the Population Division of the United Nations Department of International Economic and Social Affairs, the population had already reached 866 million in 1991. The Population Division of the United Nations Economic and Social Commission for Asia and the Pacific (ESCAP) projected 896. 5 million by mid-1993 with a 1. 9 percent annual growth rate. The United States Bureau of the Census, assuming an annual population growth rate of 1. 8 percent, put India's population in July 1995 at 936, 545, 814. These higher projections merit attention in light of the fact that the Planning Commission had estimated a figure of 844 million for 1991 while preparing the Eighth Five-Year Plan (FY 1992-96). India accounts for some 2. 4 percent of the world's landmass but is home to about 16 percent of the global population. The magnitude of the annual increase in population can be seen in the fact that India adds almost the total population of Australia or Sri Lanka every year. A 1992 study of India's population notes that India has more people than all of Africa and also more than North America and South America together. Between 1947 and 1991, India's population more than doubled.

Throughout the twentieth century, India has been in the midst of a demographic transition. At the beginning of the century, endemic disease, periodic epidemics, and famines kept the death rate high enough to balance out the high birth rate. Between 1911 and 1920, the birth and death rates were virtually equal—about forty-eight births and forty-eight deaths per 1, 000 population. The increasing impact of curative and preventive medicine (especially mass inoculations) brought a steady decline in the death rate. By the mid-1990s, the estimated birth rate had fallen to twenty-eight per 1, 000, and the estimated death rate had fallen to ten per 1, 000. Clearly, the future configuration of India's population (indeed the future of India itself) depends on what happens to the birth rate. Even the most optimistic projections do not suggest that the birth rate could drop below twenty per 1, 000 before the year 2000. India's population is likely to exceed the 1 billion mark before the 2001 census.

The upward population in India spiral began in the 1920s and is reflected in intercensal growth increments. South Asia's population increased roughly 5 percent between 1901 and 1911 and actually declined slightly in the next decade. Population increased some 10 percent in the period from 1921 to 1931 and 13 to 14 percent in the 1930s and 1940s. Between 1951 and 1961, the population rose 21. 5 percent. Between 1961 and 1971, the country's population increased by 24. 8 percent. Thereafter a slight slowing of the increase was experienced: from 1971 to 1981, the population increased by 24. 7 percent, and from 1981 to 1991, by 23. 9 percent.

Population in India density has risen concomitantly with the massive increases in population. In 1901 India counted some seventy-seven persons per square kilometer; in 1981 there were 216 persons per square kilometer; by 1991 there were 267 persons per square kilometer—up almost 25 percent from the 1981 population density. India's average population density is higher than that of any other nation of comparable size. The highest densities are not only in heavily urbanized regions but also in areas that are mostly agricultural. Population of India growth in the years between 1950 and 1970 centred on areas of new irrigation projects, areas subject to refugee resettlement, and regions of urban expansion. Areas where population did not increase at a rate approaching the national average were those facing the most severe economic hardships, overpopulated rural areas, and regions with low levels of urbanization.

The 1991 census, which was carried out under the direction of the Registrar General and Census Commissioner of India (part of the Ministry of Home Affairs), in keeping with the previous two censuses, used the term *urban agglomerations*. An urban agglomeration forms a continuous urban spread and consists of a city or town and its urban outgrowth outside the statutory limits.

Or, an urban agglomerate may be two or more adjoining cities or towns and their outgrowths. A university campus or military base located on the outskirts of a city or town, which often increases the actual urban area of that city or town, is an example of an urban agglomeration. In India urban agglomerations with a population of 1 million or more—there were twenty-four in 1991—are referred to as metropolitan areas. Places with a population of 100, 000 or more are termed "cities" as compared with "towns, " which have a population of less than 100, 000. Including the metropolitan areas, there were 299 urban agglomerations with more than 100, 000 population in 1991. These large urban agglomerations are designated as Class I urban units. There were five other classes of urban agglomerations, towns, and villages based on the size of their populations: Class II (50, 000 to 99, 999), Class III (20, 000 to 49, 999), Class IV (10, 000 to 19, 999), Class V (5, 000 to 9, 999), and Class VI (villages of less than 5, 000.

The results of the 1991 census revealed that around 221 million, or 26. 1 percent, of Indian's population lived in urban areas. Of this total, about 138 million people, or 16 percent, lived in the 299 urban agglomerations. In 1991 the twenty-four metropolitan cities accounted for 51 percent of India's total population living in Class I urban centres, with Bombay and Calcutta the largest at 12. 6 million and 10. 9 million, respectively.

In the early 1990s, growth was the most dramatic in the cities of central and southern India. About twenty cities in those two regions experienced a growth rate of more than 100 percent between 1981 and 1991. Areas subject to an influx of refugees also experienced noticeable demographic changes. Refugees from Bangladesh, Burma, and Sri Lanka contributed substantially to population growth in the regions in which they settled. Less dramatic population increases occurred in areas where Tibetan refugee settlements were founded after the Chinese annexation of Tibet in the 1950s.

The majority of districts had urban populations ranging on average from 15 to 40 percent in 1991. According to the 1991 census, urban clusters predominated in the upper part of the Indo-Gangetic Plain; in the Punjab and Haryana plains, and in part of western Uttar Pradesh. The lower part of the Indo-Gangetic Plain in southeastern Bihar, southern West Bengal, and northern Orissa also experienced increased urbanization. Similar increases occurred in the western coastal state of Gujarat and the union territory of Daman and Diu. In the Central Highlands in Madhya Pradesh and Maharashtra, urbanization was most noticeable in the river basins and adjacent plateau regions of the Mahanadi, Narmada, and Tapti rivers. The coastal plains and river deltas of the east and west coasts also showed increased levels of urbanization.

The hilly, inaccessible regions of the Peninsular Plateau, the northeast, and the Himalayas remain sparsely settled. As a general rule, the lower the population density and the more remote the region, the more likely it is to count a substantial portion of tribal people among its population. Urbanization in some sparsely settled regions is more developed than would seem warranted at first glance at their limited natural resources. Areas of western India that were formerly princely states (in Gujarat and the desert regions of Rajasthan) have substantial urban centres that originated as political-administrative centres and since independence have continued to exercise hegemony over their hinterlands.

The vast majority of Indians, nearly 625 million, or 73. 9 percent, in 1991 lived in what are called villages of less than 5, 000 people or in scattered hamlets and other rural settlements.

The states with proportionately the greatest rural populations in 1991 were the states of Assam (88. 9 percent), Sikkim (90. 9 percent) and Himachal Pradesh (91. 3 percent), and the tiny union territory of Dadra and Nagar Haveli (91. 5 percent).

Those with the smallest rural populations proportionately were the states of Gujarat (65. 5 percent), Maharashtra (61. 3 percent), Goa (58. 9 percent), and Mizoram (53. 9 percent). Most of the other states and the union territory of the Andaman and Nicobar Islands were near the national average. Two other categories of India's population that are closely scrutinized by the national census are the Scheduled Castes and Scheduled Tribes. The greatest concentrations of Scheduled Caste members in 1991 lived in the states of Andhra Pradesh (10. 5 million, or nearly 16 percent of the state's population), Tamil Nadu (10. 7 million, or 19 percent), Bihar (12. 5 million, or 14 percent), West Bengal (16 million, or 24 percent), and Uttar Pradesh (29. 3 million, or 21 percent). Together, these and other Scheduled Caste members comprised about 139 million people, or more than 16 percent of the total population of India. Scheduled Tribe members represented only 8 percent of the total population (about 68 million).

They were found in 1991 in the greatest numbers in Orissa (7 million, or 23 percent of the state's population), Maharashtra (7. 3 million, or 9 percent), and Madhya Pradesh (15. 3 million, or 23 percent). In proportion, however, the populations of states in the northeast had the greatest concentrations of Scheduled Tribe members.

For example, 31 percent of the population of Tripura, 34 percent of Manipur, 64 percent of Arunachal Pradesh, 86 percent of Meghalaya, 88 percent of Nagaland, and 95 percent of Mizoram were Scheduled Tribe members. Other heavy concentrations were found in Dadra and Nagar Haveli, 79 percent of which was composed of Scheduled Tribe members, and Lakshadweep, with 94 percent of its population being Scheduled Tribe members.

NUMBERS, DISTRIBUTION AND SEX

Numbers

Estimates vary but one often cited figure is that the number of children living independently in the streets totals between 100 million and 150 million worldwide. According to a report from the Consortium for Street Children, a United Kingdom-based consortium of related NGOs: Estimating numbers of 'street children' is fraught with difficulties. In 1989, UNICEF estimated 100 million children were growing up on urban streets around the world. 14 years later UNICEF reported: 'The latest estimates put the numbers of these children as high as 100 million' (UNICEF, 2002: 37). And even more recently: 'The exact number of street children is impossible to quantify, but the figure almost certainly runs into tens of millions across the world. It is likely that the numbers are increasing' (UNICEF, 2005: 40-41). The 100 million figure is still commonly cited, but has no basis in fact. Similarly, it is debatable whether numbers of street children are growing globally or whether it is the awareness of street children within societies which has grown.

Distribution

Street children may be found on every inhabited continent in a large majority of the world's cities. The following estimates indicate the global extent of street child populations.

- India 11 million
- Egypt 1, 5 million
- Pakistan 1, 5 million
- U. S. 750, 000-1 million
- Kenya 250, 000-300, 000
- Philippines 250, 000
- Congo 250, 000
- Morocco 30, 000
- Brazil 25, 000
- Germany 20, 000
- Honduras 20 000
- Jamaica 6, 500
- Uruguay 3000
- Switzerland 1, 000.

Gender

Although there are variations from country to country, 50% or more of street children are boys.

History

Children making their home/livelihoods on the street is not a new or modern phenomenon. In the introduction to his history of abandoned children in Soviet Russia 1918-1930, Alan Ball states: Orphaned and abandoned children have been a source of misery from earliest times. They apparently accounted for most of the boy prostitutes in Augustan Rome and, a few centuries later, moved a church council of 442 in southern Gaul to declare: "Concerning abandoned children: there is general complaint that they are nowadays exposed more to dogs than to kindness. " In tsarist Russia, seventeenth-century sources described destitute youths roaming the streets, and the phenomenon survived every attempt at eradication thereafter.

Long before the Russian Revolution, the term *besprizornye* had gained wide currency. In 1848 Lord Ashley referred to more than 30, 000 'naked, filthy, roaming lawless and deserted children', in and around London.

By 1922 there were at least 7 million homeless children in Russia as a result of nearly a decade of devastation from World War I and the Russian Civil War. Abandoned children formed gangs, created their own argot, and engaged in petty theft and prostitution.

Examples from popular fiction include Kipling's "Kim" as a street child in colonial India, and Gavroche in Victor Hugo's *Les Miserables*. Fagin's crew of child pickpockets in "Oliver Twist" as well as Sherlock Holmes's "Baker Street Irregulars" attest to the presence of street children in 19th-century London.

Causes

Children may end up on the streets for several basic reasons: They may have no choice – they are abandoned, orphaned, or disowned by their parents. Secondly, they may choose to live in the streets because of mistreatment or neglect or because their homes do not or cannot provide them with basic necessities. Many children also work in the streets because their earnings are needed by their families. But homes and families are part of the larger society and the underlying reasons for the poverty or breakdown of homes and families may be social, economic, political or environmental or any combination of these.

In a 1993 report, WHO offered the following list of causes for the phenomenon:

- family breakdown
- armed conflict
- poverty
- natural and man-made disasters
- famine
- physical and sexual abuse

- exploitation by adults
- dislocation through migration
- urbanization and overcrowding
- acculturation
- disinheritance or being disowned.

The orphaning of children as a result of HIV/AIDS is another cause that might be added to this list.

By Country

Russia: In Russia, street children usually find a home in underground pipe and cable collectors during the harsh winter. These underground homes offer space, shelter and most importantly of all, heat from hot water and central heating pipes.

Russia has 1 million street children, and one in four crimes involves underage youths. Officially, the number of children without supervision is more than 700, 000. However, experts believe the real figure has long been between 2 and 4 million.

India: India is home to the world's largest population of street children, estimated at 18 million. The Republic of India is the seventh largest and second most populous country in the world. With acceleration in economic growth, India has become one of the fastest growing developing countries. This has created a rift between poor and rich; 22 percent of the population lives below the income poverty line. Owing to unemployment, increasing rural-urban migration, attraction of city life and a lack of political will, India now has one of the largest number of child labourers in the world. Street children are subject to malnutrition, hunger, health problems, substance abuse, theft, commercial sexual exploitation of children, harassment by the city police and railway authorities, as well as physical and sexual abuse, although the Government of India has taken some corrective measures and declared child labour illegal.

GOVERNMENT AND NON-GOVERNMENT RESPONSES

Responses by Governments

Because they have not reached the age of majority, street children have no representation in the governing process. They have no vote themselves nor by proxy through their parents, from whom they likely are alienated.

Nor do street children have any economic leverage. Governments, consequently, may pay little attention to them.

The rights of street children are often ignored by governments even though nearly all of the world's governments have ratified the UN Convention on the Rights of the Child.

Governments are often embarrassed by street children and may blame parents or neighbouring countries. Non-Governmental Organizations (NGOs) may also be blamed for *encouraging* children to live in the streets by making street life more bearable or attractive through the services they provide.

When governments implement programs to deal with street children these generally involve placing the children in orphanages, juvenile homes or correctional institutes.

However, some children are in the streets because they have fled from such institutions and some governments prefer to support or work in partnership with NGO programs. Governments sometimes institute *roundups* when they remove all the children from city streets and deposit them elsewhere or incarcerate them.

In the most extreme cases, governments may tacitly accept or participate in *social cleansing* operations that murder street children.

NGO Responses

Non-government organizations employ a wide variety of strategies to address the needs and rights of street children. These may be categorized as follows:

- Advocacy-through media and government contacts agencies may press for the rights of street children to be respected.
- Preventive-programs that work to prevent children from taking to the streets, through family and community support and education.
- Institutional
  - o residential rehabilitation programs-some agencies provide an environment isolated from the streets where activities are focussed on assisting children to recover from drug, physical or sexual abuse.
  - o full-care residential homes-the final stage in many agencies' programs is when the child is no longer in the streets but lives completely in an environment provided by the agency. Some agencies promote fostering children to individual families. Others set up group homes where a small number of children live together with houseparents employed by the agency. Others set up institutional care centres catering to large numbers of children. Some agencies include a follow-up program that monitors and counsels children and families after the child has left the residential program.
- Street-based programs-these work to alleviate the worst aspects of street life for children by providing services to them in the streets. These programs tend to be less expensive and serve a larger number of street children than institutional programs since the children still must provide for themselves in the streets.

- o feeding program
- o medical services
- o legal assistance
- o street education
- o financial services (banking and entrepreneur programs)
- o family reunification
- o drop-in centres/night shelters
- o outreach programs designed to bring the children into closer contact with the agency

- Conscientization-change street children's attitudes to their circumstances-view themselves as an oppressed minority and become protagonists rather than passive recipients of aid.

Many agencies employ several of these strategies and a child will pass through a number of stages before he or she "graduates". First he/she will be contacted by an outreach program, then may become involved in drop-in centre programs, though still living in the streets. Later the child may be accepted into a halfway house and finally into residential care where he or she becomes fully divorced from street life.

RURAL POPULATION AND THEIR DEVELOPMENT

Over seventy per cent of India's population still lives in rural areas. There are substantial differences between the states in the proportion of rural and urban population. Agriculture is the largest and one of the most important sector of the rural economy and contributes both to economic growth and employment.

Its contribution to the Gross Domestic Product has declined over the last five decades but agriculture still remains the source of livelihood for over 70 per cent of the country's population. A large proportion of the rural work force is small and consists of marginal farmers and landless agricultural labourers. There is substantial under employment among these people; both wages and productivity are low. These in turn result in poverty; it is estimated that 320 million people are still living below the poverty line in rural India.

Though poverty has declined over the last three decades, the number of rural poor has in fact increased due to the population growth. Poor tend to have larger families which puts enormous burden on their meagre resources, and prevent them from breaking out of the shackles of poverty. In States like Tamil Nadu where replacement level of fertility has been attained, population growth rates are much lower than in many other States; but the population density is high and so there is a pressure on land. In States like Rajasthan, Uttar Pradesh, Bihar and Madhya Pradesh population is growing rapidly, resulting in increasing pressure on land and resulting land fragmentation. Low productivity of small land holders leads to poverty, low energy intake and under nutrition, and this, in turn, prevents the development thus creating a vicious circle.

In most of the states non-farm employment in rural areas has not grown very much and cannot absorb the growing labour force. Those who are getting educated specially beyond the primary level, may not wish to do manual agricultural work.

They would like better opportunities and more remunerative employment. In this context, it is imperative that programmes for skill development, vocational training and technical education are taken up on a large scale in order to generate productive employment in rural areas.

The entire gamut of existing poverty alleviation and employment generation programmes may have to be restructured to meet the newly emerging types of demand for employment. Rural poor have inadequate access to basic minimum services, because of poor connectivity, lack of awareness, inadequate and poorly functional infrastructure.

There are ongoing efforts to improve these, but with the growing aspirations of the younger, educated population these efforts may prove to be inadequate to meet the increasing needs both in terms of type and quality of services. Greater education, awareness and better standard of living among the growing younger age group population would create the required consciousness among them that smaller families are desirable; if all the felt needs for health and family welfare services are fully met, it will be possible to enable them to attain their reproductive goals, achieve substantial decline in the family size and improve quality of life.

Water Supply

In many parts of developed and developing world, water demand substantially exceeds sustainable water supply. It is estimated that currently 430 millions are living in countries affected by water stress; by 2020 about one fourth of the global population may be facing chronic and recurring shortage of fresh water. In India, water withdrawal is estimated to be twice the rate of aquifer recharge; as a result water tables are falling by one to three meters every year; tapping deeper aquifers have resulted in larger population groups being exposed to newer health hazards such as high fluoride or arsenic content in drinking water.

At the other end of the spectrum, excessive use of water has led to water logging and increasing salinity in some parts of the country. Eventually, both lack of water and water logging could have adverse impact on India's food production. There is very little arable agricultural land which remains unexploited and in many areas, agricultural technology improvement may not be able to ensure further increase in yield per hectare.

It is, therefore, imperative that research in biotechnology for improving development of foodgrains strains that would tolerate salinity and those which would require less water gets high priority. Simultaneously, a movement towards making water harvesting, storage and its need based use part of every citizens life should be taken up.

Food security

Technological innovations in agriculture and increase in area under cultivation have ensured that so far, food production has kept pace with the population growth. Evolution of global and national food security systems have improved access to food. It is estimated that the global population will grow to 9 billion by 2050 and the food production will double; improvement in purchasing power and changing dietary habits may further add to the requirement of food grains.

Thus, in the next five decades, the food and nutrition security could become critical in many parts of the world especially in the developing countries and pockets of poverty in the developed countries. In India one of the major achievements in the last fifty years has been the green revolution and selfsufficiency in food production. Food grain production has increased from 50.82 in 1950-51 to 200.88 million tons in 1998-99.

It is a matter of concern that while the cereal production has been growing steadily at a rate higher than the population growth rates, the coarse grain and pulse production has not shown a similar increase. Consequently there has been a reduction in the per capita availability of pulses and coarse grains. Over the last five decades there has been a decline in the per capita availability of pulses.

During the last few years the country has imported pulses to meet the requirement. There has been a sharp and sustained increase in cost of pulses, so there is substantial decline in per capita pulses consumption among poorer segment of population. This in turn could have an adverse impact on their protein intake. The pulse component of the "Pulses and Oil Seeds Mission" need to receive a major thrust in terms of R&D and other inputs, so that essential pulse requirement of growing population is fully met. Rising cost of pulses had a beneficial effect also.

Till eighties in central India wages of landless labourers were given in the form Kesari Dal which was cheaper than cereals or coarse grains. Consumption of staple diet of Kesari Dal led to crippling disease of neuro lathyrism. Over the last three decades the rising cost of pulses has made Kesari Dal more expensive than wheat or rice and hence it is no longer given to labourers as wages for work done; as a result the disease has virtually disappeared from Central India. Over years the coarse grain production has remained stagnant and per capita availability of coarse grain has under gone substantial reduction; there has been a shift away from coarse grains to rice and wheat consumption even among poorer segment of population. One of the benefits of this change is virtual elimination of pellagra which was widely prevalent among low income group population in Deccan Plateau whose staple food was sorghum.

Coarse grains are less expensive than rice and wheat; they can thus provide higher calories for the same cost as compared to rice and wheat. Coarse grains which are locally produced and procured if made available through TPDS at subsidised rate, may not only substantially bring down the subsidy cost without any reduction in calories provided but also improve "targetting"-as only the most needy are likely to access these coarse grains. Another area of concern is the lack of sufficient focus and thrust in horticulture; because of this, availability of vegetables especially green leafy vegetables and yellow/red vegetables throughout the year at affordable cost both in urban and rural areas has remained an unfulfilled dream.

Health and nutrition education emphasizing the importance of consuming these inexpensive rich sources of micronutrients will not result in any change in food habits unless there is harnessing and effective management of horticultural resources in the country to meet the growing needs of the people at affordable cost. States like Tamil Nadu and Himachal Pradesh have initiated some efforts in this direction; similar efforts need be taken up in other states also.

Nutrition

At the time of independence the country faced two major nutritional problems; one was the threat of famine and acute starvation due to low agricultural production and lack of appropriate food distribution system.

The other was chronic energy deficiency due to poverty, low-literacy, poor access to safe-drinking water, sanitation and health care; these factors led to wide spread prevalence of infections and ill health in children and adults. Kwashiorkor, marasmus, goitre, beri beri, blindness due to Vitamin-A deficiency and anaemia were major public health problems. The country adopted multi-sectoral, multi-pronged strategy to combat the major nutritional problems and to improve nutritional status of the population. During the last 50 years considerable progress has been achieved. Famines no longer stalk the country.

There has been substantial reduction in moderate and severe undernutrition in children and some improvement in nutritional status of all segments of population. Kwashiorkor, marasmus, pellagra, lathyrism, beri beri and blindness due to severe Vitamin-A deficiency have become rare. However, it is a matter of concern that milder forms of Chronic Energy Deficiency and micronutrient deficiencies continue to be widely prevalent in adults and children. In view of the fact that population growth in India will continue for the next few decades, it is essential that appropriate strategies are devised to improve food and nutrition security of families, identify individuals/families with severe forms of CED and provide them assistance to over come these problem. Operational strategy to improve the dietary intake of the family and improve nutritional status of the rapidly growing adult population would include:

- Ensuring adequate agricultural production of cereals, pulses, vegetables and other foodstuffs needed to fully meet the requirement of growing population.
- Improving in purchasing power through employment generation and employment assurance schemes;
- Providing subsidised food grains through TPDS to the families below poverty line.
- Exploring feasibility of providing subsidized coarse grains to families Below Poverty Line

Operational strategies to improve health and nutritional status of the growing numbers of women and children include:

- Pregnant and lactating women-screening to identify women with weight below 40 Kgs and ensuring that they/their preschool children receive food supplements through Integrated Child Development Services Scheme; adequate antenatal intrapartum and neonatal care.
- 0-6 months infants-Nutrition education for early initiation of lactation protection and promotion of universal breast feeding exclusive breast feeding for the first six months; unless there is specific reason supplementation should not be introduced before 6 months immunisation, growth monitoring and health care.
- Well planned nutrition education to ensure that the infants and children do a) continue to get breasted; b) get appropriate cereal pulse-vegetable based supplement fed to them at least 3-4 times a day–appropriate help in ensuring this through family/community/work place support; c) immunisation and health care.
- Children in the 0-5 age group; a) screen by weighment to identify children with moderate and severe undernutrition b) provide double quantity supplements through ICDS; c) screening for nutrition and health problems and appropriate intervention.
- Primary school children: a) weigh and identify those with moderate and severe chronic energy deficiency; b) improve dietary intake to these children through the mid-day meal.

- Monitor for improvement in the identified undernourished infants, children and mothers; if no improvement after 2 months refer to physician for identification and treatment of factors that might be responsible for lack of improvement;
- Nutrition education on varying dietary needs of different members of the family and how they can be met by minor modifications from the family meals. Intensive health education for improving the life style of the population coupled with active screening and management of the health problems associated with obesity.

POPULATION PROJECTIONS FOR INDIA AND THEIR IMPLICATIONS

Right from 1958 the Planning Commission has been constituting an Expert Group on Population Projections prior to the preparation of each of the Five Year Plans so that the information on the population status at the time of initiation of the Plan and population projections for future are available during the preparation of the Plan. Population projections have been utilised not only for planning to ensure provision of essentials necessities such as food, shelter and clothing but also prerequisites for human development such as education, employment and health care.

Over the years there has been considerable refinement in the methodology used for population projections and substantial improvement in the accuracy of predictions. The projections made by the Standing Committee on Population Projection in 1988 for the year 1991 was 843.6 million; this figure was within 0.3% of the 846.3 million reported in the Census 1991.

In 1996, Technical Group on Population Projections, had work out the population projections for the country and the states for the period 1996 to 2016 on the basis of census 1991 and other available demographic data. Population pyramids for the period 1971 to 2016.

Economic Implications

Population growth and its relation to economic growth has been a matter of debate for over a century. The early Malthusian view was that population growth is likely to impede economic growth because it will put pressure on the available resources, result in reduction in per capita income and resources; this, in turn, will result in deterioration in quality of life.

Contrary to the Malthusian predictions, several of the East Asian countries have been able to achieve economic prosperity and improvement in quality of life inspite of population growth. This has been attributed to the increase in productivity due to development and utilisation of innovative technologies by the young educated population who formed the majority of the growing population.

These countries have been able to exploit the dynamics of demographic transition to achieve economic growth by using the human resources as the engine driving the economic development; improved employment with adequate emoluments has promoted saving and investment which in turn stimulated economic growth.

However, not all countries, which have undergone demographic transition, have been able to transform their economies. Sri Lanka in South Asia underwent demographic transition at the same time as South East Asian countries but has not achieved the economic transition. It is now realised that population growth or demographic transition can have favourable impact on economic growth only when there are optimal interventions aimed at human resource development and appropriate utilisation of available human resources. For India the current phase of demographic transition with low dependency ratio and high working age group population, represents both a challenge and an opportunity.

The challenge is to develop these human resources through appropriate education and skill development and utilise them fully by giving them appropriate jobs with adequate emoluments; if this challenge is met through well planned schemes for HRD and employment generation which are implemented effectively, there will be improved national productivity and personal savings rates; appropriate investment of these savings will help the country to achieve the economic transition from low economic growth-low per capita income to high economic growth-high per capita income.

It is imperative to make the best use of this opportunity so as to enable the country and its citizens to vault to the high income- high economic growth status and stabilize at that level.

Interstate differences

The projected values for the total population in different regions. There are marked differences between States in size of the population and population growth rates, the time by which replacement level of fertility is to be achieved and age structure of the population. If the present trend continues, most of the Southern and the Western States are likely to achieve TFR of 2.1 by 2010.

Urgent energetic steps to assess and fully meet the unmet needs for maternal and child health care and contraception through improvement in availability and access to family welfare services are needed in the States of UP, MP, Rajasthan and Bihar in order to achieve a faster decline in their mortality and fertility rates. The five states of Bihar, Uttar Pradesh, Madhya Pradesh, Rajasthan and Orissa, which constitute 44% of the total population of India in

1996, will constitute 48% of the total population of India in 2016. These states will contribute 55% of the total increase in population of the country during the period 1996-2016. In all the states performance in the social and economic sector has been poor. The poor performance is the outcome of poverty, illiteracy and poor development which co-exist and reinforce each other.

The quality and coverage under health services is poor and the unmet need for FW services is about 30%. Urgent energetic steps are required to be initiated to assess and fully meet the unmet needs for maternal and child health care and contraception through improvement in availability and access to family welfare services in the states of UP, MP, Rajasthan and Bihar in order to achieve a faster decline in their mortality and fertility rates.

The performance of these states would determine the year and size of the population at which the country achieves population stabilisation. There are also marked differences between States in socio-economic development. Increasing investments and rapid economic development are likely to occur in the States where literacy rates are high; there is ready availability of skilled work force and adequate infrastructure. In these States, population growth rates are low. If equitable distribution of the income and benefits generated by development is ensured, substantial increase in per capita income and improvement in quality of life could occur in these States in a relatively short time. In majority of States with high population growth rates, the performance in the social and economic sector has been poor. The poor performance could be the outcome of a variety of factors including paucity of natural, financial or human resources.

Poverty, illiteracy and poor development co-exist and aggravate each other. In order to promote equity and reduce disparity between States, special assistance has been provided to the poorly performing States.

The benefits accrued from such assistance has to a large extent depended upon:

- The States' ability to utilise the available funds; improve quality and coverage of services and facilities, increase efficiency and improve performance
- Community awareness and ability to utilise the available services.

In spite of the additional assistance provided, improvement in infrastructure, agriculture and industry have been sub-optimal and the per capita income continues to be low in most of the poorly performing States. These States also have high birth rates and relatively low literacy rates. It is imperative that special efforts are made during the next two decades to break this vicious self perpetuating cycle of poor performance, poor per capita income, poverty, low literacy and high birth rate so that the further widening of disparities between States in terms of per capita income and quality of life is prevented.

The higher population growth rates and low per capita income in poorly performing States are likely to have a major impact on several social sector programmes. The health status of the population in these States is poor; the health sector programme will require inputs not only for improving infrastructure and manpower, but also increasing efficiency and improving performance. The Family Welfare Programme has to address the massive task of meeting all the unmet needs for MCH and contraception so that there is a rapid decline in mortality and fertility rates. Due to high birth rate, the number of children requiring schooling will be large. The emphasis in the education sector on primary education is essential to ensure that the resource constraints do not result in an increase in either proportion or number of illiterates. Emphasis on prevocational and vocational training in schools will enable these children to acquire skills through which they will find gainful employment later.

Migration

The available data from census shows that until 1991 both internal and international migration has been negligible. The Technical Group while computing the population projection upto 2016, has assumed that the component of migration between major States and from India will be negligible. This assumption may not be valid if there is further widening of the disparity between States in terms of economic growth and employment opportunity.

Given the combination of high population growth, low literacy and lack of employment opportunities in the poorly performing States, there may be increasing rural to urban migration as well as interstate migration especially of unskilled workers. Such migration may in the short run assist the migrants in overcoming economic problems associated with unemployment.

However, the migrant workers and their families may face problems in securing shelter, education and health care. It is essential to build up a mechanism for monitoring these changes. Steps will have to be taken to provide for the minimum essential needs of the vulnerable migrant population.

Labour, Employment and Manpower

Population, which is engaged in any economic activity and population seeking work constitute Labour Force. India has the second largest labour force in the world. Projection of labour force is pre-requisite ensuring optimal utilisation of available human resources. Manpower development is then taken up to provide adequate labour force, of appropriate skills and quality to different sectors so that there is rapid socioeconomic development and there is no mismatch between skills required and skills available. Planning also attempts to provide enabling environment for employment generation in public, private and voluntary sectors in urban and rural areas. Labour force in India will be increasing by more than 10 million per annum during 1997-2012. It will be imperative to plan for and achieve adequate agricultural and industrial growth to absorb this work force. Most of the persons entering the labour force will be educated and have some skills.

Increasing literacy and decreasing birth rates may result in more women seeking economically productive work outside home. It will be important to generate appropriate and renumerative employment at places where labour force are available so as to reduce interstate and urban migration in search of employment. Attempts should be made to eliminate bonded labour, employment of children and women in hazardous industries and minimising occupational health hazards.

Planners face the challenge to have sustained high economic growth rate in sectors that are labour-intensive to ensure adequate employment generation for productively utilising this massive work force. If the massive work force of literate, skilled, aware men and women in age-group 20-60 years get fully employed and adequately paid they could trigger off a period of rapid economic development. As they have very few dependant children and elders there will be increased savings and investments at household level; this in turn will improve the availability of resources for accelerating economic growth. The current stage of demographic transition thus provides the country with the opportunity window for using human resources as the engine to power economic development and improving the quality of life of all the citizens.

Sex Ratio

The reported decline in the sex ratio during the current century has been a cause for concern. The factors responsible for this continued decline are as yet not clearly identified. However, it is well recognised that the adverse sex ratio is a reflection of the gender disparity. Higher childhood mortality in girl children is yet another facet of the existing gender disparities and consequent adverse effect on survival. In the reproductive age group the mortality rates among women are higher than those among men.

The continued high maternal mortality is one of the major factors responsible for this. Effective implementation of the Reproductive and Child Health Programme is expected to result in a substantial reduction in maternal mortality. At the moment, the longevity at birth among women is only marginally higher than that among men. However over the next decade life expectancy among women will progressively increase. Once the reproductive age group is crossed, the mortality rates among women are lower as women outlive and outnumber men in the age group 65 and above. The needs especially of the widowed women have to be met so that quality of life does not deteriorate.

The census 2001 will collect and report vital data on sex disaggregated basis; this will be of help in identifying and taking up appropriate interventions in correcting gender disparity; continued collection, collation, analysis and reporting of sex disaggregated data from all social sectors will also provide a mechanism to monitor whether girls and women have equal access to services. There are substantial differences in sex ratio at birth and in different age groups between states.

The SRS based estimates of average sex ratio at birth for the period 1981-90 for the major States. The observed sex ratio of 110 is higher than the internationally accepted sex ratio at birth of 106. There are substantial differences among states in the reported sex ratio at birth. There had been speculations whether female infanticide, sex determination and selective female foeticide are at least in part responsible for this. The Government of India has enacted a legislation banning the prenatal sex determination and selective abortion. Intensive community education efforts are under way to combat these practices, especially in pockets from where female infanticide and foeticide have been reported.

Increasing Longevity

The projected populations of India in the three major age groups. Over the coming decades the country will be facing a progressive increase both in the proportion and number of persons beyond 60 years of age. Over the next 20 years the population of more than 60 years will grow form 62.3 million to 112.9 million; the subsequent decades will witness massive increase in this age group. Increasing longevity will inevitably bring in its wake increase in the prevalence of non-communicable diseases.

The growing number of senior citizens in the country poses a major challenge and the cost of providing socio-economic security and health care to this population has to be met. Currently several region and culture specific innovative interventions to provide needed care to this population are underway; among these are efforts to reverse the trend of break up of joint families. If these efforts succeed, it will be possible to provide necessary care for rapidly increasing population of senior citizens in the subsequent two decades within the resources of the family and the country. Majority of the people in their sixties will be physically and psychologically fit and would like to participate both in economic and social activities.

They should be encouraged and supported to lead a productive life and contribute to the national development. Senior citizens in their seventies and beyond and those with health problems would require assistance. So far, the families have borne major share in caring for the elderly. This will remain the ideal method; however, there are growing number of elderly without family support; for them, alternate modes for caring may have to be evolved and implemented. Improved health care has "added years to life". The social sectors have to make the necessary provisions for improving the quality of life of these senior citizens so that they truly " add life to years."

HEALTH IMPLICATION OF THE DEMOGRAPHIC TRANSITION

It was earlier assumed that population growth during demographic transition will lead to overcrowding, poverty, undernutrition, environmental deterioration, poor quality of life and increase in disease burden. Experience in the last few decades have shown that this may not always be correct. India is currently in the phase of demographic transition when the increase in population is mainly among younger, better educated and healthy population with low morbidity and mortality rate. The challenge for the health sector is to promote healthy life styles, improve access to and utilisation of health care so that the country can achieve substantial reduction in mortality and morbidity.

Occupational health and environmental health programme need be augmented to ensure that working population remain healthy and productive. If these challenges are fully met, it is possible to accelerate reduction in morbidity and mortality rate in this age group and improve health indices of the country. With growing number of senior citizens there may be substantial increase in health care needs especially for management of non-communicable diseases. Increasing availability and awareness about technological advances for management of these problems, rising expectations of the population and the ever escalating cost of health care are some of the problems that the health care system has to cope with. Health care delivery systems will have to gear up to taking up necessary preventive, promotive, curative and rehabilitative care for growing population of senior citizens.

Population projections and their implications for the FW programme

There will be a marginal decline in the population less than 15 years of age. The health care infrastructure will therefore be not grappling with ever increasing number of children for providing care and they will be able to concentrate on:

- Improving quality of care;
- Focus on antenatal, intranatal and neonatal care aimed at reducing neonatal morbidity and mortality;
- Improve coverage and quality of health care to vulnerable and underserved adolescents;
- Promote intersectoral coordination especially with ICDS programme so that there is improvement in health and nutritional status;
- Improve coverage for immunization against vaccine preventable diseases.

The economic challenge is to provide needed funds so that these children have access to nutrition, education and skill development. The challenge faced by the health sector is to achieve reduction in morbidity and mortality rate in infancy and childhood, to improve nutritional status and eliminate ill-effects of gender bias.

There will be a massive increase of population in the 15-59 age group. The persons in this age group will be more literate and have greater access to information; they will therefore have greater awareness and expectation regarding both the access to a wide spectrum of health care related services and the quality of these services.

Under the Reproductive and child health care programme efforts are underway to provide:

- Needed services for this rapid growing population
- To broaden the spectrum of services available and
- To improve quality and coverage of health care to women, children and adolescents, so that their felt needs for health care are fully met.
- To improve the participation of men in the planned parenthood movement.

The components of the comprehensive RCH services are given in the text box. While providing the package of services, efforts will have to be made to improve the quality of services, make services more responsive to users' needs, ensure that health workers and health care providers have the necessary skills and supplies they need and there is a strong and effective referral system to manage all the risk cases.

Family welfare Programme is attempting to improve the logistics of supply of drugs and vaccine to make sure good quality drugs are available at appropriate time.

Simultaneously the IEC efforts are being directed to:

- Ensure responsible reproductive/sexual behaviour;
- Improve awareness about reproductive health needs;
- Promote community participation and optimal utilisation of available services

Essential Reproductive and Child Health Services

Though it is desirable that the entire package of services indicated under comprehensive RCH care is made available to all those who need it, it will not be possible to immediately implement such a comprehensive package at primary health care level on a nationwide basis. After consultation with experts a package of essential reproductive health services for nationwide implementation at primary health care settings has been identified.

Essential components recommended for nationwide implementation include:

- Prevention and management of unwanted pregnancy,
- Services to provide antenatal, intra-natal and post-natal, and neo-natal care
- Services to promote child health and survival,
- Prevention and treatment of RTI/STD.

Most of these services are already being delivered under the Family Welfare Programme. However, there are wide variations in the quality and coverage of services not only between states but also between districts in the same state.

The focus under RCH Programme is therefore on the improvement in the quality and coverage of the services over and above the existing level in all districts/states in an incremental manner so that there is over all improvement maternal and child health indices.

POPULATION GENETICS: POPULATION AND CLINE

At the beginning of the 20th century, anthropologists questioned, and eventually abandoned, the claim that biologically distinct races are isomorphic with distinct linguistic, cultural, and social groups. Shortly thereafter, the rise of population genetics provided scientists with a new understanding of the sources of phenotypic variation. This new science has led many mainstream evolutionary scientists in anthropology and biology to question the very validity of race as a scientific concept describing an objectively real phenomenon. Those who came to reject the validity of the concept of race did so for four reasons: empirical, definitional, the availability of alternative concepts, and ethical (Lieberman and Byrne 1993).

The first to challenge the concept of race on empirical grounds were anthropologists Franz Boas, who demonstrated phenotypic plasticity due to environmental factors (Boas 1912), and Ashley Montagu (1941, 1942), who relied on evidence from genetics. Zoologists Edward O. Wilson and W. Brown then challenged the concept from the perspective of general animal systematics, and further rejected the claim that "races" were equivalent to "subspecies" (Wilson and Brown 1953).

Clines

One crucial innovation in reconceptualizing genotypic and phenotypic variation was anthropologist C. Loring Brace's observation that such variations, insofar as it is affected by natural selection, migration, or genetic drift, are distributed along geographic gradations or clines (Brace 1964). In part this is due to isolation by distance. This point called attention to a problem common to phenotype-based descriptions of races (for example, those based on hair texture and skin colour): they ignore a host of other similarities and differences (for example, blood type) that do not correlate highly with the markers for race. Thus, anthropologist Frank Livingstone's conclusion, that since clines cross racial boundaries, "there are no races, only clines" (Livingstone 1962: 279).

In a response to Livingston, Theodore Dobzhansky argued that when talking about race one must be attentive to how the term is being used: "I agree with Dr. Livingston that if races have to be 'discrete units,' then there are no races, and if 'race' is used as an 'explanation' of the human variability, rather than vice versa, then the explanation is invalid." He further argued that one could use the term race if one distinguished between "race differences" and "the race concept."

The former refers to any distinction in gene frequencies between populations; the latter is "a matter of judgment." He further observed that even when there is clinal variation, "Race differences are objectively ascertainable biological phenomena... but it does not follow that racially distinct populations must be given racial (or subspecific) labels." In short, Livingston and Dobzhansky agree that there are genetic differences among human beings; they also agree that the use of the race concept to classify people, and how the race concept is used, is a matter of social convention. They differ on whether the race concept remains a meaningful and useful social convention.

In 1964, biologists Paul Ehrlich and Holm pointed out cases where two or more clines are distributed discordantly—for example, melanin is distributed in a decreasing pattern from the equator north and south; frequencies for the haplotype for beta-S hemoglobin, on the other hand, radiate out of specific geographical points in Africa (Ehrlich and Holm 1964). As anthropologists Leonard Lieberman and Fatimah Linda Jackson observed, "Discordant patterns of heterogeneity falsify any description of a population as if it were genotypically or even phenotypically homogeneous" (Lieverman and Jackson 1995).

Patterns such as those seen in human physical and genetic variation as described above, have led to the consequence that the number and geographic location of any described races is highly dependent on the importance attributed to, and quantity of, the traits considered. For example, if only skin colour and a "two race" system of classification were used, then one might classify Indigenous Australians in the same race as Black people, and Caucasians in the same race as East

Asian people, but biologists and anthropologists would dispute that these classifications have any scientific validity. Scientists discovered a skin-lighting mutation that partially accounts for the appearance of Light skin in humans (people who migrated out of Africa northward into what is now Europe) which they estimate occurred 20,000 to 50,000 years ago. The East Asians owe their relatively light skin to different mutations. On the other hand, the greater the number of traits (or alleles) considered, the more subdivisions of humanity are detected, since traits and gene frequencies do not always correspond to the same geographical location. Or as Ossario and Duster (2005) put it: Anthropologists long ago discovered that humans' physical traits vary gradually, with groups that are close geographic neighbours being more similar than groups that are geographically separated. This pattern of variation, known as clinal variation, is also observed for many alleles that vary from one human group to another. Another observation is that traits or alleles that vary from one group to another do not vary at the same rate. This pattern is referred to as nonconcordant variation.

Because the variation of physical traits is clinal and nonconcordant, anthropologists of the late 19th and early 20th centuries discovered that the more traits and the more human groups they measured, the fewer discrete differences they observed among races and the more categories they had to create to classify human beings. The number of races observed expanded to the 30s and 50s, and eventually anthropologists concluded that there were no discrete races (Marks, 2002). Twentieth and 21st century biomedical researchers have discovered this same feature when evaluating human variation at the level of alleles and allele frequencies. Nature has not created four or five distinct, nonoverlapping genetic groups of people.

More recent genetic studies indicate that skin colour may change radically over as few as 100 generations, or about 2,500 years, given the influence of the environment.

Populations

Population geneticists have debated as to whether the concept of population can provide a basis for a new conception of race. In order to do this, a working definition of population must be found. Surprisingly, there is no generally accepted concept of population that biologists use. It has been pointed out that the concept of population is central to ecology, evolutionary biology and conservation biology, but also that most definitions of population rely on qualitative descriptions such as "a group of organisms of the same species occupying a particular space at a particular time" Waples and Gaggiotti identify two broad types of definitions for populations; those that fall into an *ecological paradigm*, and those that fall into an *evolutionary paradigm*. Examples of such definitions are:

- Ecological paradigm: A group of individuals of the same species that co-occur in space and time and have an opportunity to interact with each other.

- Evolutionary paradigm: A group of individuals of the same species living in close-enough proximity that any member of the group can potentially mate with any other member.

Richard Lewontin, claiming that 85 percent of human variation occurs within populations and not among populations, argued that neither "race" nor "subspecies" were appropriate or useful ways to describe populations (Lewontin 1973). Nevertheless, barriers—which may be cultural or physical—between populations can limit gene flow and increase genetic differences. Recent work by population geneticists conducting research in Europe suggests that ethnic identity can be a barrier to gene flow. Others, such as Ernst Mayr, have argued for a notion of "geographic race". Some researchers report the variation between racial groups (measured by Sewall Wright's population structure statistic F_{ST}) accounts for as little as 5% of human genetic variation[2]. Sewall Wright himself commented that if differences this large were seen in another species, they would be called subspecies. In 2003 A. W. F. Edwards argued that cluster analysis supersedes Lewontin's arguments.

These empirical challenges to the concept of race forced evolutionary sciences to reconsider their definition of race. Mid-century, anthropologist William Boyd defined race as: A population which differs significantly from other populations in regard to the frequency of one or more of the genes it possesses. It is an arbitrary matter which, and how many, gene loci we choose to consider as a significant "constellation" (Boyd 1950).

Lieberman and Jackson (1994) have pointed out that "the weakness of this statement is that if one gene can distinguish races then the number of races is as numerous as the number of human couples reproducing." Moreover, anthropologist Stephen Molnar has suggested that the discordance of clines inevitably results in a multiplication of races that renders the concept itself useless (Molnar 1992).

The distribution of many physical traits resembles the distribution of genetic variation within and between human populations (American Association of Physical Anthropologists 1996; Keita and Kittles 1997). For example, ~90% of the variation in human head shapes occurs within every human group, and ~10% separates groups, with a greater variability of head shape among individuals with recent African ancestors (Relethford 2002).

Conversely, in the paper "Genetic similarities within and between human populations" Witherspoon *et al.* (2007) show that even when individuals can be reliably assigned to specific population groups, it is still possible for two randomly chosen individuals from different populations/clusters to be more similar to each other than to a randomly chosen member of their own cluster. This is because multi locus clustering relies on population level similarities, rather than individual similarities, so that each individual is classified according to their similarity to the typical genotype for any given population. The paper claims that this masks a great deal of genetic similarity between individuals belonging to different clusters. Or in other words, two individuals from different clusters can be more similar to each other than to a member of their own cluster, while still both being more similar to the typical genotype of their own cluster than to the typical genotype of a different cluster.

When differences between individual pairs of people are tested, Witherspoon *et al.* found that the answer to the question "How often is a pair of individuals from one population genetically more dissimilar than two individuals chosen from two different populations?" is not adequately addressed by multi locus clustering analyses.

They found that even for just three population groups separated by large geographic ranges (European, African and East Asian) the inclusion of many thousands of loci is required before the answer can become "never". On the other hand, the accurate classification of the global population must include more closely related and admixed populations, which will increase this above zero, so they state "In a similar vein, Romualdi et al. (2002) and Serre and Paabo (2004) have suggested that highly accurate classification of individuals from continuously sampled (and therefore closely related) populations may be impossible".

Witherspoon *et al.* conclude "The fact that, given enough genetic data, individuals can be correctly assigned to their populations of origin is compatible with the observation that most human genetic variation is found within populations, not between them. It is also compatible with our finding that, even when the most distinct populations are considered and hundreds of loci are used, individuals are frequently more similar to members of other populations than to members of their own population"

GEOGRAPHICAL DISTRIBUTION OF ANIMALS

Animals are a major group of mostly multicellular, eukaryotic organisms of the kingdom Animalia or Metazoa. Their body plan eventually becomes fixed as they develop, although some undergo a process of metamorphosis later on in their life. Most animals are motile, meaning they can move spontaneously and independently. All animals are also heterotrophs, meaning they must ingest other organisms for sustenance.

ETYMOLOGY

The word "animal" comes from the Latin word *animal* (meaning *with soul,* from *anima,* soul). In everyday colloquial usage, the word usually refers to non-human animals. Frequently only closer relatives of humans such as mammals and other vertebrates are meant in colloquial use. The biological definition of the word refers to all members of the Kingdom Animalia, encompassing creatures ranging from insects to humans.

Characteristics

Animals have several characteristics that set them apart from other living things. Animals are eukaryotic and are mostly multicellular (although see Myxozoa), which separates them from bacteria and most protists. They are heterotrophic, generally digesting food in an internal chamber, which separates them from plants and algae. They are also distinguished from plants, algae, and fungi by lacking rigid cell walls. All animals are motile, if only at certain life stages. In most animals, embryos pass through a blastula stage, which is a characteristic exclusive to animals.

Structure

With a few exceptions, most notably the sponges (Phylum Porifera) and Placozoa, animals have bodies differentiated into separate tissues. These include muscles, which are able to contract and control locomotion, and nerve tissue, which sends and processes signals. There is also typically an internal digestive chamber, with one or two openings. Animals with this sort of organization are called metazoans, or eumetazoans when the former is used for animals in general.

All animals have eukaryotic cells, surrounded by a characteristic extracellular matrix composed of collagen and elastic glycoproteins. This may be calcified to form structures like shells, bones, and spicules.

During development it forms a relatively flexible framework upon which cells can move about and be reorganized, making complex structures possible. In contrast, other multicellular organisms like plants and fungi have cells held in place by cell walls, and so develop by progressive growth. Also, unique to animal cells are the following intercellular junctions: tight junctions, gap junctions, and desmosomes.

REPRODUCTION AND DEVELOPMENT

Nearly all animals undergo some form of sexual reproduction. They have a few specialized reproductive cells, which undergo meiosis to produce smaller motile spermatozoa or larger non-motile ova. These fuse to form zygotes, which develop into new individuals.

Many animals are also capable of asexual reproduction. This may take place through parthenogenesis, where fertile eggs are produced without mating, or in some cases through fragmentation.

A zygote initially develops into a hollow sphere, called a blastula, which undergoes rearrangement and differentiation.

In sponges, blastula larvae swim to a new location and develop into a new sponge.

In most other groups, the blastula undergoes more complicated rearrangement. It first invaginates to form a gastrula with a digestive chamber, and two separate germ layers — an external ectoderm and an internal endoderm. In most cases, a mesoderm also develops between them. These germ layers then differentiate to form tissues and organs.

Food and Energy Sourcing

All animals are heterotrophs, meaning that they feed directly or indirectly on other living things. They are often further subdivided into groups such as carnivores, herbivores, omnivores, and parasites.

Predation is a biological interaction where a predator (a heterotroph that is hunting) feeds on its prey (the organism that is attacked). Predators may or may not kill their prey prior to feeding on them, but the act of predation always results in the death of the prey.

The other main category of consumption is detritivory, the consumption of dead organic matter. It can at times be difficult to separate the two feeding behaviours, for example where parasitic species prey on a host organism and then lay their eggs on it for their offspring to feed on its decaying corpse.

Selective pressures imposed on one another has led to an evolutionary arms race between prey and predator, resulting in various antipredator adaptations.

Most animals feed indirectly from the energy of sunlight. Plants use this energy to convert sunlight into simple sugars using a process known as photosynthesis. Starting with the molecules carbon dioxide (CO_2) and water (H_2O), photosynthesis converts the energy of sunlight into chemical energy stored in the bonds of glucose ($C_6H_{12}O_6$) and releases oxygen (O_2). These sugars are then used as the building blocks which allow the plant to grow. When animals eat these plants (or eat other animals which have eaten plants), the sugars produced by the plant are used by the animal. They are either used directly to help the animal grow, or broken down, releasing stored solar energy, and giving the animal the energy required for motion. This process is known as glycolysis.

Animals living close to hydrothermal vents and cold seeps on the ocean floor are not dependent on the energy of sunlight. Instead chemosynthetic archaea and bacteria form the base of the food chain.

Origin and Fossil Record

Animals are generally considered to have evolved from a flagellated eukaryote. Their closest known living relatives are the choanoflagellates, collared flagellates that have a morphology similar to the choanocytes of certain sponges. Molecular studies place animals in a super group called the opisthokonts, which also include the choanoflagellates, fungi and a few small parasitic protists. The name comes from the posterior location of the flagellum in motile cells, such as most animal spermatozoa, whereas other eukaryotes tend to have anterior flagella.

The first fossils that might represent animals appear towards the end of the Precambrian, around 610 million years ago, and are known as the Ediacaran or Vendian biota. These are difficult to relate to later fossils, however.

Some may represent precursors of modern phyla, but they may be separate groups, and it is possible they are not really animals at all. Aside from them, most known animal phyla make a more or less simultaneous appearance during the Cambrian period, about 542 million years ago.

It is still disputed whether this event, called the Cambrian explosion, represents a rapid divergence between different groups or a change in conditions that made fossilization possible. However some paleontologists and geologists would suggest that animals appeared much earlier than previously thought, possibly even as early as 1 billion years ago.

Trace fossils such as tracks and burrows found in Tonian era indicate the presence of triploblastic worm like metazoans roughly as large (about 5 mm wide) and complex as earthworms.

In addition during the beginning of the Tonian period around 1 billion years ago (roughly the same time that the trace fossils previously discussed in this article date back to) there was a decrease in Stromatolite diversity which may indicate the appearance of grazing animals during this time as Stromatolites also increased in diversity shortly after the end-Ordovician and end-Permian rendered large amounts of grazing marine animals extinct and decreased shortly after their populations recovered.

The discovery that tracks very similar to these early trace fossils are produced today by the giant single-called protist *Gromia sphaerica* casts further doubt on their interpretation as evidence of early animal evolution.

ASSUMPTIONS AND FRAMEWORKS TO EXPLAIN POPULATION GROWTH

A number of assumptions are made about population growth, its effects (positive or negative), and therefore this affects how we it and how to tackle it, if at all. Summarizing from Robbins, assumptions include the following:

- Population growth leads to negative effects such as
- Economic decline
- Stagnation
- Global poverty
- Hunger
- Environmental devastation
- Political unrest
- Decreasing death rates in poorer countries, due to medical enhancements, better nutrition, improved sanitation etc led to population increases.
- High mortality balanced by a high birth rate led to stable populations before the rapid growth in the eighteenth century.
- Religious beliefs that promote large families and lack of education for women in poorer countries hamper the ability to control populations.
- Only Western forms of birth control techniques and educational programs will slow birth rates.

These assumptions ignore many socio-economic factors that affect population growth and decline patterns. However, some major frameworks provide support for these perspectives that make them such popular assumptions:

Malthusian Perspectives

Thomas Malthus in 1798, wrote the famous *Essay on the Principle of Population*, saying that while populations increase at a geometrical ratio, resources for survival, especially food, increase with a ratio that is only arithmetic. As a result, without "moral restraint" and other checks to control fertility, populations will increase, use up our resources and result in things like famine, war and disease to balance resources and population.

While his theories sound nice and simple (and easy to grasp and therefore popular), a number of criticisms have emerged from various perspectives. One of them includes the actual concerns that Malthus was addressing and is summed up by the following:

[P]opulation growth was not, for Thomas Malthus, the major issue. What concerned him was the rising number of poor in England, why they should exist and what should be done about them.

Poverty, according to Malthus, was not a consequence of expanding industrialism, enclosure laws that evicted people from common lands, or the need of manufacturers for a source of inexpensive labour, but arose from the laws of nature, the discrepancy between the powers of reproduction and the ability to expand food production. People were poor because of there were too many of them, and because they kept having children in spite of their poverty. Providing relief to the poor, argued Malthus, would simply encourage them to have more children. Instead, they should be forced to delay marriage (Malthus was opposed to all forms of birth control). …

The Malthusian position assumes that if poverty exists it must be because of overpopulation, which is the fault of those people who, because of a lack of moral standards, refuse to change their reproductive behavior. There also may have been in the Malthusian position a fear that the army of the poor gathering in cities such as London would stimulate revolution, much as it did in France in 1787.

In that light, Malthus was in essence blaming the "victims". This also lent itself well to those who pursued eugenic theories to back notions of racial superiority via genetic traits etc. That is not to say that all, or even most, Malthusians were eugenicists and racists. However, Malthusian principles do have a class bias in them which makes it hard to accept as a complete explanation, as it then questions other perspectives on how global issues are looked at. This is also a sentiment that continues today, among many who are wealthy, even in poorer nations:

"[An] incredible thread that often runs through the thoughts of the comfortable is the notion of "blaming the victim." The poor are miserable because they have too many children, the reasoning goes. Once they start family planning and control their procreational urges, they'll be on their way to upward mobility. "The better off have always had this attitude toward the poor," [Dilip] D'Souza says. "But now it is respectable to say this." — *Amitabh Pal, The Great Divide; India Confronts Globalization, In These Times, September 3, 2001*

For today, as during Malthus's time, it also allows the underlying models of political economics, exploitation etc to continue, because those are not seen as the issue. Instead, the poor are to blame in some ways.

Demographic Transition

Another theory on populations is known as the demographic transition which says that birth and mortality rates are linked, so that for example, a high rate of both leads to stable population growth, while an imbalance of high birth rates compared to mortality rates would lead to accelerated growth. Advances in medicine, health, modern contraceptives are attributed to declines in population growth in developed countries today. However, as Robbins (who was quoted above) continues and points out on demographic transition theorists, there were numerous assumptions which he says has a "clearly ethnocentric bias":

- Fertility rates in pre-industrial, non-Europeans would not or could not be controlled.

- Only Western methods of birth control and contraception would stabilize population growth.
- It is assumed that the resistance of people in poor countries to adopt Western standards of fertility is because of irrational thinking, outmoded religious values, traditional/fatalistic world views etc, while fertility control in seen as rational and modern.

Much of this ignores variations in fertility that arise from various economic and social factors and that pre-industrial societies were actually healthier than we generally believe.

Economic development is seen as another answer. However, the *type* of economic development must be questioned.

Later in this chapter, a look at consumption patterns and the current forms of economic development are shown to be more damaging to the environment than just population numbers alone and that these consumption patterns are seen in wealthier nations, not the poorer ones where people prescribe the overpopulation cures.

What Affects Population Growths And Declines, Anyway?

While the basic factors affecting population growths and declines are obviously found in births and deaths, there are also additional socioeconomic and cultural factors affecting birth and death rates, such as:

- Fertility (affected by the space of time between children, which itself is affected by cultural norms or cultural taboos as well as consumption patterns)
- Migration (which can influence regional patterns of growth and decline, as a population where many migrate away can lead to a lower population and a reduced pressure of population. Rising birth rates may result if marriages then occur earlier, which is likely. If more men migrate, there are fewer women that will marry which could also lower birth rates instead)

Socioeconomic factors often affect fertility rates and migration patterns themselves, such as (but not limited to):

- Removing or reducing land rights
- Increasing concentration of ownership of land
- Economic/trade policies that increase poverty (such as Structural Adjustment policies that can result in):
- Lack or reduction of education
- Lack or reduction in health care
- Lack of rights for women
- and so on.

Robbins continues to show how in prehistoric hunter/gathering societies, fertility rates were generally low and increased when they settled. He continues to then contrast that with the case of French Canadians, which had a high percentage of men, leading to earlier marriages and high fertility. While it had the highest fertility rates in the 18th century, it now has one of the lowest, even though it is a predominantly Catholic society.

He also details the Irish potato famine and the relation to populations. Here he shows another circumstance where the control of land by British landlords led to an initial doubling from 4 million to 8 million between 1780 and 1840 due to increasing available land for Irish people to use for their own needs.

Potato was really the main crop grown and when a fungus struck in 1845 and affected entire harvest of the following year, about 1.1 to 1.5 million deaths occurred as well as an annual exodus of 200,000.

The average age of marriage also increased. By 1901, the population was down to 4.5 million. He also points out that while an eighth of the population starved, shiploads of food, protected by armed guards, made their way to the ports of England, where people who could afford the food would purchase them.

This was an example of how economic and political factors affected populations.In these circumstances, fertility rates were changed according to the different environmental, social and/or economic circumstances, not necessarily because of improvements in health etc.

Furthermore, similar environmental, socioeconomic changes etc may not always lead to same result in terms of population growth and sizes, because of so many other complex factors involved, as well as the complexity of these factors themselves. For example, in Ghana, population related studies showed that in some cases due to high costs of education and health, the cost of too many children led to some poor families choosing to have fewer children. In this scenario, family planning programs were very effective and successful.

Gender Empowerment

Empowering women, providing better education etc are also related to economic circumstances to some extent, as mentioned by Robbins, who quotes Handwerker in a study on changes in patterns of family relations:

Handwerker (1989:210) concluded that changes in patterns of family relations, not large-scale population control programs of the sort advocated by the Cairo Population Conference, will determine fertility. It is not knowledge of contraceptive techniques or a population problem per se that inhibits women from having smaller families, but an issue of power relations. Family planning programs, said Handwerker:

Should not be expected to bring about fertility transition because they can neither create the jobs, nor provide the education necessary for many jobs that would permit women to achieve meaningful control over their own lives. The "right" to have a small family is not a real option for women who are dependent for basic material well-being on their children. — Richard H. Robbins, Global Problems and the Culture of Capitalism.

Education and empowerment for women is definitely important. It is not to say there should be none. It is to recognize that as well as providing better education, the economic environment must be improved upon so that education can be made use of.

Bibliography

Allen, Kathleen M. S., Stanton W. Green: *Interpreting Space: GIS and Archaeology*, London and New York: Taylor & Francis, 1990.

Balshaw, Maria, and Liam Kennedy: *Urban Space and Representation.* Sterling, VA: Pluto Press, 2000.

Belden C.: *Landscapes of the Sacred: Geography and Narrative in American Spirituality*, New York: Paulist Press, 1988.

Berry, J.K. : *Beyond Mapping, Concepts, Algorithms and Issues in GIS*, Fort Collins, CO: GIS World Books, 1993.

Blij, Harm Jan, De: *Geography: Realms, Regions, and Concepts*. Hoboken, NJ: John Wiley, 2008.

Bolstad, P. : *GIS Fundamentals, A first text on Geographic Information Systems, Second Edition*, White Bear Lake, MN, Eider Press, 2005.

Burch, William R. Jr.: *Human Ecology: An Environmental Approach*, Belmont, Duxbury Press, 1994.

Burrough, P.A. and McDonnell, R.A. : *Principles of Geographical Information Systems*, Oxford University Press, Oxford, 1998.

Carrillo, J., Lung, Y., and van Tulder, R. : *Cars, Carriers of Regionalism*, Palgrave Macmillan, New York, 2004.

Costanza, R.: *Ecological Economics*, Columbia Uni. Press., New York, 1991.

Cronon, William: *Changes in the Land: Indians, Colonists, and the Ecology of New England*. New York: Hill and Wang, 1983.

Dibbern, Jens : *The Sourcing of Application Software Services, Empirical Evidence of Cultural, Industry and Functional Differences*, Physica Verlag Heidelberg, 2004.

Duckworth, W L H : *Morphology and Anthropology : A Handbook for Students*, Cosmo, Delhi, 2006.

Elangovan K. : *GIS, Fundamentals, Applications and Population Geography*, New India Publishing Agency, New Delhi 2006.

Gay, Kathlyn: *Saving the Environment: Debating the Costs*, New York, Franklin Watts, 1996.

Harvey, David: *Explanation in Geography*. London: Edward Arnold, 1969.

Harvey, Francis : *A Primer of GIS, Fundamental Geographic and Cartographic Concepts*, The Guilford Press, 2008.

Hofrichter, Richard: *The Theory and Practice of Environmental Justice*, Philadelphia, New Society Publishers, 1993.

Jackson, Peter: *Maps of Meaning: An Introduction to Cultural Geography.* London and Boston: Unwin Hyman, 1989.

James S. Duncan: *Writing Worlds: Discourse, Text, and Metaphor in the Representation of Landscape.* London and New York: Routledge, 1992.

James, T.: *The Best Poor Man's Country: A Geographical Study of Early Southeastern Pennsylvania.* Baltimore: Johns Hopkins Press, 1972.

Johnston, R.J: *Geographies of Global Change: Remapping the World.* Blackwell Publishers, London, 2002.

King, Anthony D.: *Buildings and Society: Essays on the Social Development of the Built Enviroment.* London: Routledge & Kegan Paul, 1980.

Lewis, Earl. *In Their Own Interests: Race, Class, and Power in Twentieth-Century Norfolk, Virginia.* Berkeley: University of California Press, 1990.

Lewis, Peirce. *New Orleans: The Making of an Urban Landscape.* Cambridge, MA: Ballinger Publishing Co., 1976. Annotation

Liam Kennedy: *Urban Space and Representation.* Sterling, VA: Pluto Press, 2000.

McDonnell, R.A. : *Principles of Geographical Information Systems*, Oxford University Press, Oxford, 1998.

Michael P.: *The Making of the American Landscape.* Boston: Unwin Hyman, 1990.

Michael, H.: *City Form and Natural Process: Towards a New Urban Vernacular.* London: Croom Helm, 1984.

Neil, H.: *The Land of Contrasts: 1880-1901,* The American Culture 5. New York: G. Braziller, 1970.

Peet, Richard: *Modern Geographical Thought.* Oxford: Wiley-Blackwell, 1998.

Peter, G.: *The Slow Plague: A Geography of the AIDS Pandemic.* Oxford and Cambridge, MA: Blackwell Publishers, 1993.

Pilgrim R.: *Post Harvest Handling of Minor Exotics*, St. George's, Grenada, 1996.

Ramann, E. : *The Evolution and Classification of Soils*, Asiatic Pub, Calcutta, 2006.

Ray Allen: *The Far Western Frontier, 1830-1860.* The New American Nation Series. New York: Harper, 1956.

Ritchie, J.: *Landscape and Material Life in Franklin County, Massachusetts, 1770-1860.* Knoxville: University of Tennessee Press, 1991.

Soja, Edward: *Postmodern Geographies: The Reassertion of Space in Critical Social Theory.* Verso, London, 1989.

Stephen, D.: *Fields of Vision: Landscape Imagery and National Identity in England and the United States.* Cambridge: Polity, 1993.

Victor, A. : *Geography of Art and Culture,* Contributions to Economic Analysis, Elsevier, 2004.

Watkins, Eric: *The Middle Eastern Environment*, London, The British Society for Middle Eastern Studie, 1995.

Wolf, Aaron T.: *Hydropolitics along the Jordan River, Scarce Water and its Impact on the Arab-Israeli Conflict*, NYC, United Nations University Press, 1995.

Index

❑❑❑